STEVENS' COURSE IN PUPPETRY

STEVENS' COURSE IN PUPPETRY

Martin Stevens

With Additional Tips by
Rick Morse, Ronnie Burkett
Jim Menke, & Luman Coad

Plus a Reprint of a 1947 Popular Mechanics Pamphlet

CHARLEMAGNE PRESS
Garden Bay, BC, Canada

STEVENS' COURSE IN PUPPETRY
Copyright © 1997 by the Martin Stevens Trust

"Stage Your Own Puppet Show"
  courtesy Hearst Publications Inc.

Canadian Cataloguing in Publication Data

Stevens, Martin, 1904-1983.
  Stevens course in puppetry

ISBN 0-921845-16-2

1. Puppet theatres. 2. Puppet making. 1. Title. 11, Title: Course in puppetry.

PN1972.S731997   791.5'3   C97-910665-6

CHARLEMAGNE PRESS
4348 Coastview Drive
Garden Bay, BC
V0N 1S1 Canada

CONTENTS

	Preface	v
Session 1	Developing the Concept	1
Session 2	"The Plays the Thing"	9
Session 3	"What is a Puppet?"	17
Session 4	Designing the Stringpuppet	25
Session 5	Designing the Handpuppet	33
Session 6	Developing the Voice	39
Session 7	Crafting the Stringpuppet (Part I)	49
Session 8	Crafting the Stringpuppet Part II)	57
Session 9	Crafting the Stringpuppet (Part III)	65
Session 10	Crafting the Head (Part I)	75
Session 11	Crafting the Head (Part II)	87
Session 12	Stringing and Manipulation	95
Session 13	Creating the Handpuppet Stag3	109
Session 14	Creating the Stringpuppet Stage	119
Session 15	Scenery, Props, and Lighting	127
Session 16	Music, Rehearsals, & Performing	134
Session 17	Animated Faces	143
Session 18	Finding the Audience	151
Session 19	Working in Television	159
Session 20	Personalized Sessions	169
Appendix A	"Stage Your Own Show"	183
Appendix B	"Marionette Stage"	203

Preface

Martin Stevens introduced the Stevens' Correspondence Course in Puppetry in 1959. The first *Puppetry Journal* ad offering thirty sessions for $25 may have been a typographical error because the next Journal's full page ad stated there would be twenty sessions for $25. It was an intriguing offer to study with one of the mainstays of the Puppeteers of America.

Until the mid-1950s, the Puppeteers of America Festivals were three day affairs of performances and meetings. Nearly every year Rufus & Margo Rose, Romaine & Ellen Proctor, and Martin & Olga Stevens would perform. A Puppetry Institute was held the week prior to the Festival in which students worked with these three couples to learn the multiple skills of an accomplished puppet performer. Here was a chance to study at home and at a slower pace with one of the leading puppeteers.

"Steve," as Martin was affectionately called, was separated from Olga and living in New York City when he wrote the Course. Among the initial group of registrants was Marge Kelly of Topeka, Kansas, who eventually became Margi Stevens.

The Course was different from the usual how-to books which began with create a puppet then come up with a show. Steve's approach was to begin with the idea of a production, then create the puppets to suit the concept. This method changed the way many participants worked.

A few of the sessions have added tips by Rick Morse, Ronnie Burkett, and myself, but the entire original text in Steve's inimitable style, including the liberal use of commas and dashes, as been preserved.

Throughout the Course Steve stressed doing it the easy way. "...if you picture a show that stirs you, that excites you, that makes you smile every time you think about it, you will automatically move toward all the multitude of details that must be encountered on the way to that mutual enjoyment. And the bonus! The bonus of such a procedure is that it all becomes fun!"

Isn't that what first attracted us to puppetry? Well ....have fun!

Luman Coad
July, 1997

Postscript

Steve once said very few people ever submitted questions for their personalized twentieth session. Several are included in this publication but to make this Course as complete as possible, I would greatly appreciate learning of any others. Many thanks.

Luman

Session 1 **Developing the Concept**

Dear Registrant:

Here we go. We're going to do something new here - a whole bunch of plain talk about Puppetry. We'll talk about her as she has been, as she exists, and as she might be. Or become. I'll try not to be stuffy or pedantic – a thing any writer can so easily fall into – but I shan't try not to be opinionated: I don't think I'd be worth anything to you if I didn't express my opinions. You can get that kind of writing anywhere. One of the very great virtues of subscribing to a course such as this is that you can hear what is being thought without the censoring of "public opinion" or "organization policy" or "well, it really wasn't good, but he's a nice guy, and there's no point in hurting his feelings." Sure, there's no point in hurting his feelings, and if I'm real careful, maybe I can avoid a libel suit, but there are a lot of things that should be said to you about this art form and its practice, and I propose – as clearly as I can see them – to say them.

I am honored to know most of the professional people in this field, and along with my bias I expect to bring you the consensus. Nearly all of them are interested in the same aims that animate the Puppeteers of America – the increasing of the individual ability to the betterment of the entire art AND its income, and I depend on them for the up-to-the-minute reports on how it is in their areas of activity. I want you to have all the latest information on things that are important to the way you work.

As to technical physical data, I propose to offer you all the details of "how to" as I have found them most effective, not an endless parade of all the ways everyone ever made this or that detail. The P. of A. has a bookstore, and your town probably has a library with the WONDER-full books out of which I learned so much when I was beginning. If you haven't already read these grand compendia, you probably will, but in the mean time, the information you get in this course will work beautifully, and I guarantee you, with the least physical effort on your part. In addition, it will leave out methods (also in the books) which do not work, and have misled generations of enthusiastic innocents up blind alleys.

The length of each session will vary according to its contents, but the measure of the success of the course FOR YOU will be the application you make of each session as it comes. I can only put the means in your hands – you must put it into action in your own show. But I assure you, the thinking and the understanding part of this course will be of far greater importance to you than the sawing and hammering part.
For Puppetry is primarily Showmanship, and it is THIS the customer pays to see, rather than the skill of the sewing room or the carpenter shop. Here we go, then: let's see how to supply the customer with what he paid his money for!

Enthusiastically yours,

Martin Stevens

What is a Show?

Offhand, a person wouldn't think a question like that would need asking, considering there never was a time when so many shows were seen by so many people, for so many reasons. But the commonness of such remarks as "most TV shows are a waste of time," or "that's only a `B' picture," or "after investing $100,000 and all that time, they opened on Broadway and closed in three nights," indicate that if the people whose business it is to know what a show is frequently fail to "deliver," it behooves us to at least inquire into what a "show" is to us.

Grant that an audience (whose business is not producing shows) doesn't know what a show is, but knows what it likes, why does it like it? Because in seeing this endless parade of shows it has been educated, all unconsciously, to expect certain ingredients – the mores of that particular type of show – and when these ingredients are missing, the audience is unsatisfied. It doesn't go out saying, "The timing was off," or "The basic premise was wrong," or "There was no logical resolution of the problem," or the myriad other things that we, as show producers must know and must incorporate; they simply go away unsatisfied, and in our case it leads to their making remarks like, "No thanks: I saw a puppet show once."

The point here is simple and important: the minute you charge money to see your show, you are in the position of Metro-Goldwin-Mayer, Ringling Bros, Barnum & Bailey, and the Helen Hayes Theatre: you obligate yourself to deliver to them a satisfying experience in the theatre on their terms – that is, the terms they have been unconsciously taught to expect from a theatrical experience. They are paying money for showmanship. And what is showmanship? Why bless my soul that's what this Course is about! All we'll talk about, all we'll do, all we'll learn and practice will be directed to that one goal: the gratification of the audience by our conscious use of the skills of showmanship.

Let us proceed with your show. Whether it is a School Assembly performance, an off-Broadway try, a night club act, or a classic drama performed in concert with the symphony orchestra, it must do two things: it must start where the audience is – its culture, theatrical experiences and acceptances – and satisfy those, then take them one step farther – in appreciation, understanding, delight. Always, however, it just starts with the audience's condition. You can't force the audience to appreciate *Oedipus Rex* if its taste is *Peter Rabbit*. *So* it is required of you to gauge your audience – know it. If you are just starting out, or if you are inclined to enter a new field, study that field; go where they go, see what they see, become experienced in what pleases them, what satisfies them, the kind of things they rave about as they leave, and for days after. If you are already doing a show that isn't getting quite the response you think it should, go back and look at the audience again. "Remember," said Charles Kettering, the most successful inventor of his day, "you and I get no place in the world except as we serve the fellow who pays for our dinner." And the knowledge and practice of showmanship is how we serve our audiences.

What is a show? A show is an experience shared by a showman and an audience. The most beautiful production in the world performed in an empty theatre is not a show. A show involves the audience emotionally in what is happening to the characters on the stage. It has to care about the success or failure of the characters involved, whether it is Medea murdering her children or a chorus girl getting out of step, a clown falling off a table or the Princess guessing Rumpelstiltskin's name. Just as one of these themes will intrigue an audience more than another, so one of them will intrigue you more than another. You can't do a showmanlike job on a theme you can't care about. So let us consider what show you would most like to do.

There are many ways to do this considering; material you already have on hand and feel you must use; commitments you have already made; but for just now, try this:

Sit quietly back, make yourself comfortable and relaxed. Don't think about any of the usual considerations of puppetry as you practice it, but just let your mind drift through the field. Don't try for anything, just float. Think about puppetry. Picture a stage, a show, lights, an audience. Picture yourself in this surrounding. See a show. What is it like? What is it doing? How is the audience responding? You will bring up images which please you, which amuse and intrigue you. Don't "try" to do anything with them - just follow along as they unfold. This is day-dreaming by intention and your intention is for you to have a pleasant time. You will find that this is very pleasant, for you are not making something happen to a purpose – you are happening. When you have gotten quite into the enjoyment of it, expand your dreaming to include the audience, the theatre, the surrounding circumstance. All these are enjoying your pleasure with you. And now perhaps you have opened a new vista for yourself, an activity in an area of puppetry which you had not previously considered, but one in which you could be enthusiastically productive. For as was said before, a show is the participation of the showman and the audience in a mutual enthusiasm.

This method of relaxed creativity is valuable in any direction your show activity needs to take – the promotion show for the Community Chest, the program for and by the Cub Scouts, the night club act or whatever. For lay it down as a rule: if you are bored by the prospect, your audience will certainly be. When you come to the point in your reverie where you are smiling with satisfaction, you can start making notes. These, at this time, aren't "going anywhere" either, but are merely the first steps toward materializing the delight you have envisioned – pinning the pleasure down, so to speak, for future use.

Now, if you are enthused, you can start the process of actualizing the dream. And how do you do that?

There is a lovely myth to which many of us subscribe: the Cinderella myth. The publicists for the movies make much of it: lovely girl being a car-hop who never gave a thought to being in the movies is suddenly discovered by a Big Producer and overnight becomes a Star of the First Magnitude. Strudel! In the majority of instances, as you will recognize if you're an avid movie fan and give it a little remembering, the "stars" are more frequently second- third- even fourth-generation show-folk who had the craft drummed into them from the time they started to breathe. Not that they inherited talent with their chromosomes, understand – simply that their minds, their thoughts were directed in these channels over and over again. The same thing works with you and me: what we put our minds on, becomes real!

So with the picture you just dreamed up: if you are enthusiastic about it, your enthusiasm, your emotion, will generate attention – attention to everything that has to do with the realization of that picture. Over and over again in my experience, as I have turned my enthusiastic attention on a new show – *The Passion Play, Joan of Arc, Macbeth* – everything I needed in the way of material or information came into focus; people appeared who could help me, opportunities for showing the play, for publicizing it, for understanding it, for going toward that magic moment when the houselights dim and everybody is ready to have fun! This is the meaning of the phrase: "This above all, to thine own self be true…" for if you picture a show that stirs you, that excites you, that makes you smile every time you think about it, you will automatically move toward all the multitude of details that must be encountered on the way to that mutual enjoyment. And the bonus! The bonus of such a procedure is that it all becomes fun! When people after a show say to me, "My, it must take a lot of patience to do all this," I am always surprised, for it doesn't take any patience at all. Every detail, every moment is a joy, for from the inception of the idea – that intentional day-dreaming – down to the checking of the last minute prop placement before the curtain goes up, I'm "on my way to a party," and what could be pleasanter than that.

Now as you can see, by looking at this show of yours with enthusiasm, and knowing that it isn't a show unless it has an audience, the next logical thing is to think into what kind of audience could have fun with you. So studying the audience's habits, tastes, demands, becomes a part of the fun, rather than a chore. It is true that the audience is going to "hire" you, but once they are in their seats you are the host, and it behoves you to know as much about your guests as is necessary to give them the greatest possible satisfaction.

None of this is hard. This course might be called The Easy Method, for I assure you that after doing it the hard way for years, I am interested only in what will get the desired results in the pleasantest way possible. And of course you will do a better job, for yourself and for the audience if you do it without strain. In the course of this study, we will touch on all the varied outlets for puppet activity (with the possible exception of puppets in mental therapy, which does not come under the head of showmanship or entertainment) and we will see the differences in their several requirements, but underlying them all is a basic quality, an attitude, a requirement, and it is this with which we are primarily concerned. Puppetry, like any of the arts, has its fundamental laws but, as in the case of painting, no two painters paint alike. Some people taking up puppetry read one or more books, swallow them whole, and permit themselves to be bound by them the rest of their careers. We hope to avoid this by explaining why certain things get certain reactions, and then helping you apply them in your particular way.

To recapitulate what has been said:

We have discussed what a show is, and discovered it is not merely an exhibition of the puppeteer's skills, but a mutually enthusiastic experience of puppeteer and audience.

We have said that you can, without strain, picture the most delightful excitement, and that this is a bona fide for you to go forward to presenting it, as it is yours.

We have seen that the enthusiasm with which you view this pleasantry generates the creation of it, not only in the physical appurtenances, but in the selection and understanding of that other participant, the audience, and that the whole thing can be achieved gaily.

Now read through this session again, and then sit quietly back and do a bit of pleasant and relaxed picturing. If you already have a show, or know what you're going to produce next, do it anyway. This is a preliminary for further picturing we're going to do when we get to plays, scripts, et cetera, and I want you to get into the habit of knowing that you can make great creative strides while expending no effort whatever.

These Sessions will be of varying lengths – as this goody is not sold by the yard. If one of them comes up with more pages than its predecessor, don't figure it has more importance because of that: it may just have required more words to say less, while a more vital one may take fewer.

Some Sessions will be mostly illustrations, some will have none, like this one. In each case you will receive what appears to me to be the clearest, simplest, and most valuable exposition of the material possible.

Now go have some pretty pictures.

Session 2 "The Play's the Thing"

When people meet each other, what do they say to each other? They say, "A pleasure to meet you, Mr. Smitherfoots, and what do YOU do?" Notice that the initial concern isn't how tall you are or who is your tailor or where you have been – the question is, "What do you DO?" This is of first importance to you as a puppet showman. There has been some very curious advertising for puppet shows, such as "The marionettes in this production require twenty-seven miles of fishline," and, "During this tour, the Company will travel 96,000 miles." Well, that's nice, but what am I going to see if I go to this show (which at this point is unlikely!) In other words, what's DOING?

Motion isn't Enough

When we make our first puppet and it comes alive in our hands, it is an entrancing experience – no doubt about it. I remember it well! The trouble is that some of us never come out of our trance. It is quite true, that some people when they work puppets are playing with dolls, and that's perfectly all right – for them. But here we are studying Puppetry, which is showmanship, and quite another thing. Puppetry is not doll-play, which is an individual doing a "let's pretend" between himself and a toy. Nor is Puppetry (as one practitioner informed me) "largely a matter of sculpture." Puppets are only incidentally works of art; being an ornament isn't their prime function. Nor should they be merely means to a "jiggle-show" which, alas! they often are. They are encouraged in this by some no doubt sincere people who inform us that "Puppets have to have lots of action. Jump `em around! Keep `em lively! If you don't, you'll lose your audience." But, as `Sportin' Life' says, "It ain't necessarily so." One of the best things a puppet can do is stop stock-still and `give it a good think.' But notice that by the action of stopping (whatever he is doing) and thinking, he is DOING something. And this brings us back to you: what is your puppet doing? What is the play?

What to Do

You have now "done your home-work" on Session One, and dreamed up the feeling of your next show. Because of the latitude of interests of those taking this course, these intentions will cover the whole range of entertainment, from a carnival Punch & Judy to a TV spectacular. Before we have finished, we will touch such details as are pertinent to the majority of these interests, but because most of you will be concerned with what is usually termed a "play," we'll start with that. This is logical and proper, for the structure of a play is important to you whether you are a ventriloquist, a variety artiste, a night club performer, or a maker of TV commercials. In my capacity as Script Consultant for the Puppeteers of America, I constantly received requests for plays: "Where can we get such and such a kind of play," and preferably by next Thursday. Answering them briefly and directly is not usually possible – which is one of the reasons for presenting this course. The P. of A. has gone to considerable effort and expense to compile a list of available plays which members can get for a small fee. The junior League also has a list of available plays which may be used by paying a royalty. That great and good institution known as the Public Library (to which I owe so much!) is a source, and of course there are the play publishing concerns which have an endless list of plays for the ordinary or "people" theatre. My experience has been that of spending days and days and DAYS of effort searching and reading and considering and rejecting, and finally deciding that the only way I would get the play I wanted was to write it myself!

Do It Yourself, Kit!

Does this frighten you? It needn't. You've never written a play? Good! You won't be led astray by a bunch of misconceptions. Don Vestal once asked Gertrude Stein to write a puppet play and she said she would. "Have you ever seen a puppet show?" asked Don. "No," replied Miss Stein, "so I shall write the very best one," or words to that effect. Or as the old joke goes: "Can you play the piano?" "I don't know – I've never tried!" You just might be a whiz at it!

How to Write a Play

Let's take this real easy. Remember, this is the Easy Method. Suppose you were to go through all that searching I reported having done on the previous page, and you finally decided, "Well, this is as near to what I had in mind as I'm likely to get," and you start to produce it. When you get down to the actual production, you'll have to alter it to fit your own needs, inclinations and abilities anyway. So why not just be bold and take a crack at it right off the bat? What can you lose?

You probably haven't considered this, but you already know an awful lot about plays. Remember, when you're not on the stage, you're in the audience, and the YOU are those people we talked of in Session One, who can tell satisfaction from dissatisfaction when they've seen a show. The only thing we're going to do now is explain to you what it is you liked and why you liked it.

A play is merely the exposition of the experiences of a character who wants something very much and tries to get it. Something or someone hinders him, and for a time makes it seem that he will never get his desire. But then a decision he makes, and an action he takes, overcomes the hindrance and he gets what he wanted. It's that simple! Classically stated, "Boy meets Girl, Boy loses Girl, Boy gets Girl." Just look at any play with which you're familiar and see how it goes. **Cinderella. Red Riding Hood. Snow White.** Name your own. Now take a soap commercial: Lady has lovely hands, Lady uses strong detergent and loses lovely hands, Lady uses OUR detergent and gets lovely hands! Take a welfare campaign: Human has right to health and happiness, Human loses health and happiness, but through YOUR contribution, Human gets health and happiness. See how it works! Punch has life, liberty, and the pursuit of happiness. Hangman threatens to remove all three. Punch hangs the Hangman and regains life, liberty, and the pursuit of happiness. The Messiah has life, the opposition kills him, and he returns to life.

Application

The formula holds whether Community gets Chest, or Child get Gold Star, or Part get Support, or Charlie McCarthy puts one over on Edgar Bergen. You have in Session One dreamed up a circumstance in which you were seeing the ideal puppet show for you. How elaborate or how simple it was doesn't change this basic premise. You're starting with something: maybe a puppet you have already made; maybe a whole cast of puppets you inherited or bought; maybe a story you remember vaguely from `way back. Whatever your starting point, this is the direction in which you proceed.

Now there are those who say they cannot write the play out first and then match the puppets to it; they must have the puppet or puppets first and see where they go on the stage. All right – that's a way of doing the same thing. In either case, the dreaming exercise you did in Session One is still the process. The only difficulty with this method is that if your puppets are already built, you must accommodate your dreaming to their limitations. However, if you have already built shows in this way, you may prefer to continue so. Only now you will incorporate consciously this basic ingredient, the "formula", as the direction your dreaming will take.

For me, a puppet is not a "thing in itself" which is to be catered to and have plays written for it: a puppet is the physical appearance of an idea I have, and is to express that idea. This is why I recommend doing the dreaming first – knowing who is going where and how he is to get there, and then making the puppet as the perfect embodiment of who and how to.

Imagination

Many of my students, when first confronted with the idea that they might write a play, make a great shuddering disclaimer: "But I have no imagination!" Of course this is not true of anyone. You do have imagination and you use it all the time. The possibility that you have not used it in this way for this purpose in no way demonstrated that you have none. Have you ever made up a story for a child? Wondered what happened to someone? Lied to someone? Felt empathy for someone in a disaster? There, you see? You have as much imagination as you need to tackle giving form to this – the delightful show you have already pictured in your mind. Remember – that took imagination, too!

Let's Not Go "Hog Wild"

While we have stated the basic premise of a play, let us not give such free rein to our imaginations that we "gallop off in all directions." Here is a golden rule:

One Idea to One Play!

What does this mean? It means, tell your audience at the start where you are going, and then go there! If Red Riding Hood is going to her Grandma's house, let her go there – don't let her meet Sinbad and go wandering off after the Roc's egg. If you do, we – the audience – will be confused about whose show it is and who we're supposed to cheer for, and we'll lose interest. For a play is just like a ball game: we, the audience, choose sides. We want to be "for" the good guy and "agin" the bad guys.

Make the "Goody" Good

Whatever it is the hero wants, make him want it with all his heart. It is vitally important to him. If it isn't, so what's the difference if he loses it. He won't care, and I won't care. And if what he wants so much is for someone else's benefit – so much the better. That makes him noble. And as I – the audience – am identifying with him, that makes me noble, too.

Make the "Baddy" Bad

Equally important is to oppose the hero with a force so much stronger than he is that he has hardly a chance of winning through. Out-number him. Never give him a break. Put him in such a hold that it looks quite hopeless. This puts me – the audience – in the hole with him, and I'm rootin' like crazy for him to do something – ANYthing – to get us out of there!

Let Him Do It

Now we've reached such a crisis in our hero's affairs that he's got to win but- he has to win by his own virtue. None of this last minute villain-tripped-and-broke-his-neck stuff, or a-fairy-happened-to-be-passing-and …. Oh no. He can't just be lucky and fall out of trouble. Our boy has to think of the solution and DO something about it. (What do you DO, Mr. Smitherfoots?") He has to outwit the villain. Or if it takes outside assistance, he has to have earned that assistance previously. This is why **The Musicians of Bremen** never "got off the ground" as a show - they didn't set out to be heroes; the band of robbers just **happened** to be in the house. And whatever else you may think of **Hansel and Gretel,** he did fool the Witch with the bone, and he did dispatch her into the oven she had prepared for them.

How I Proceed

Everybody works out his own system, of course. The way I do it is to take my "jumping off point" – the idea of a character, or a situation, or a truth I want to express, and relax into a pleasant expectancy which makes for good dreaming. Notice: no strain! Making notes as I go along, I see who my character is. What he's like. What he wants. Why it is imperative that he get it. How he goes after it. What stops him? Why did they want him not to have it? What does he do to get "out of the hole"? The more I dream over this, back and forth, the more details occur to me, and I make brief notes on them all. They're not in sequence – they're set down just as they appear in my mind. Finally I have "seen" the action of the show pretty clearly. Notice I have seen it, and not heard it. I have seen what the characters are doing! Not heard what they are saying. Here is where you establish the ACTION, which is a play, as opposed to an essay.

Aut Scissors At Nullius

Now I take my scissors and snip all my notes apart, and rearrange them in the order in which they will occur. Too many repetitions? Throw some away. Gaps in the action? Now I can see them, visibly in front of me. Fill them in. Still no dialogue. Not until I have the entire action of the play, the motivations, the resolution that is reasonable and comes out that way because it could come out no other, and I am not only satisfied but enthusiastic about it, am I ready to put words in their mouths!

Now I know who is going to be in my play, and what he is going to do, down to the last detail. I look at each character, and see what he must be like in order to do these things. I make a character analysis of him, and out of this grows the picture of what he looks like, how he behaves, how he talks. NOW I'm ready to write the dialogue. I'm familiar with the play, the characters, and the things they say come out right and spontaneously! They're not saying words now just to fill up the time, but to express their intention, the direction of their action. They're going somewhere. They're DOING something! See the fun?

One more very important detail, and you're ready to go:

DON'T SURPRISE YOUR AUDIENCE

Does that surprise you? It's true. Surprise the characters in the play, but not the audience. If your hero on his way to the castle is to step into a bear trap, have the villain set the bear trap in advance, where we can see him do it. Maybe even snap it shut once with a clang! so we see what a danger it is. THEN when the hero walks innocently toward it, we have an involvement, a caring. Identifying with him, we have something at stake. I've seen audiences so involved like this they couldn't contain themselves and cried out, "Don't DO it!" but if we're unprepared, and he just walks along and steps into a bear trap, we're puzzled – what happened? – and we miss the participation we, the audience, deserve. Remember Session One: a show is us as well as you!

Now have some rare delight: write your play. If you're timid, and your play is so big it still scares you, write a little teeny play – just for fun. As I've demonstrated, this principle holds for a thirty second commercial as well as for a five hour *Hamlet,* so do it. For your own pleasure of discovery. For fun. I assure you you'll do fine! And it will be YOUR play, an expression of YOUR enthusiasm, and so a show you can perform enthusiastically-which in turn makes us, the audience, enthusiastic too. When you're not writing your own, study TV shows and movies: see how these principles are employed by your fellow showmen. They're all there, and they always work.

Do it.

Session 3 What is a Puppet?

We've had some detailed analyses of What Is A Show and What Is A Play. Now let us consider the medium we propose to use in doing our play as a show: the puppet.

When conversation lags at a social gathering, one can usually give it a shot in the vocal chords by asking the simple question: "What Is Art?" In any average gathering, this is good for hours of animated discussion, for each has his own definition suited to his own needs. And in a sense, all of them are right – for their time, place, and condition. Yet despite this lack of agreement, Art continues to flourish, and intentional communication or the lack of it is achieved. We may assume there can be no one definition of any practical value for all artists of all time.

So with our question. Avid people (of whom I have been one) will "fight to the death" to uphold their concept in the face of all others. So hurrah! Let us believe they knew what they thought, and what they wanted a puppet to be to them. That's all to the good. So perhaps we should rephrase our question to read

What is a Puppet to You

"A puppet is a stunt." Well, some puppets are just that, and if that is your intention for it, good. Make it the very best stunt of its kind in the world. However, if your stunt is just that, it is very soon over, and your audience can turn it off with, "Yes, very clever. They do it with strings, you know," and that's all of that. But the most straight-forward stunt, when given the addition of The Formula (see Session Two) immediately transforms the stunt-figure into the Hero who wants something, who fails to get it, who gets it. Why does the aerialist almost fall off the high wire? Why does the juggler drop the plate? Why does the magician "forget" the magic word for a moment? To add this personal ingredient, the opposition to success, and then its achievement.

"Puppets are people." Well, I don't think they are.

"Puppets are works of art." They can be, but mostly they aren't.

"Puppets are dolls." Not in this Course, they're not!

What are they, then? I'll tell you what I think they are, but first I must recall the great Walter Wilkinson's definition of Art: "Art is the personal contribution to the evercontinuing conversation about Life." Isn't that a beauty? Now we have a practical definition, which is applicable to the Art of Puppetry as an Art of Theatre, and it immediately puts the puppet in perspective.

In order for our first definition of A Show to hold true, you, the showman have your comment on life – in the form of a theatrical idea, and you have to get it across – to communicate it to us, the audience, who want to be "in on this thing" with you. For this communication you will use all the craft of theatre, but your principle tool as a puppet showman is a puppet. A puppet, then, is an expression of your idea – the visible, moving form it takes.

A Puppet is the Shape of an Idea in Motion

And if your idea is fuzzy your puppet will be fuzzy, your show will be fuzzy, and our audience reaction to you will be fuzzy. This, then, is why we start a Course in **Puppetry** not with "First shred some old newspaper," but with the first two Sessions telling you what to look for in yourselves and then asking you to look at it. If you have "done your homework" by now you should have a pretty clear picture in your mind of what you intend us to see, having in some degree already "seen" it yourself. And now you can think about designing the puppet. You know where your show is going, who is needed to go there, who is needed to get in his way. These are the "designing" factors, and as you dream through the show in your imagination you can see who's the big guy and who's the little guy – and how big and how little. By seeing them act in your mind, you can see whether they stoop or strut, leap or tippy-toe, and these things are what determine their design.

How to Design a Puppet

A child was asked, "How do you draw?" and he answered, "I see something on the paper and I put a line around it." All right, so you "can't draw a straight line." Who can? But you can do this: Take a big piece of paper (I use wrapping paper) and, using the bottom edge of it as the stage floor, make a series of vertical lines, equal to the number of your characters. Now make a horizontal mark at the top of the tallest one. Ditto the shortest one. You already have a scale for the relative sizes of the rest of the puppets. Remember, handpuppets don't have to be all one size any more than marionettes do.

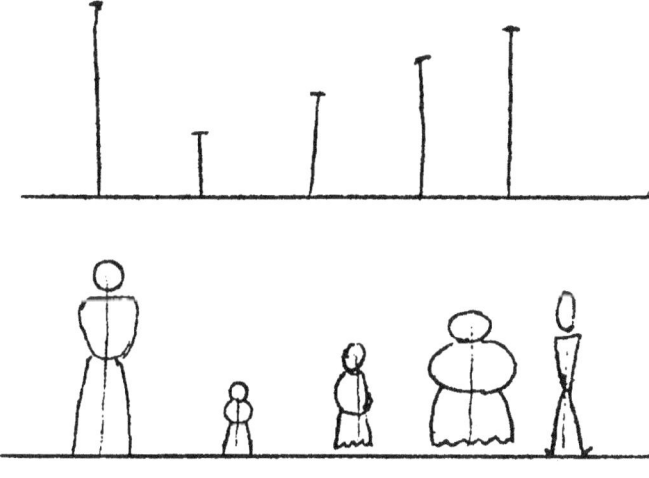

That's a very respectable variety. We know who each one is, so let's make them a bit more like themselves.

Not bad at all. There's the Giant, and Jack, and his Mother, and the Giant's Housekeeper, and that skinny guy who traded Jack the beans. NOTICE! See what you brought with you: as I mentioned each of the above, you mentally applied characteristic details to each one out of your own imagination. And that's the way it's done. Simple. Want an exercise to show you how good you are? Rename them any other five characters you please, and see your imagination alter them and fill them out, just as it did the first time.

At this point we'll have to split up and consider handpuppets and stringpuppets separately because the methods of designing and making them differ. As handpuppets must of physical necessity depart more from the average human dimensions than stringpuppets, let's

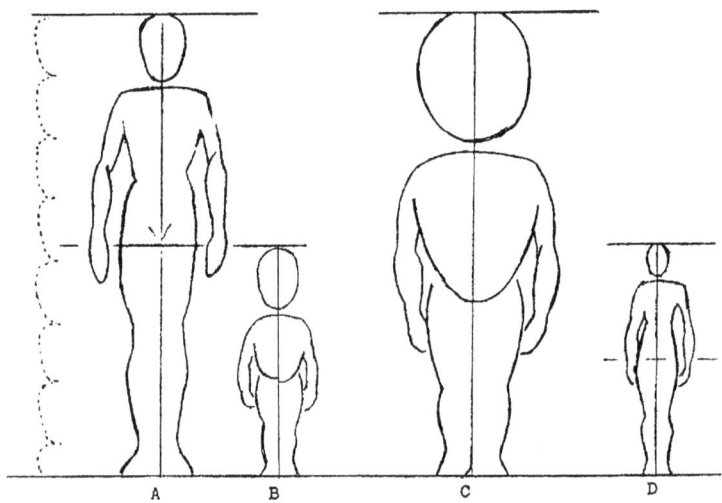

Consider the Human Dimension

Any art store can supply you with inexpensive books with diagrams of anatomical proportion – so can the blessed public library – so can your encyclopedia – so will I. But mine will be of the greatest simplicity, because you have the very best model right in your house: YOU. It is really astounding how many "realistic" puppets look as though their creators had never really seen a person – and it is true that they haven't. As The Toymaker said to the puppet Stripes, "You never looked."

Don't you make that mistake. As we go along, get out your tape measure and really look at yourself.

These are "average" proportions. A is an "average" adult male. Seven and a half heads high. Shoulders two heads wide. Crotch in the middle of his overall height. Fingertips hang halfway between his hip and knee. (Don't ask me where his hip is; where's yours?) Such other measurements as are necessary we'll pick up as we go along. Right now, here's

Something Important!

Look at B. That is obviously a child. It can't be a "small man" or it would look like D. Actually, we recognize it as a child because of its proportion. Look at that head in relation to the body: hardly more than three and a half heads high. And his crotch considerably below center. You accept this and your audience accepts this as the difference between kids and grown folks without ever thinking about it. We see this proportion and we know they're "little people" meaning kids. The point is that you mustn't take everything you hear about puppets as gospel without examining it: like "Make their heads big so they'll be easier to see." It ain't so.

"All we want is the facts, Ma'am." Take an audience of 1500 people (as big as I ever agree to play to.)

Why Do They Look So Big

Obviously because of proportion; the room you see is in the right proportion to the "people" you see, the chairs are right for them to sit on - the door the familiar proportion to go through. But if the door is too little for Alice to crowd through or the table too high for her to reach, we have established her relative sizes by proportion.

If you look across the street at your neighbors on the porch, you similarly have no difficulty determining how big they are even though you can't see the details of their faces. In that auditorium seating 1500, you can't see the detail of the faces beyond the tenth row – they might as well be blocks or spheres for all the good that dimple you so cleverly worked into the chin is concerned – BUT the proportion can be seen from the last row in the balcony. Now look at figure C: it has a GREAT BIG head compared to A, but although it is the same height would you say it was the figure of a man? Huh uh – that's a child's figure, and it doesn't matter from what distance or how clearly I see it, it will still not be a man's figure to me. And because at this distance (I can afford only the cheaper seats) I can't see that it has wrinkles and a sallow skin, but I know that's no man.

Don't think I'm saying you shouldn't use exaggeration or distortion MERCY no! Our ability to do that is one of the chief excuses for doing puppets. What I'm saying is simply,

Know What You're Distorting

And do it by intention rather than by accident or ignorance. Relative proportion is one of the things that can be seen from the rear of the auditorium, but that means not only the relative size of the various puppets, but the various features in each puppet. When you say "He has a big head," he has it in relation to the average of other similar-sized people. If it's a little bigger he may look like the Chinese God of Longevity, but if it's a LOT bigger he's got to look like a dwarf or a baby. If, on the other hand, you want him to look bigger, make his head smaller! Look at classic sculpture. Look at "high fashion" drawing. Look at Jack's Giant again, and make his head smaller; it adds tons to his weight.

Look at It

You know how Junior draws his first picture of you – something like the sketch here. You'd think anyone who'd been as close to you as junior has could see that your eyes weren't at the top of your head. And so he could if he had been "seeing," but most of us don't actually look at things. Not as the things themselves. We look at them with our emotions, our conditioned reflexes, our desires and repulsions. We look at the **idea** of a glamor girl, or a ballerina, or a foreigner, or the "other woman" and mostly we see what we expected. So with some people's puppets which all look alike - their maker hasn't seen any farther than that.

In this wonderful culture, everything we need is immediately at hand (well, NEARly everything). One thing we HAVE got is pictures of people. Look at them. See the human being. Swimmers. Golfers. Chorus girls. Track teams. Basketballers. Happily for us they hold still in pictures so we can study their relative proportions. Don't look at their names, their personalities, their activities – just look at how they're put together. Unless you are a longtime student of anatomy, you may really be surprised. Compare them. How actually does this one differ from that.

Don't Make a File

Clipping pictures of "representative types," inaugurating an elaborate filing system, and cross-indexing for future reference isn't necessary. What we're aiming at here is an enlargement of you, not your source material. The material is always available for reference – but we're working on your creativity, and your home work is to enlarge your own interior resources, out of which you create. When you think of Rodin, and his magnificent creativity, I'm sure you never think of him going to his file and pulling out the picture of the decathlon champion of umteen-forty-two. He had stuff inside him out of which he created – and you have too, or you wouldn't have enrolled in this course. This exercise in seeing is to increase your inner resources, and is one which you will continue the rest of your life, to your enrichment and the enrichment of your audiences.

You Can Draw

Most people protest, "Oh, I can't DRAW!" This "ain't necessarily so," Everyone has drawn something at one time or another, just as junior drew your picture. It's a much more natural means of expression than writing these symbols which we call words; the earliest writing WAS drawing pictures. Remember on page nineteen where the kid answered the question "How do you draw?" This exercise is to help you see.

In the next session you will have specific instruction on how to go about drawing. It's so simple I don't understand why everyone doesn't have it as his ordinary equipment. One picture IS worth a thousand words, and a good intelligible picture is so easy to make.

But you can't make a picture if you don't know what it is a picture of. SEE it. Right now, look at the human being, and (maybe for the first time) actually SEE how he is put together. I assure you, it's a pleasure.

Whether your trend is toward the factual or the fictional, whether your fun is something old or something new, something borrowed or something blue (which means "dirty" in theatre parlance) you have to have a frame of reference – a jumping off place – the thing seen in order to be the thing portrayed. Don't feel you are "wasting your time" by just getting comfortable and leafing through a copy of *Life* or *Time*. There are HUMANS there, to be seen, to be absorbed, to be comprehended. And whether you're doing people or animals or Outer Space Creatures, you must always refer back to this primary consideration: What Are People Like.

Session 4 Designing the Stringpuppet

Now, if you've been "looking" at people, intending to see them instead of your preconception of them, you have more resources than you had when you finished reading Session Three. Let's put 'em to work.

How to Draw

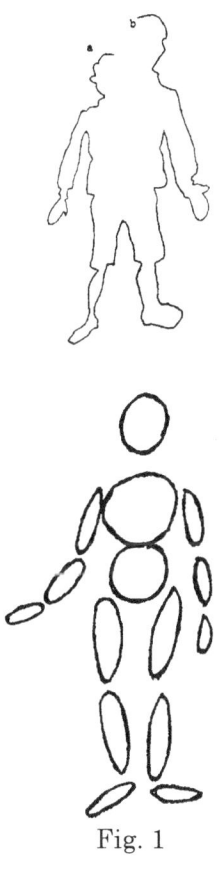

Fig. 1

That effort on the left is not how to. When you start at a and "put a line around it" until you get to b, you're likely to have some trouble with proportion. Figure 1 is a way for you to start thinking about the human figure. These are the main "chunks" of it as taught in art schools and happily they happen to coincide with the parts of a puppet. Our purpose now is to get them into the proportions characteristic of the character in your show. You need a big hunk of wrapping paper, a soft pencil, a big piece of that wonderful eraser called Art Gum, a good straight yardstick, and eventually a triangle. For this first exercise try fastening your paper on a smooth wall, where you can stand up to it. Your arm will be free to make loose, easy strokes. Have the light on your left. And remember this is fun.

When schools used to teach the "Palmer Method" of handwriting (do they still?) We were told to do this exercise to loosen up our arm muscles and get them into the act, and overcome hard little writing with our cramped fingers. That's how we want to start this drawing. Make a bunch of these circular things six or eight inches high, using your arm for the motion. Relax at it. See how easy it is. Now let's start drawing the puppet. You decide who yours is going to be. I think I'll do Jack. Establish your height – top and bottom lines – and your middle (the relative length of trunk and legs.)

So far you have in your mind, and on your notes, descriptions of Jack, but now we want to see him, physically, so as you proceed, think about Jack.

Pitching Horseshoes

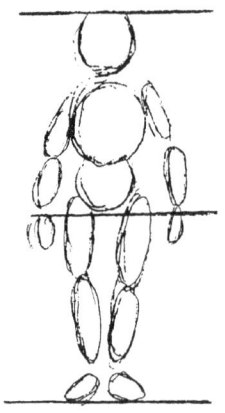

Fig. 2

Some long-ago teacher of mine said, "Throwing a line is like throwing a horseshoe. When you get a ringer you know it, and when you don't, you throw another one." Do that now with your design, thinking of what you know about Jack as you go. Make loose, free-arm ovals – of the general size and shape of Jack's head, chest, arms, legs – just throwing nice easy ovals at the general direction it feels he ought to take. When you have done, walk across the room, thinking of Jack as you "saw" him in your reverie. Now turn and look across at the "oval mock-up" you've just drawn, and immediately you will see where it matches your thought and where it doesn't. Some of the many lines you've made will be way off – one shoulder too high – hips too wide – head too large or too small – arms too long or too short. But some of the lines will be "ringers." They look like Jack. Now with your nice soft pencil, emphasize these lines. You're no longer facing a blank piece of paper and wondering where to go next – but you "have something to go on." If you get lost in the lines you have made and feel fuzzy about it, go away from it – have lunch or read the paper, but leave the drawing there on the wall. If you think of it at all while you're away, don't think about the drawing: think about Jack as you see him in your mind. THEN when you see him next, whether you go there to, or just look up suddenly and see the drawing, you'll spot his short-comings AND his rightnesses and can continue to pin them down with that soft pencil.

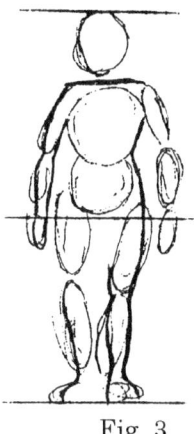

Fig. 3

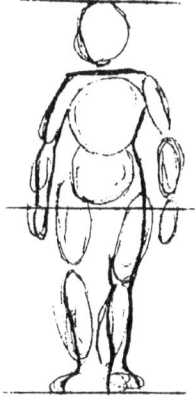

Fig. 4

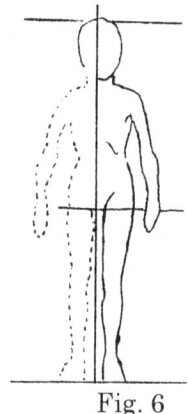

Fig. 6

Now the Art Gum. Get rid of a lot of those original lines you just threw at the paper. Keep the ones you've approved, add some more as you see them. Pretty soon you'll have the **little** rascal where you want him. When you do – don't take him down: go see a movie or an art exhibit or anything to get what you've just done out of your mind's eye. Don't look at him until tomorrow.

Now it's tomorrow, and you take a fresh look at him. What's this – you see something else that can stand a little bettering. Good: that's what the "going away from it" is for. Now if you're satisfied, draw a vertical line (accurately, using your triangle and yardstick) up through what appears to be his center, and erase one half of him. Now take the paper down, and crease it along the vertical line. Fold the erased half under, and beneath it place a sheet of carbon paper, carbon side up. (Figure 5)

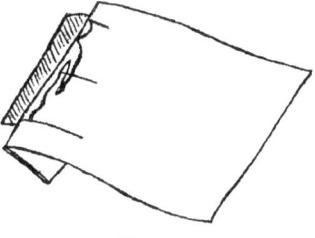

Fig. 5

What's all this for? Well, you're making a marionette, and for it to work well and dependably, it must be in balance. However good your eye is, you will have drawn differences in the two sides (you can see them in Figure 4). Now if you will take a hard pencil and trace the pencilled half still showing in Figure 5, you will make a duplicate of it underneath which, when opened, will be a drawing with both side alike.

Only - "YEEPS! What's that? Who's that fat boy? That isn't what I had in mind at all! How did it happen?" Simple: look at Figure 4. One side is bigger than the

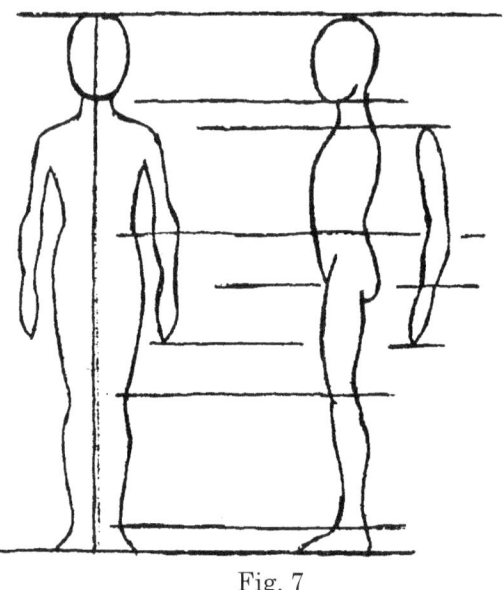

Fig. 7

other, and when we duplicate it we just get more boy. If we'd erased it and used the other side, we'd have got a skinny boy. If we'd left it as it was and made the puppet from it, he would have been lopsided. So a good thing we discovered it now. Looking at the difference between what we have and what we had in mind, slim him down again – on both sides – till he looks right – erase half, and trace him again. There now – that better?

Now we're ready for the side view. Run horizontal lines (being sure they are accurately at right angles to the vertical one!) across the paper from chin, shoulder, hip (which is approximately elbow), knee, crotch (which is slightly higher than bottom of buttock), and ankle. Your own looking at all those photos has told you much about what the side of the figure looks like. An anatomy chart can tell you more. An arrangement of mirrors will enable you to look at you.

Here note a thing which is usually ignored: when a person stands erect, his chin is directly over the balls of his feet. Don't require of your puppet that he try to stand with his heels ahead of his nose.

For simplicity, I like to draw the arm in the side view where I have indicated it: it makes a less complex drawing and it's simpler to trace later when I make a template for the actual puppet.

So far I have mentioned nothing about Jack's clothes. The reason is twofold: first, the person is more important than his wardrobe, and human emotions are the same in any sartorial period. I want to get you in the habit of building your characters from the inside outward from your original dreaming of them. Their bodies are built by you solely to be able to move with that meaning, and their clothes are only something to carry it further. Second, we are very fortunate with stringpuppets in that when they are made, we have something to make clothes for. There's a body there to drape. This is not true of handpuppets, as we shall see when we get to them.

A stringpuppet must move easily and predictably between the pull of the string and the pull of gravity. He must have his physical appearance as well as his characteristic movement built into his body before he gets his clothes, and his clothes must not hamper the movement of his body. If, for instance, we used "stock figures" – all of them alike – and then tried to "dress" their character differences into them, it would be almost impossible to keep the padded clothing from impeding the free movement and so defeating the character. All the detailed "dreaming" we did in the beginning pays off all down the line.

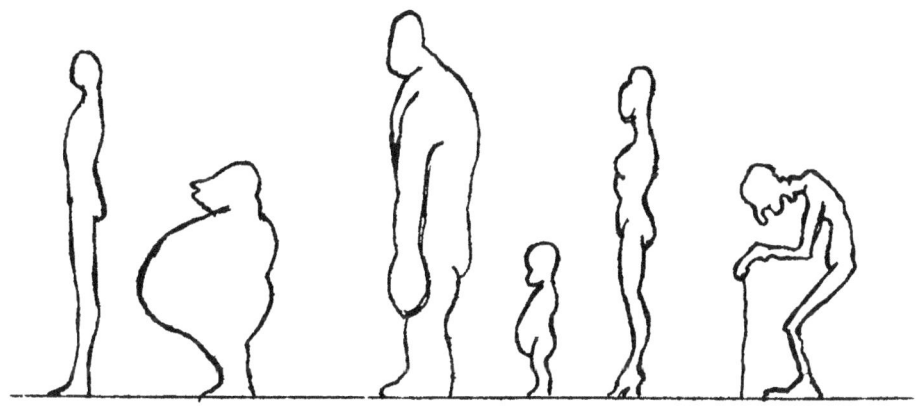

Fig. 8

Obviously such variations in figure as the above need to be foreseen and provided for in the original planning and subsequent construction, rather than being tacked on and padded out as an afterthought. Yet, as can be seen, all of them are variations of the same human structural plan which is the taking-off place for any flight of fancy we may care to indulge. So consider your time well spent whenever you use it to be more familiar with anatomical construction and movement. What was good enough study for DaVinci can't hurt us.

As you become a better actor-puppeteer you will become a better designer, for if you don't know what the feeling-person is like, you can hardly expect to portray him with your mind, your voice, or your hands.

A Real Good Tip

Take a tip from the way Disney does it. When the Disney studios are creating a new character, various members of the personnel assign themselves roles, and proceed to act them out – physically, vocally, emotionally. Walt himself is a great and enthusiastic performer of such creative activity according to report, and to walk into a story conference and find this man being a duck and that one a frog and the other a whinnying horse would surely relieve you of any inhibitions YOU might have about appearing ludicrous in any face other than the one you customarily show to your associates. If the first thought of doing this embarrasses you – lock yourself in your room to do your pretending in private. Go through some of the action of the character. Make your room into a stage arrangement comparable to your puppet stage, and roar, squeak, quack, stomp, mince, or whatever seems to you proper for the character in the situation. As you do it, notice what your body is doing – swelling chest, aching gut, clenching fist, defending arms, clutching hands, grimacing face. All of us have similar emotions, and you can use yours to express the Invading Martian or the Love Life of the Amoeba.

Bonus

I cannot refrain here from pointing out to you that the method of loosely throwing ovals at the paper is the best "method" of "drawing" I've ever been taught (I'll never forget how surprised and released I was when my teacher told me every line I set down didn't have to be considered a success or a failure) and that the more you do it, the better, easier, and happier your puppet designs will come out – but in addition, you can have a whee of a time just for yourself – just for FUN! Whether you become a "Great Artist" (whatever that is) or not, you can increase your own appreciation and delight by practising it, and delight a lot of other people as well. Do take a poke at it – just for fun!

There you are: get yourself a flock of wrapping paper, (if you don't know – there's some you can draw on easily, and some that's too slick) soft pencil, hard pencil, Art Gum, and something to fasten the paper to the wall ("masking tape" is wonderful!), a yardstick, a triangle, carbon paper and you're "in business." Lay out all the puppets in your proposed show. Approach it easily, confidently. But don't - DON'T settle for less than you had in mind, because you don't have to.

Session 5 Designing the Handpuppet

Now let's look at handpuppets. I confess that for many years I was a string man, and all the enthusiastic things the handpuppet people said sounded to me far fetched, unreasonable, and several other things like that. But for the past several years the only show I have had is a handpuppet show, and I love the little rascals dearly. If you're a string enthusiast, I urge you to just consider handpuppets for a while – just as an open inquiry. Might be you can enlarge yourself.

Please get and read "Fist Puppets" a book by Bessie Ficklen. Years ago, in the very depth of my string mania, I picked it up and couldn't stop reading it. You can learn stuff from it.

While there are practically no limitations on the size and shape of stringpuppets, there are some reasonably definite ones on handpuppets. In the first place, how big is your hand? Put a piece of paper up on the wall again, draw a horizontal line near the bottom to indicate the stage floor level, and prepare to draw the outline of your own hand above it.

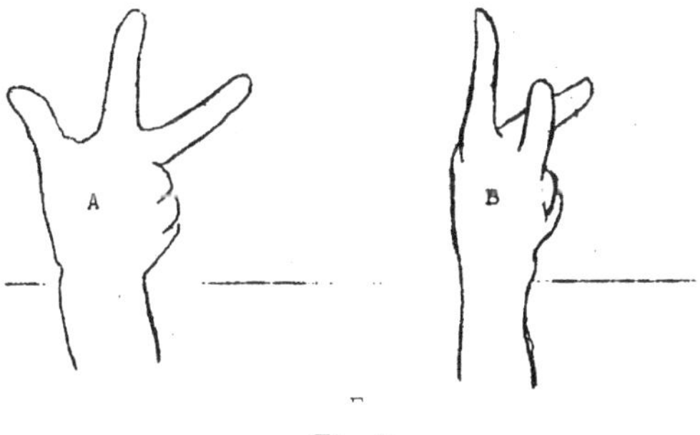

Fig. 9

First let us consider how one manipulates a handpuppet. Usually the index finger goes into the neck, the thumb in one hand, and the middle finger (next to the index) into the other hand. But some people prefer using the "pinkie" or little finger for the other hand. I use the middle finger, but it is entirely a matter of which feels better

to you. In these drawings, I'll use the middle finger.
Put your own hand up against the paper, in the position in which you will manipulate, and draw a line around it. It will look something like A. Turn your hand sideways, and draw a line around it. A & B are now your taking-off points. These are the conditions with which you have to work, and as you will agree from your study of the human anatomy, this doesn't really look too much like a man. But it will before we get through.

Where Do We Go From Here?

Go back to where you had finished your dreaming about the character in your play, complete with notes, and start thinking about designing as instructed for the marionette. ALWAYS keep before you the picture-feeling about the character. Now we have

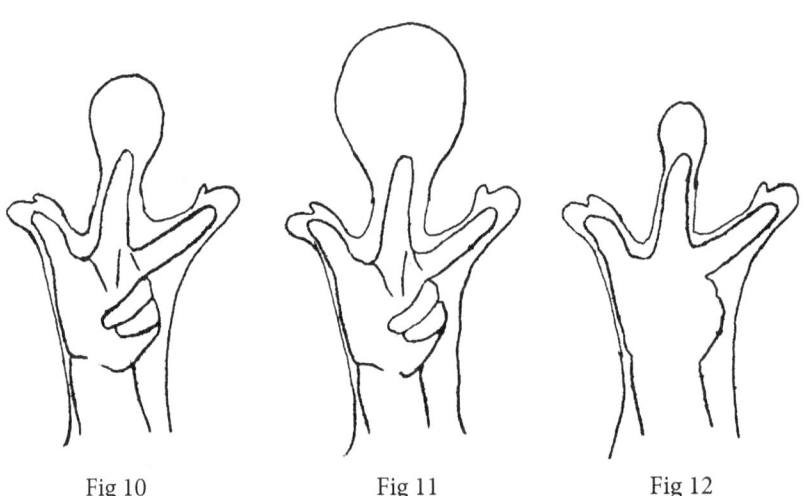

Fig 10   Fig 11   Fig 12

to do something about accommodating your dream-up to the hand which is inside it. First of all, let us consider the size of the head which will best meet the requirements imposed by the size of your hand.

Figure 10 might be an acceptable size for a head, considering we have such a narrow span for the arms. Handpuppets' arms are short – no two ways about it. Suppose we make the head bigger, as in Figure 11. Remembering relative proportion as described in Session Three, we know that a bigger head makes a smaller body. Suppose we make the head smaller, as in Figure 12? Here they all are on one page: take your pick. It's your puppet, and you have the picture in your mind of what he should look like.

Fig 13

If you have the facts of these relative effects in your mind, then you can do what you **intend** – rather than just settling for what "happens." (I once knew a puppeteer who started out to make a fish and wound up with a bird – so he just changed the script to accommodate it, and went about taking bows for the clever bird he'd made! Personally, I'm too egotistical for that: I want to take bows on what I've done. Art – I maintain – is not accidental.)

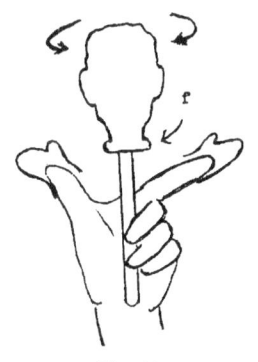

Fig 13

Attempts have been made to overcome the short-arm distortion by putting the hands on cuffs (cardboard, buckram which, to me, emphasizes their inability to put their arms down at their sides, and the fact that their "elbows" aren't in the right places. Also it cuts down the efficiency with which handpuppets do that wonderful thing – pick things up! Except in cases where the design of your puppet **demands** long arms, try some other way around the difficulty. In the session on costume we'll talk about it some more.

While still in the primary designing stage, where the manner of manipulation determines the method of procedure, here's a seldom used but at times most effective way of manipulating a handpuppet. Instead of the finger going up into the head, a permanent dowel comes down out of

- 35 -

it, and is held and rotated against the palm by the second and third fingers. The flange `f on the bottom of the neck allows it to be retained in the top of the costume, yet free to rotate, independently of the body. In the former style of puppet, the nod for "yes" can be as bold or as delicate as you please, without much involving the rest of the body, whereas a "no" gesture requires the entire body to turn with the head. With the control shown in Figure 14, the circumstance is exactly reversed: the "yes" requires more participation of the body, but the "no" is practically like yours. And there are times when the ability of a puppet to simply turn his head and look is most effective.

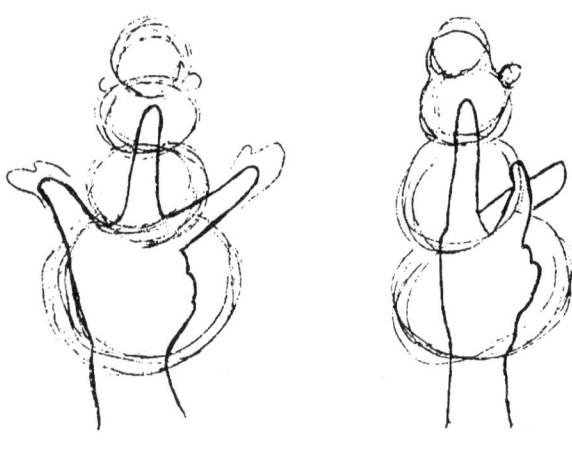

Fig. 15

Just for fun, fasten a 3/8" dowel (or a big fat pencil) in any puppet head you have around, and try this out. It might be the very solution to a manipulation problem for you. And of course it allows you to use your thumb and index finger in manipulating the hands, which some folk find much better.

Now we can return to our designing. Whatever way you have chosen to manipulate, you now have the front and side profiles of your hand drawn on your paper. Keeping your character ever in mind, proceed as with the designing of the stringpuppet, tossing easy loose ovals at the paper. The difference here is that now you must take into account the covering of your hand. And because there is really a lot of very strenuous activity goes on under there, your puppet can't be so small that it binds your hand. (I have sometimes had to hire very small puppeteers with little teeny hands, to get a small enough puppet into the show!)

When we did this "layout" for the stringpuppet, we were starting what amounts to a blueprint for a subsequent "machine". Here we do not have the same goal of precision, but are "firming up" in our minds the actual physical body of the character, and the relative sizes of his parts. By doing it now, and then making the puppet to those sizes, we save the frustration that comes with spending days on a detail and then discovering when we go to apply it that it's so big or so little as to be useless and all that time and effort is wasted. I've done it.

To Leg or Not to Leg

That is the question, as regards handpuppets. Offhand, I would say not but then at least half my handpuppets have them. Originally it was because they had to climb a tree and sit on a limb, and that's pretty hard to do if you haven't any legs to hang over. Since then, the legs are very handy when the puppet wants to sit down on the playboard and talk to the audience, or just take his ease. George Latshaw did the most wonderful things once with a puppet's legs: sat him in a chair, and with the puppet's hands, crossed his legs, or threw one up over the chair arm, or sat sidewise with both legs over the arm. And if you like to look at precedent, traditional of Mr. Punch has legs, and no one else in the cast has! When you can afford one person to one puppet, you can make an individual stage (6" square) of plywood, fastened to a stick, and by placing it up under the handpuppet's feet and twisting it right and left as he progresses, make him walk with his legs. If his feet slip on the little stage, put fine sandpaper on it. By moving his body in rhythm with his feet, it's quiet effective.

Fig. 16

So whether you have legs on your handpuppet or not depends entirely on how you feel about it. You see, this IS a creative endeavor, and you are the creator. That's what make its so much fun.

While we are on the subject of creation, let's pause for a moment and look at it. If there is one thing that distinguished us from the rest of the animal kingdom, it is this beautiful fact that we can dream up things. When we are little, most of us are not encouraged in the development of this magnificent faculty – the emphasis being on a great social necessity; conformity – so we won't get our teeth bashed in. But in the process, our ability to create new forms, new attitudes, new conceptions is largely ignored. Happily for us, the ability is always there – in you – ready to be used. Which is why when you started this course, you were asked to just sit back the ENJOY you vision.

Now, as you have already taken some tentative pokes at the visual shape of your characters, both mentally and physically (with the loose easy ovals on paper), take a little time out to flex your creative muscles. Remember, this isn't what we commonly call "work" – this is CREATION! And you remember how they say The Lord did it – He didn't "work" at it – He simply said, "Be thou," and it was! So with you: look again at each of your characters. How can they be a little MORE of themselves? A little more sympathetic, a little more brutal, a little dopier, a little more heroic. You have the basic ingredient of a play – this exercise is for underscoring, for "beefing up" the image. Go see an animated cartoon (not the antiques that fill in the endless hours on TV most of the time, but some a LITTLE more recent) and see how **bad the bad guy** is, and how sweet the sweet young maiden. Don't misunderstand: you are not to "lift" them off the screen or the comic book and put them on your stage! There has been quite enough of that (How many times have we seen the ostrich ballerina from Disney's *Fantasia?)* but look at them with an eye for WHY they made those shoulders extra large, those teeth extra long, those glances extra simpering. The whole of this craft of expression is laid out in panorama before you – waiting only for you to SEE it, and make it yours.

When you've done this, and can say, "Oh yes – THAT'S what that was for," look again at your drawings in that light, and see where you can "punch it up." Now is the time to do it, before you start molding the material of the actual puppet – while it's still in the plastic state of your mind's eye. NOW you can make his head a little pointeder, his hands a little bigger, his paunch a little fatter or leaner – to the better expression of your idea, and with no investment of energy. Who every saw an easier instruction?

Ssession 6 **Developing the Voice**

Now we will work on voice. As I sit here to write this I'm grinning with delight because what you are about to learn is so important to you – so valuable, not only to your show but to your entire social being, that if you don't use anything else in the Course but this, you will have got more than your money's worth.

You Are an Actor

There are people in the profession of puppetry who wouldn't know a screw-eye from actors. There are people in this profession who make the most delicious puppets – whose shows are an unconscionable bore! This is too too bad, not only for the audience but also for those of us who want audiences for our endeavors. For when they have displayed their ineptitude at the cost of the customer's time and money and boredom, you and I can't get in there to do a show for at least another generation. Some of the highest and mightiest of our august predecessors have done this, provoking the deathdealing remark, "No thanks – I've seen a puppet show."

Then what is it that makes the difference? It's YOU, and your understanding of the craft, and your practice of it. And the most immediate and important tool in this craft is your appreciation of what acting is, and how to do it.

So we can't study "voice" in this connection without also studying acting. Then let's do it!

Actors don't "live" their parts. They act them. If they "were" the character in fact, we'd get nobody to do *Hamlet* for instance, for everyone would have to kill everyone, and pretty soon there wouldn't be any actors. No no! You aren't the character – you just act like him. How? This way:

They say of an actor, "He was so natural in the part." He was not. He was artificial. (Webster: artificial. Opposed to natural; made or contrived by art.) And contrived by intention – by knowing how, and proceeding toward the effect. He seemed natural because of his art.

Don't let the word "art" throw you. Webster says: "Art: Skill in performance, acquired by experience and observation." Simple as opening a can of peas.

He seemed natural because:

      a) He knew how the character felt.
      b) He knew how to speak.
      c) He knew how to behave onstage.

Well, what have we been talking about all this while? And how can you get these skills? "Know-how" and practice. These instructions are "know-how." Practice is up to you. The people you admire in this profession practice these things which are now available to you. And if you will apply yourself to them, you too will have the "skill in performance" that Webster designates as art.

We started out this Course by having you "dream up" the situation. So by now you know "who does what to whom and who has to pay for it." Unlike an actor in a play who acts and is acted upon and that's it, you are ALL the characters (as playwright) and must know how they all feel. But take it apart: take each character separately and be him. Remember, each character in the situation does what he thinks is best for him at that time.

Nothing you have dreamed up is beyond your comprehension and you are able to evoke in yourself his feelings. It's easy. Recall a time in your own life when you were in a spot such as he is in. Now you know how he feels. You can evoke the same feeling. When Mamma scolded Jack for being such a fool as to trade a good cow for a handful of beans, you know what that felt like. I certainly do. When the Housekeeper felt guilty about double-crossing the Giant by hiding Jack? When the Giant felt outraged at being robbed. You've felt all there is – you have only to re-evoke it. This is what an actor does. There's nothing mysterious about it. And the way YOU re-act is what gives authenticity to your portrayal! That's what makes the character seem "natural."

How to Speak

Isn't it strange that there should be a section like this? "How to speak" indeed! I've been speaking all my life! Yet, as a long-time teacher of speech, it is very interesting that most of my pupils, when told to listen to their voices, look at me in blank astonishment. The fact is that we do not hear – just as in the early sessions I pointed out that we do not see! You know yourself that if Minnie knew how she sounded on the telephone, she'd do something about it! But, unless we've studied voice, it usually applies to us, too! So, as with our imagining, and our designing of puppets, let's see what we can do with our voices – consciously.

Have you access to a tape recorder? Go to it and talk into it – at some length – then play it back and listen to your voice. Not to the words, but to the sounds you made. If you haven't ever done this, you'll be surprised. One reason is that when we ordinarily hear ourselves talk, we hear it from inside our heads, as well as outside, and that makes a difference. The audience, of course, has to hear us from outside, and as we are aiming at it, we should know what it is the audience is hearing. As a puppeteer, speaking is at least half your equipment, so let's see what the machinery of speech is and how you can manipulate it by intention.

How It Works

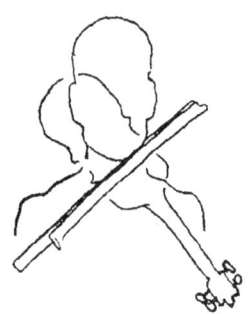

Your voice works like a fiddle, only better. Your breath can be compared to a fiddlebow, which vibrates your vocal cords comparable to the strings – which "re-sound" in your face bones the fiddle body. This is a most apt illustration which I wish you to keep in mind. Hum, lightly touching your front teeth together. Feel them vibrate? Take hold of the bridge of your nose, and hum loudly. Feel it vibrate? That's where your voice is, in your mouth and sinuses – not in your throat. You can hum high and low by just wishing to, without conscious muscular effort. That's automatic. Forget your throat.

How Do You Make Words?

Hum, opening your mouth a little so the sound comes through it. Sounds like "huh," doesn't it? A fiddle can do that much. But you make words by shaping that basic "huh" into vowels and pinching them off into consonants with your tongue and lips.

VOWELS are sounds you make with your mouth open (e, a, ah, o, u.)

CONSONANTS are sounds you make by shutting off or interfering with the vowels. (m, p, k, etc.)

Vowels can be loud. Yell "Hay!" and you'll be heard a block away.

Consonants can't be loud. Try to yell "Psst!"

The wider you open your mouth, the better your vowels can be heard.

Some vowels can be heard better, and said more easily than others.

Practice!

Practice saying these strong, easy vowel sounds (before a mirror, to see that you open your mouth) so you'll always be heard:

Hold the tip of your tongue firmly down behind your lower front teeth.

Say "Meee" and think of being pleased.

Say "May" and smile.

Say "Mah" so relaxed you'll probably yawn.

Say "Mo" thinking of a round hole. Be sure to shape your lips into one.

Say "Mooo" like a cow. Shove that round hole of your lips forward like a tunnel to do this.

Where was the tip of your tongue during that? That's right: keep it firmly down behind your lower front teeth on vowels.

Do It!

Set a special time each day – maybe when you brush your teeth (you're in front of the mirror then) – to say or sing these vowels, making each distinct from the other. Your speech rides on them, and if they're weak, piddlin' little sounds, you haven't GOT a voice.

And remember – when you practice these vowels:

Your Voice is Upstairs!

Not in your throat. If you throat gets tired while you're doing it, you're doing it wrong. THINK of it happening in your head, in your ears, in your mind.

Sing these "me-may-mah-mo-moo" sounds, increasing the volume of sound, and the length of time you sing each one. That vibration you felt before is your voice, and what you are doing with this exercise is increasing the vibration. This increased vibration is what will fill an auditorium without the aid of a loudspeaker system, and from behind the drapes of your proscenium.

Unfortunately, you can be heard without being understood. Hence the emphasis on these five sounds which are the most resonant and the easiest to say, and the practice on making each one distinct and different from the others. Don't start out with an "A" and wind up with an "E" (as in "plaaaaaeeeee" for "play"). Make the "A" an "A" all the way.

Consonants are partitions between vowels that make them into understandable words. Make them distinct. Particularly the ones on the ends of words. Use them, and you can be heard all over the theatre in a whisper, and understood. Ignore them, and you may bellow your head off without making sense.

To "act" with your voice, you must get lots of air into you quickly, and control how it comes out in your voice. Don't swell up your chest like Superman. That's good for health, bad for speech. Let your chest alone.

Breathe with Your Belly

Suck in a deep bellyful of air, making your belly stick out. Now slowly slowly let the air out. Slower than that. Feel your belly muscles pulling back into shape? Those muscles control your breath. They need exercise. Do this:

Take air in deep and **quick;** let it out slow. Do this every time you think of it.

Take a quick bellyful of air; now say the alphabet, or the Lord's Prayer, or your favorite poem – all of it – on that one breath. You can't say it all? Then practice it often every day.

Take another breath. Say "Hah!" sharply. Bark it! Punch out a row of "Ha ha ha ha!" barks. Alternate doing this with saying the long passage on one breath. Every day. You are controlling your breath.

And what's all this for? It is to enable you to always have a sufficient amount of air, the use of which you control. I am sure that at some time or other you have run out of breath before you finished the sentence, and the resultant little squeak you made at the end could hardly be called voice or speech. Do these breathing exercises every day and you'll develop a new kind of control of your speech machinery. By taking in a bellyful of air before you begin a speech, you'll have plenty of it to work with, to make good vibrant sounds throughout the length of the speech, and with plenty of punch to wind up on.

Now you have conscious control of the machinery of making sound; what are you going to sound like?

Just as you trained yourself to see anatomy, you must now

Train Yourself to Listen

Consciously **hear** voices. Describe to yourself how one voice differs from another. Your mate, your child, your parent. Your favourite movie actor. Contrast the voices of the leading performers in a TV show. Listen to a particular voice: now imitate it. Listen to yourself say a part of whatever quotation you've been practising breath control with. Remember how you sounded. Now say that part again, **exactly** as you said it before.

Did you hit it? Say it in a different way; remember it; repeat it. Did you do it? Think of something else for five minutes. Now recall how you said it, and say it again, that way. You hit it? Good. You are now controlling your speech.

Take Every Opportunity to Sing

If you consider yourself one of the people who "can't sing," don't reject the above instruction. You are not trying out for the Met. You are training yourself in voice production. Start each phrase with a bellyful of air, and sing those five vowels. Make up your own tune, or sing them to some tune you know. What you are after is the ability to make those resonant vowels distinct from each other, whenever you think of them, and of any duration and volume. Tongue tip pressed against roots of lower front teeth – mouth as wide open as possible! Repeat:

Mouth as Wide Open as Possible!

By now you have begun increasing your vocal ability. There are some things we cannot achieve, due to the physical construction we have. (I, for instance, can't do a believable natural woman's voice. However, many women do completely satisfactory men's voices.)

Now you can graduate in your "listening exercises" to hearing and reproducing the "character" caricature noises such as are employed by Disney. Many character voices used by actors for TV commercials (voices of soap bubbles, germs, grime, dogs talking, and such) can give you opportunities for testing your mimicry. When you hit on one you can use, do it repeatedly until you have become thoroughly at ease with it. REMEMBER: the character of the voice is created in the mouth and sinuses – NOT IN THE THROAT! Try to do it in your throat and you'll get mighty tired. **Think** it upstairs. You'll be astounded at what variations in pitch, volume, and quality you can achieve by first hearing it clearly in your mind, and then **thinking** it into action.

What you have read so far indicates very necessary work for you to do to develop your natural equipment, and it is to be done every day. We shall leave the subject at this point in our instruction, to give you the opportunity to work on this much, while continuing with other phases of puppetry. When we return to its application to your show, you should have these exercises in hearing, breathing, and producing vibrant, intentional sounds so well mastered that you do them without thinking about them.

Session 7 Crafting the Stringpuppet (Part I)

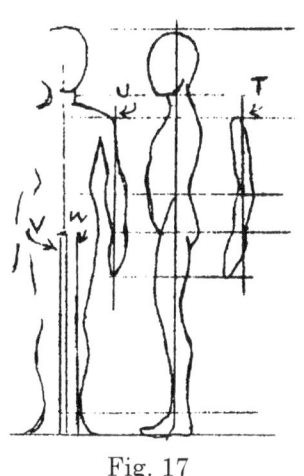

Fig. 17

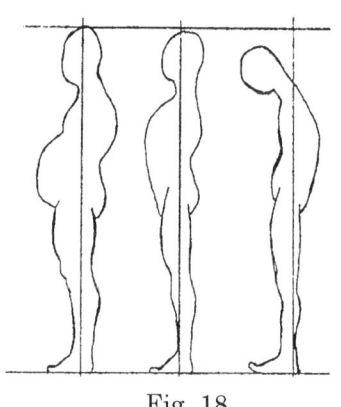

Fig. 18

Now while you are working on your voice, let's take up where we left off in Session Four. Presumably you made drawings for all your cast of characters for this play at that time, and haven't looked at them much while you were studying the intervening sessions. This is all to the good, for when we make something we get our eyes and our ears so full of it that for a while we don't really see it as it is. Now, however, you can take a fresh look at your drawings. Does it look as good to you as it did before? Perhaps it would benefit from a little more here, a little less there? Now is the time to make the last minute changes, for now we're going to freeze it into a machine.

Now "clean up" all the lines; erase all those that aren't exactly what you want. End with a clean line drawing like Figure 17. Now drop a vertical line exactly at right angles to the horizontal ones – down what appears to be the middle of the bulk of the side view S. You have to do this with your eye. This is an irregular piece of wood, and the line goes where you'll have half the weight of the wood on either side. Guess at it. You already have the front view split up this way. What we are after here is a means of Counterbalancing. In a stringpuppet it means that when he is cut apart and jointed and then supported by strings, whenever you release the pull in one direction or another, it will return him to the characteristic stance you planned for him in the beginning. This has been done with lead weights, but as we can make it happen by the way we place the joints, why bother with lead. In Figure 18 we have three types of figure. In each of them, the line of balance does just that: balances the front half of his bulk against the back half. His shoulder strings, waist joint, and hip joints will all be on this line.

This line serves another purpose, along with T, U, and W, on Figure 17: they are traced onto the templates when we make them. Still on Figure 17, look at the two parallel vertical lines marked V. Originally there was one line separating his legs. Now you make two – each an 1/8" away from center – so now the inside lines of his legs are 1/4" apart. This space is very necessary, and sometimes must be even greater, for when you put pants on him, there must be room for the cloth – or the friction will be so great he shan't be able to walk.

Templates

This nice word merely means a pattern from which you are going to cut the wood to make the puppet. Any light weight cardboard or very heavy paper will do (I like the laundry's shirt-boards, or old suit boxes). What we want now is six cardboard templates; front and side of trunk, one arm, and one leg. Notice how I have rounded off the top of the trunk A. Flattened the inside of the arm at the shoulder B. Cut off the bottom of the trunk C & E, and the front and back faces of the top of the thigh D. The juncture of the trunk and thigh are the center of the body, or crotch. The right angle C–D is sufficient to allow him to walk or sit. If he is to kneel, a much wider angle must be provided.

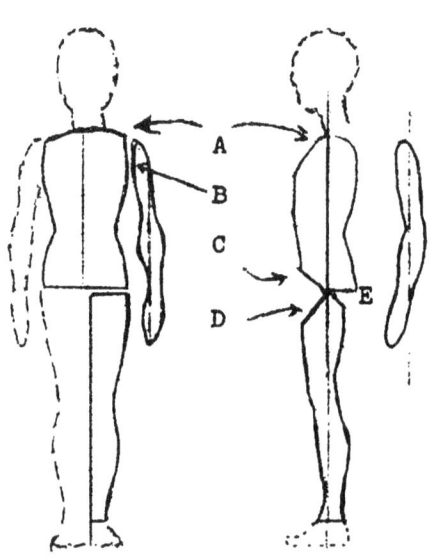

Fig. 19

With carbon paper, trace these six outlines on cardboard, and on each be sure to include the vertical lines S, T, U

- 50 -

and the one in the center of the front view of the trunk. If you have made the inside of the leg perfectly straight, that will do for the vertical line on this view.

Carefully cut out the six cardboard templates.

Now about wood. California sugar pine is my favorite. It's a soft wood with practically no grain, easy to carve, but with enough body to endure. Bass wood is good, but a little harder to come by in lots of areas. What you want is wood with the above qualities, and if your local lumber yard doesn't have it, go to a Pattern Works. This is a wonderful place where skilled carvers make wood models of all those things you get that are cast in plastic and metal. They have beautiful carvable wood, and they'll let you buy what you need for your puppet.

To know how much wood you need: measure the length and width of the templates of the front and side views of the trunks and add a half inch to each dimension. This is the minimum. Do the same with the templates of the arm and leg. But remember you need two of each. That's all, except that when you get it from the man, ask him for a couple of scraps big enough for the feet; they always have a marvellous scrap bin!

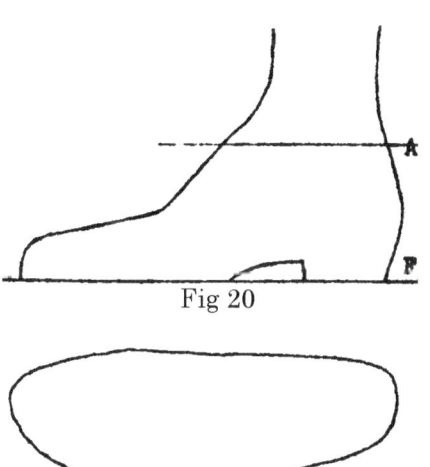

Fig 20

Fig 21

Unless you have a shop of your own, give your dimensions to the lumber man or pattern worker and have him cut the wood you buy to size. On his power saw he can do it in a minute or two, and it will be "squared up" which is vital to the next process.

We still have the feet to arrange for. Your drawing indicates the length of them, and the distance from the floor F to the ankle A. This is the thickness of the wood you need. Now look at the bottom of one of your shoes, or bedroom slippers. On a piece of cardboard indicate the length of the drawn foot, and draw the shape of your shoe (Figure 21) This is the only template you will need for the feet, and this is the procedure whether your puppet is barefoot or wears shoes.

A word here of encouragement: it is likely that some of you reading this find complexities that are bewildering. Let me assure you that these arise solely out of unfamiliarity. The phrase, "Familiarity breeds contempt" does not mean contempt for the thing which is familiar, but contempt for what at first acquaintance was insurmountable complexity. The process to which you are being exposed may seem full of intricacies, but follow it through on one **puppet** and you will find them the simplest and most direct way to easy achievement of the expression of your intention. To me, at this point, they are as easy and natural as shaving, or making toast: I do them without thinking, and they turn out predictably well. Once you use them, they will for you, too, and that includes the exercises in seeing, and hearing, and the production of speech. Just read carefully, and proceed with confidence and enthusiasm.

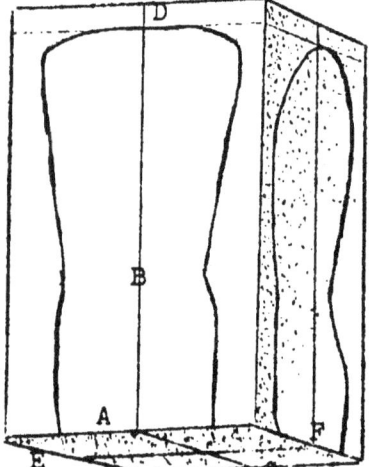

Fig. 22

On the "squared up" block of wood which you have procured for the trunk, lay the front template with its bottom on the bottom of the block A. Make sure that the center line on the template B is parallel to the edge of the block C. Carefully draw a line around the template. Mark on the block where the line B touches it at A and D.

Do the same thing with the template of the side view, making the same kind of mark at the top and bottom of the center line. Now on the bottom of the block run a line from A to G, and from F to E, accurately parallel to the edges of the block. (This is for future use.)

Do the same with the templates of the arm and leg on the blocks you have provided for them. Caution! You have made a template for the front of a left arm. You use it for the right arm by turning it over. Ditto the leg. But be careful in making your tracings of the templates: it's frustrating to wind up with two left legs!

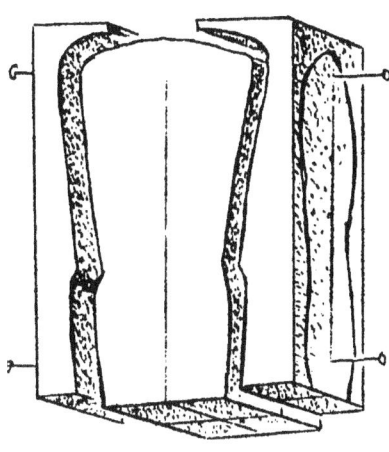

Fig. 23

Now you have the wood all marked out for a trunk, two arms, and two legs. Take the two pieces of wood you have for the feet (being sure the thickness is precisely that of A to F (as in Figure 20) on YOUR drawing) and trace around the template for the soles of two feet. Whee! We're ready to go. Where? To a bandsaw! No sense in living in the much vaunted "modern age" if we don't take advantage of its modernity. Do you have a bandsaw? Good. If not – does your friend have one? Good. If not, the Pattern Works where you got the wood has one, and probably can be available for the job. In big cities, there are "Make-It-Yourself" workshops where you can avail yourself of power tools at a small fee. If you can arrange it at all, the very best thing is to use the saw yourself; other people just don't realize how important precision is on that one little curve you worked so hard to design!

This bandsaw thing is no "big deal" to be afraid of Works practically like a sewing machine. Couple of practice runs and you'll be an expert. A small saw blade (one eighth inch) will allow you to make smaller curves than a big one, of course, and aside from that, all you have to do is keep your fingers out of it. So now you cut out the front profile. Simple. You'll wind up with three pieces (Figure 23). You have to saw out the side view too, so take those two pieces you sawed off, and nail them back on – with thin brads or wire nails – turn the block over, and saw out the side view. It's pie! NOW you can throw away the scraps.

Do the same thing with the arms and legs, and you're back to the feet again. Only one cut on these – just the soles. The rest you whittle.

Now what have you got? Actually you have in three dimensions the figure you drew on paper, and there's almost nothing you can do from here on out that will make it depart from your beautiful conception. That's why we've been so precise all this time!

Now You Carve

At this point I'd be a little timorous about you if you weren't my pupil but as you are, you already have the background for what follows: you have SEEN this creature! Someone once said about sculpture: "You just take a block of wood, and throw away what you don't want." That's mighty good, for that's just what you're going to do. You have in your hand these various parts, each of them being in wood what your drawing was when it had all those original ovals on it: you have a place to work FROM! Each piece of wood has two profiles of what you intended. If you did no more than round off the sharp edges, you'd come up with an approximation of your intention. You can't lose!

If you have carved before – fine. If not, let's "at it." Get a great big pocket knife, a pocket-sized Carborundum stone, and a little can of oil. Most hardware stores have free pamphlets on how to sharpen tools. If your store should not have, ask the man, or have him direct you to the man, who can tell you how to keep a good sharp edge on your knife.

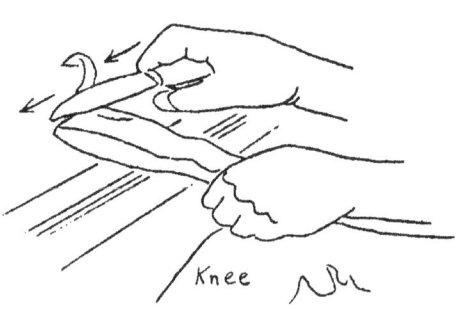
Fig. 24

I have all the tools that ever were invented for working wood – but in my hip pocket I have a Boy Scout knife, with which I would undertake to make the most elaborate puppet conceivable.

If you have carving tools with which you are familiar, by all means use them. But if not, start with this.

Reason I said a "great big pocket knife" is because if you're a stranger here, this is going to exercise a lot of new muscles, and you need a big handle to make your work easier.

"Whittle From Ya Never Cut Ya"

That's what my Grandma used to say. Sit at a worktable that won't jiggle. Take a leg firmly in one hand, and lay one end of it on the edge of the firm table. Now the word "whittle" doesn't really apply here: it's sort of carefree, whereas what you're doing is careful. In attacking your wood, don't "saw," and don't try to "push" your way through. SLICE! Not a big slice – just a little one. Take it easy – little at a time – slice slice slice – then stop and look at it. When you move to another area, you may find that your knife bites in deeper than you intended, and if that direction were pursued, it might have a tendency to split! So turn the piece around, and slice at it from the opposite direction. The knife slices, the table edge gives the needed resistance, your holding hand gives firmness, and you might even tuck your knee up under your holding hand to give it support.

All these are tools – the sawed leg, the knife, the table, your hands – but what's going on here is you seeing a form and making it happen. Stop and look at it regularly. You don't quite know if it's right or not? Then look at your own leg. Where are the bones, the fullnesses and the flatnesses? Be familiar with anatomy in your own consciousness, and you'll see immediately what is needed for the thing you're carving. Your initial exercises in "seeing" are paying off – for no one can put it down on paper so you can merely transfer it to your puppet: you are a creator – and this thing can only be created your way! You're UNIQUE! And so is the thing you're creating. The only important thing is that it must be created the way YOU see it – or it's nothing.

OOPS! What happened? Aw – you pushed a little too hard and it split off! Why that's all right; it happens to the best of woodcarver. A little of Mister Dupont's DUCO Household Cement (happily available everywhere!) will stick it tightly together, and then you just carve right over it.

If this is your first try at carving, you may feel it is a trifle less excellent than the best carving you've seen, but be of good cheer: it's amazing how quickly you'll get the knack. It's a natural knack. Meantime –

        REMEMBER WHAT GRANDMA SAID

Session 8 Crafting the Stringpuppet (Part II)

Your carving material has been limited to seven pieces (trunk, two arms, two legs, two feet) so they'll all match, rather than carving an upper arm, a lower arm, a hand, a thigh, a shin, a foot, et cetera. Carving them in toto makes them match, and later you can cut them apart. Beside that, they're too small to hold and carve individually.

Preserve the "line of balance" on the trunk. I use my triangle (because it's flexible) to draw the line (Fig. 22) from A to D, and F upwards (forgot to put a letter on the top there!) and whatever else I slice off, I leave the pencilled line (or if I inadvertently slice part of it of, I put it right back) for it is very important when I get to Jointing.

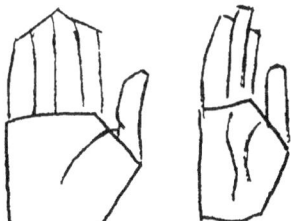

Fig. 25

How are you doing on your carved hands. Little problem? Look at your own hands. SEE them! Helps to see a pentagon as the base from which the thumb and fingers spring. This is another phase of the principle of "something to take off from."

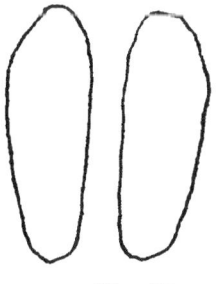

Fig. 26

Let's look at feet. Here these two pieces of wood shaped like the bottom of your shoe. Assuming you have carved the legs, put these two feet down on your work table about 1/4" apart, with their inside profiles parallel. Now stand the legs on the feet, with the top edges of the legs in line. Holding them in place, make a mark 'A' on the front of the ankle and the top of the foot. Make a similar mark on the back. Now run a line around the ankle (on the foot piece, of course) at B. Here you have the indication of

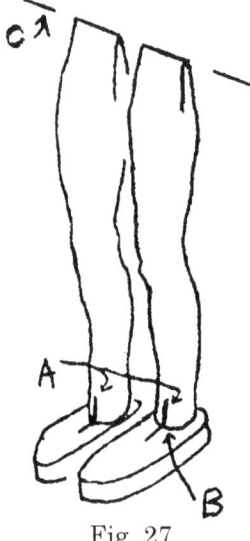

Fig. 27

where you are to start carving down and away into the foot shape. How do you do that? Why, you have a model waiting for you: your shoe! LOOK at it. Absorb it. Copy it in wood! I love carving shoes – they always come out so well.

But WAIT! Stringpuppets have a tough enough time trying to walk under the best of circumstances, so let's give 'em a break. Instead of the sole and heel being flat on the stage, give them a rocker to walk on. Yeah – like a rocking chair! Round off the heel – round up the toe! It's wonderful how much this helps! And don't worry about the audience noticing it – I've been doing it for years and nobody ever saw it – but my puppets personally thank me for it.

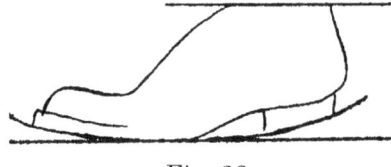

Fig. 28

Let's say now we're all carved! Yeeps! This is getting exciting! Naturally you want to sand it – and there are those who say the smoother it is, the better the parts slip under the cloth – no friction impedance, y'know! Even knew a person who **waxed** his puppets!

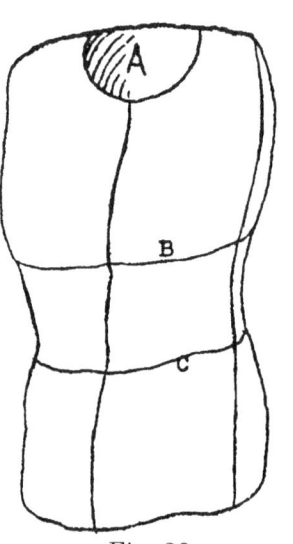

Fig. 29

In the trunk scoop out a hollow A for the neck. It will need to be bigger and deeper than you think, so when you get "enough" done, do some more – otherwise the neck will bind, and we can't have that! Now being sure your lines of balance on front, back, and sides are in place, saw the trunk apart at B and C. Just straight sawing across with an ordinary sharp saw, making the cuts reasonably parallel.

Now we get to use those lines of balance we've been so carefully preserving all this time. On the top of the middle block (Figure 30) draw a line from the front balance line to the back

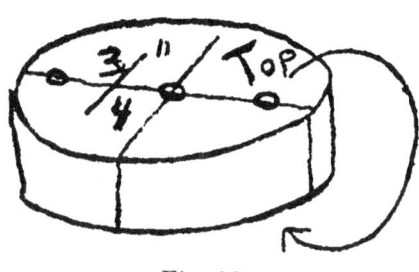

Fig. 30

one, and the same from side to side. Better mark this face "Top". Where the lines cross is where the hole will go for the spine string. Make a mark 3/4" from this center dot on each side. Now turn the middle block over and do the same marking on the bottom. Do this all precisely. Now with a sharp point (I use an ice pick) indent each of these six dots, to help start the bit when you drill the holes.

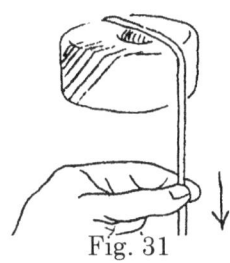

Fig. 31

Let's talk about string. All this puppet's joints except his neck are to be made of string! No fibre, tin, leather, cloth, plastic. None of that hard to handle stuff. ANYbody can thread a string through a hole! Get a ball of this string at the hardware store. It's called "chalk line" – carpenters and plumbers use it. It's a good, strong, reasonably hard string, and just the right thickness for us. [Note: Use a braided, not twisted cord, approximately 1/8" or less thick.]

DUCO Household Cement. Squirt a bit on your thumb and finger, and slide it down a 3 or 4" end of the string to make a "needle" of it. It dries in a very few minutes, and enables you to poke it through the holes you're going to drill.

A hand-drill you must have, of course, and the cheapest one you can get will do fine, but it must be the type illustrated, as you will see when you read how we use it – and boy! do we use it! While you're at the hardware store, have the man sell you a "bit" for a hand-drill – the size to allow the string to go through the hole it makes easily, but not sloppily. Then get another bit two sizes bigger.

While you're downtown, get a box of round toothpicks. Not flat ones – round ones. They're very important to this method.

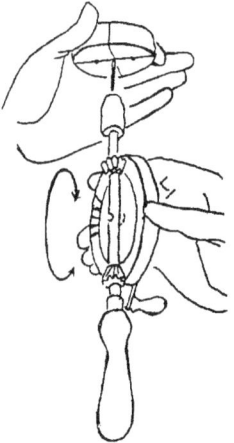

Fig. 32

The following instruction on handling the hand drill is by courtesy of that great puppet showman and craftsman, Rufus Rose. I know of no one process that has given me more pleasure through the years than this. Master it, and you'll have a mighty handy skill.

Instead of fastening the middle block in a vise and using two hands on the drill as usual, hold the block in your left hand, and when the drill bit is in the indentation you made, rock the wheel back and forth. It's that simple! There'll be lots of this drilling before the puppet is done, and all the parts are too irregular to hold well in a vise, anyway.

STOP!

Don't drill all the way through! Just a little over half way. Do the same with the other two holes. Now turn the block over and drill through from the other side. This eliminates the problem of how to come out at the marked point!

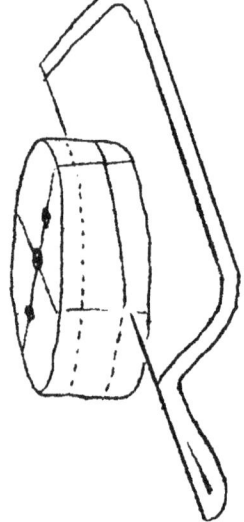

Fig. 33

You now have three holes precisely drilled in the middle block. Now make two pencil lines around the outside of the block marking it off in approximately thirds, and saw on each line to within 1/2" of the center hole. (I use a "coping saw" from the dime store for this, but any saw you can use will do.)

Fig. 34

When this is done, carefully break off the top and bottom layers to where you have stopped sawing. They'll be so thin they'll crack off easily – but so will the middle one, so be careful. Carve the remaining hunk of wood (dotted line) to a flat point around the center hole – flat because the chest and hips are to "ride" on them when it's strung. Sand the

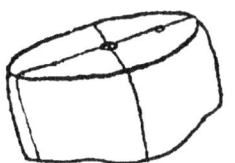

Fig. 35

rough edges very smooth, and we're through with it for a while. Oops! Better mark which is front and back before you forget; they look pretty silly when their middles are installed upside-down and backwards.

Now do the same cross-marking on the top of the hip piece, and the bottom of the chest, and indicate the side holes 3/4" away from center an each. (Figure 35) Indent the center dot on the bottom of the chest piece, and drill a hole diagonally through it and out the back of the chest. Where it emerges, scoop out a little hole to eventually accommodate a knot in the string. Refer to Figure 19, Session 7.

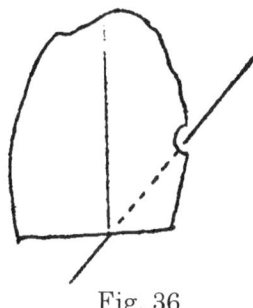

Fig. 36

On your drawing you indicated a right angle between C and D. Saw that line off the front of the hip piece as indicated here, but LEAVE ON the cross line on the bottom, on which you have indicated the center dot. Sand it down, retaining the line. Figure 38-A indicates how the mark looks in the front of the hip piece, and Figure 38-B indicates what you have left when you've sawed off the piece.

Drill a hole through the center dot (starting from both sides as before).

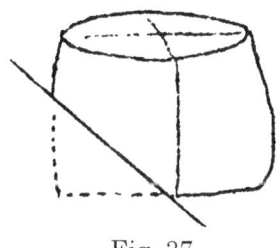

Fig. 37

We'll do something different with the two side holes on the top of the hip piece: drill the left hole on an angle from a out through the newly-sawed face b. Gouge out a niche to receive the eventual knot C1 (Figure 40). Do the same with the right hole, emerging at b. An inch away, start another hole at c and drill it out the side at d.

Let's make holes for ankle joints next. Lay your two carved legs on their backs, with their inside edges together. Draw a line across the bottoms a, about a third the distance from front to

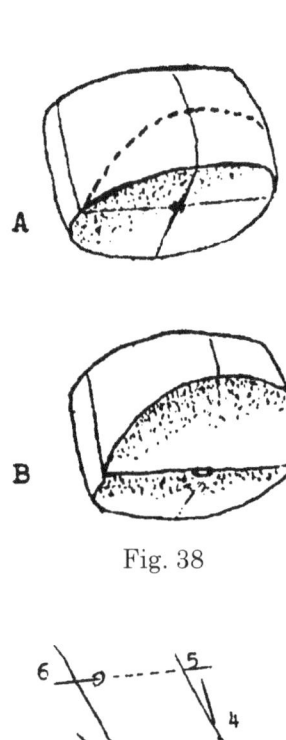

Fig. 38

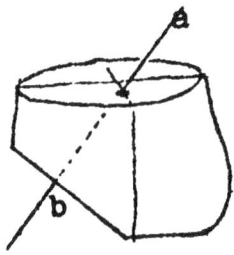

Fig. 39

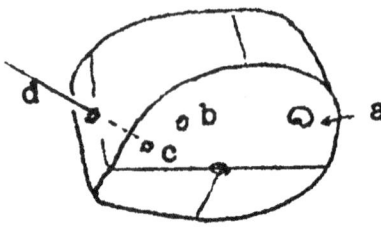

Fig. 40

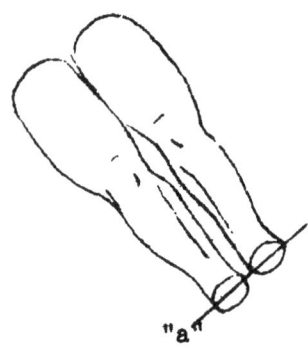

Fig. 41

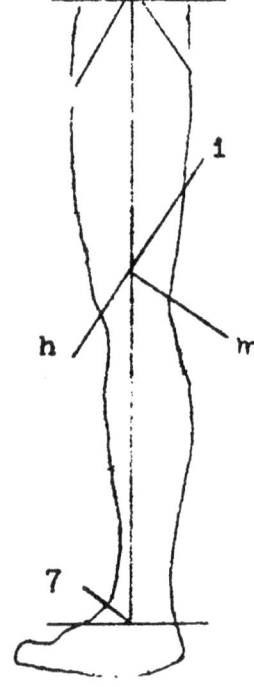

Fig. 42

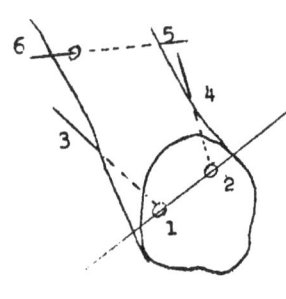

Fig. 43

Fig. 44

back. Indent a couple of dots (1 & 2, Figure 43) as near the edge as you think you can drill holes without splitting the wood. Drill from 1 up through the flat bottom surface and out the side at 3. Go in again at 2 and out the side at 4. Go in again at 5 and drill a hole straight across the leg and out at 6. Slice off the front of the ankle (7, Figure 41) up TO the front edges of the holes 1 & 2, but not INto them. This is to let the foot turn upward.

Set the legs back on the feet as in Figure 27, and make dots on the top of the feet to correspond to the

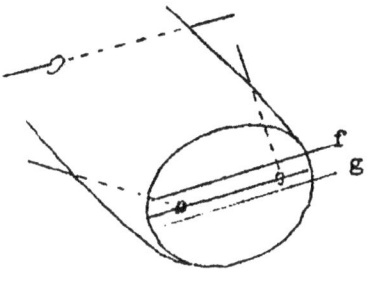

Fig. 45

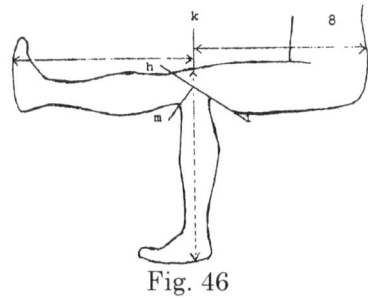

Fig. 46

holes you just drilled in the ankles. Drill holes in the feet at these dots. Turn the foot over (Figure 44). Carve a small V-shaped trench between the two holes, to countersink the string later on.

To the top of the leg, now. You should still have the balance line on the outside of each leg. Stand them up together as in Figure 27 but without the feet this time, and draw a line from side to side across the tops (as you did across the bottoms in Figure 41.) Do the same thing you did in drilling holes in the ankles: holes as near the edge as you can without splitting the wood, in on the flat top, out on the sides, and then a hole straight across (as in 5 to 6 in Figure 43).

Again look at Figure 42. The diagonal cuts on the front and back. First draw two parallel lines almost at the edges of the holes, as indicated at f and g, then slice away the front and back edges. Carefully don't cut into the holes.

Where do we cut the leg so the knee joint will be in the right place? When questions like this arise, go to your private model: you! If you will sit in a chair with your feet on the floor, you will find that the distance from the back of your buttock to the front of your knee equals the distance from the top of your knee to the floor. Put the leg and foot on your table, with the top of the leg at the point on the hip piece where it will be joined. Measure the overall distance, halve it, and place a mark on the knee-cap k. This will not mark the bottom of the upper half of the leg, but approximately the point at which the lower leg will fasten to it. So (Figure 42) the line h–i will bisect the vertical balance line, which will bring the h end of it somewhat lower.

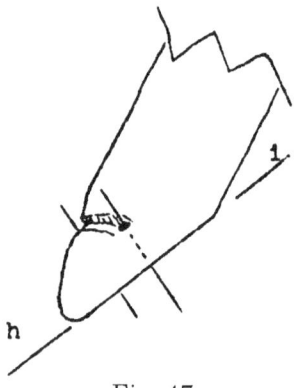

Fig. 47

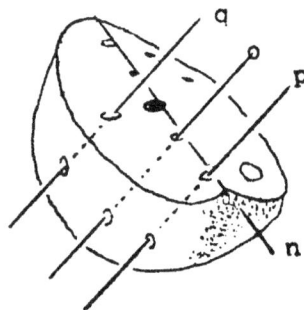

Fig. 48

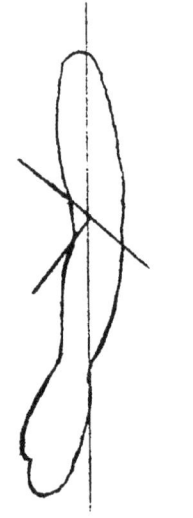

Fig. 49

Saw the leg in two along h–i. Drill holes in the top of the lower leg just as you did in the ankle and the top of the upper leg. Slice away the back of the top of the lower leg on the line m. Put the two halves of the leg together, face down, and mark dots on the h–i face of the upper leg to match the holes you have just drilled in the top of the lower leg.

Drill holes at right angle into the face h–i. Join them with that little V-shaped trench you used before to bury the string in the bottom of the foot. (The trench is on the top of the knee – not on the h–i face.)

Lay the top of the leg against the bottom of the hip piece, the outside of the leg flush with the outside of the hip piece, and mark on the cross line where the matching holes o & p are to go. Drill these holes on the angle indicated, so they come out the back of the hip piece (where your hip pockets are.) Repeat this with the other leg, on the other side. Double check each leg is on its proper side, and fronts are to the front.

Opposite center hole (for spine string) drill hole q same angle – and out the back.

Nothing left now but the arms, and the elbow joint is made just like the knee. I've left it for last as it is the most delicate of all the drilling, and by now you are an expert. Now re-read this Session, being sure you understand each operation, and then do it, as precisely as you can. It's easier that way than going back and doing it over. In Session Nine, we'll put him together, huh?

Session 9 Crafting the Stringpuppet (Part III)

You have stiffened an end on your string. Cut off about three feet, and knot the other end.

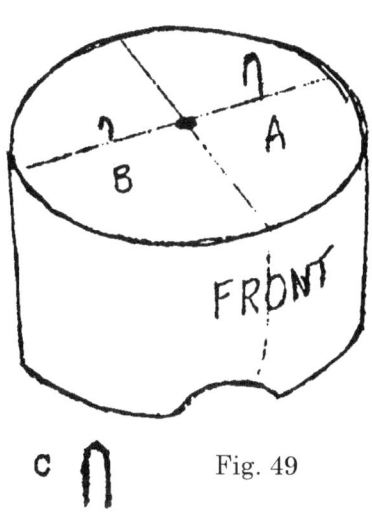

Fig. 49

With the larger of your two drill bits enlarge the side holes in the middle piece (Figure 33). Figure 49 is the bottom of the chest piece. A & B are the side dots you haven't done anything to yet. The little thing at C is the actual size of a staple made by clipping off the head of a wire nail, grinding a point on the end, then bending into a U-shape. These staples are to accommodate a string which will let your puppet trunk twist only so far as you wish. At A set one foot of the staple on the dot, the other toward the back of the chest piece. Drive the staple in until (B) there is just room for the string to slip easily through. Notice that a line between these two staples would run **behind** the center hole.

The Art of Snubbing

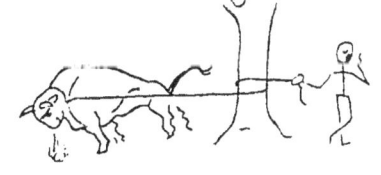

You are familiar with the fact that a raging bull can be easily held by taking a turn around a tree with the rope. This is known as "snubbing" and it's the handiest thing in the world in stringing puppet joints. If you've ever tried to tie a knot in a string at preCISEly the right point (I'm talking in sixteenths of an inch now) you know it's almost impossible; yet that's the kind of precision we need, and snubbing will give

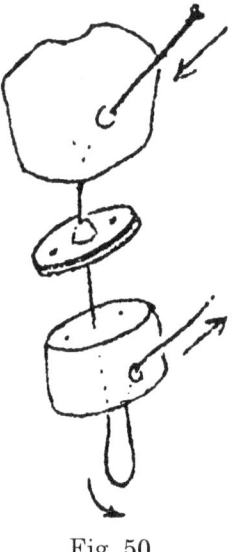

Fig. 50

Fig. 51

it to us. First, put the spine string in this three-piece trunk. Start the string in through the hole in the back of the chest piece. Through the center hole in the middle piece, making sure it's right side up and front side to. Through the top of the hip piece, out the bottom, in the bottom and out the back of the hip piece, like a tail. Don't pull it up tight: leave at least an inch between each part.

Cut a round toothpick in half.

When you put the string through that last hole, you were snubbing it: now the pull of the weight won't be directly on the fastening (the guy's hand on the bull's rope) but on the extra turn around the wood. Takes very little to hold it now, so press a toothpick into the hole the string came out of. This is all the fastening necessary, and it's beautiful, for in all the different joints you can bring the string to any degree of tension or slackness you wish, and it is instantly and easily held there. Furthermore, if you don't like what you got, it's so easy to take out and redo!

Don't press any of the toothpicks in too hard until the whole thing is strung (I "press" them in with the flat of a screwdriver - hammers are likely to break them), and when you cut your string, leave several inches hanging out to get hold of for future adjustments. When you're sure it's right, then press the toothpick in as far as it will go, and trim it and the string flush with the surface. [Note: A drop of white glue on the cut end of the toothpick will ensure it doesn't work its way out.]

The stopper (the string which stops the torso from twisting farther than you desire) follows the path indicated in Figure 52, going through the two staples on the chest piece, behind the

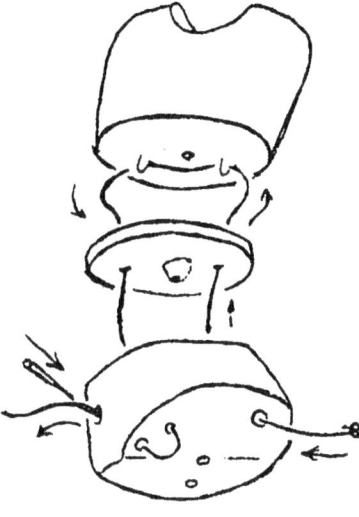

Fig. 52

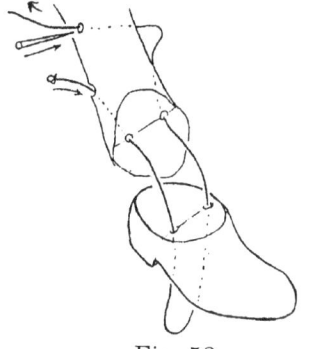

Fig. 53

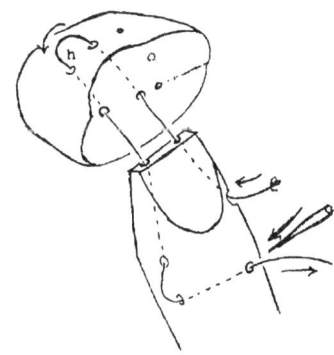

Fig. 54

spine string (which I've not drawn in here for simplicity's sweet sake). Down at the bottom we use the old snubber again.

NOW you can tighten up the spine string 'til all the parts touch. Now tighten the "stopper" string. If it's too loose, he can twist completely around; if too tight, he can't twist at all. See how much YOU can twist, and try that on him.

Let's attach a foot. By now you should be getting ahead of me, but I've drawn this joint in detail because it's the same one you use on the knee and elbow. On this, as on the other joints, if you pull it up too tight it won't do anything. On the other hand don't have it so loose that when you lift his knee, his foot hangs vertically down to the ground and he walks as though he were stepping in and out of buckets. YOUR foot doesn't do that.

Ankles, knees, and elbows all jointed? Okey, here go the hips. As you can see, there's nothing to it! This joint, like the others, can be tighter or looser as you please. If it is reasonably taut, he'll walk well, his legs won't "interfere" as they pass each other. But if you want him to sprawl you'll have to loosen him up.

This is the perfect system for getting both legs the same length. What a joy! And if you have been following directions, you still have that quarter inch or better between the legs that you drew on the original plan.

Hey! there's nothing left but the shoulder joint! And I've never seen one to beat this. Drill into the shoulder on that balance line, straight

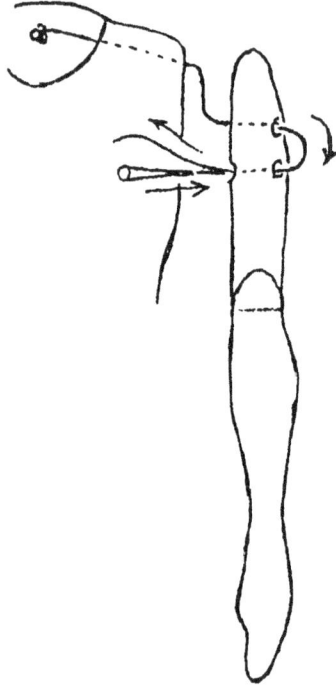

Fig. 55

Fig. 56

through into the neckhole. Put the arm up against it, and make a mark on the inside of the arm 1/2" or 3/4" lower. Then drill two holes in the arm as indicated. Gravity will hold the arm where it's supposed to be when at rest, but when it moves, it does all the things your shoulder does: slides around the rib cage, lets him reach across his own body, and accommodates itself to the cloth between it and the body. It's a beaut!

Got it all together? How does it seem? Move it a bit, keeping in mind what it has to do in the show. Now is the time to make alterations if any are necessary, not after it's dressed. Does it bend over far enough? Sit comfortably? Kneel, squat, reach where it's supposed to? Some of this can be altered by tightening or loosening the strings, some by removing a little wood at a joint.

When it "behaves" we can clean it up, In Figure 54, see h. I automatically make a little trench to countersink those snubbing strings flush with the surrounding surface, even when they're under clothing. Of course it is necessary when they're exposed. Press in all the toothpicks, cut both toothpick and string flush with surface.

The result still isn't smooth enough for close-up still photos, so here's a quick "cover-up." Out a piece of gummed paper (or any paper if you want to put your own stickum on it) a little longer and wider than what you want to cover. Then snip little cuts into it all around. Wet it, and press it over the area to be covered. The snipped edges overlap to let the paper conform to the curved shape under it. With just a little practice you will become a Great Concealer. By the time you've painted over it, even YOU will forget it's there. And it's so much easier than plastic wood and such to get through if you have at some future date to make repairs.

All tidied up? Then let's put the nails in for stringing (not jointing-stringing, but manipulating-stringing). I use the tiniest wire nails (not "brads") I can find. The two for the shoulders must be placed on the line of balance, above the hole you made for the shoulder string. The back string on the bottom of the back of the chest piece. One in each knee. For hands I prefer to drill a hole and run the string through and fasten it. (A hole, of course, as small as the string.)

And that, my dear friends, is one way to make a puppet.

How To Get a Head

When my father put together his first puppetshow, he got two doll heads from the dime store, repainted them somewhat, sewed kimonos on them, and that was it. (He soon gave up puppetry, said it was too much work.)

"But Is It Art?"

There are those among us who shudder over "store bought" help, who squeam at puppets made of soup strainers and dishmops, urp over naturalistic or "representational" puppets. Why? Because these methods are not conducive to "Art."

Pooie. Art is a statement about something, by you, and the way you say it, the choices you make, are perfectly legitimate "creations." When you rearrange your livingroom, or decide what color to paint the factory, you are making an artistic comment. "Artists" aren't a special breed of people they're just people who have seen more and exercised more in certain directions. If you spent most of your time rearranging the living room, or repainting the factory, you'd become interior and exterior decorators. And that's what you've been asked in this course to spend a little more time seeing.

We all see relatively the same world in toto, but each of us SELECTS different things from it. So no two puppet heads are alike. Which is wonderful. If you see eggs or blocks for heads, and felt and thumbtacks for features, hurrah for you! If the couple of ways I'm going to talk about here in the matter of making heads fail to please you, bully for you! You are exercising choice in expressing your "comment about Life" and that's art. You're an artist, and NO one can express your comment exactly like you. Proceed easily and confidently, and say "no" whenever you disagree. Just so you know what you're disagreeing with. Then, your art is YOUR art!

Your "jumping off place" on the head is the head as she exists. I'll show you what it's like in its average condition and then indicate ways in which it can be stretched and shrunk this way and that way, and from then on it's your baby. I'm going to detail two ways of manufacture which are totally different from each other, but whether you make your heads either of these ways or out of dry ice, you still must take off from the same starting place. (Digression. Someone asked what an artist was

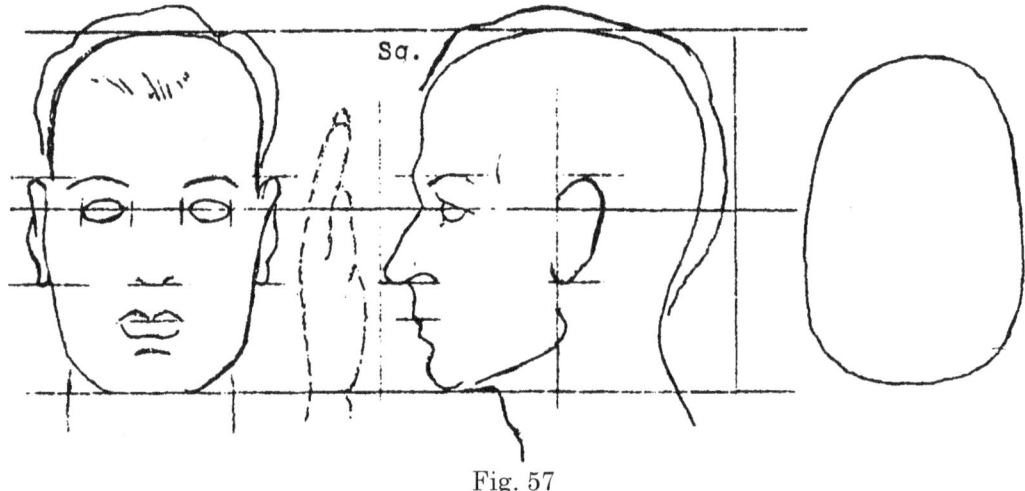

Fig. 57

"for!" Someone answered that an artist was to help people see what was around them. That's what you're doing.)

But you have to see it first. There are certain dimensions which are "average" And let's be clear about the words "average" and "normal." They don't mean "specific" and "right", they just mean that if you put ALL the people together, they'd come out something like this. Even our bodies can't help being creatively original. So if your measurements aren't exactly those given above, don't think you're a freak.

Eyes, contrary to junior's first impression, are about in the middle of the head. Their width is about a fifth the width of the face, with an eye's width between them. Noses are about halfway from eyes to chin, and mouths at about a third of the remaining distance. Ears usually have their tops even with the eyebrow, and their bottoms with the bottom of the nose. If you draw a square over the side view, you'll see that most of the "action" takes place in the lower left hand quarter. That means an awful lot of stuff is head. Don't make your puppets all "face."

Interesting comparison: a face, from hairline to chin, is about as long as a hand. From the front, necks are about as wide as jaws.

Look at people and at photographs, but go out of your way to look at sculpture. Carvings, figurines, that bust on the mantle, pick them up, turn them over, look at them from all directions. They'll hold still for it and won't be selfconscious, as people might. SEE how deep an eye is set behind the bridge of a nose, how surprisingly wide cheek-bones are right in front of the ears. What shape is the skull when seen from above. Has your doctor got a skull you could look at? What's the shape of the inside of your hat?

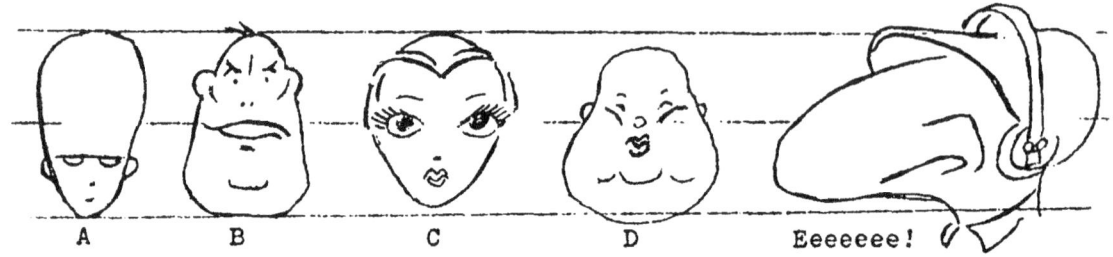

Fig. 58

Vive La Difference!

All through this Course I've been dinging away at "proportion." How big is this as compared to that. This is your big tool - it's what you have to work with. And you study the "average" so you can "take off" from it. Do you want a "highbrow"? Okey, make him a highbrow, by giving him more and more brow until he's practically ALL brow. (A) Shrink the rest of his features into relative unimportance: all his energy is in thought, so food, smell, muscle, even sight will have no great attraction for him -hence mouth, nose, jaw, eyes will be "played down."

Is he a giant with a "bird-brain?" Reverse the process. No skull capacity at all big muscular jaw (B), big mouth for the food intake necessary to stoke that hulk. Are her "eyes like limpid pools"? (C) Make `em big enough to swim in! Is he fat? (D) Lay it on him with a trowel! Sink his eyes, his little button nose, even his pursy mouth in mounds of lard. Emphasize his girth by making his extremitie, hands, feet, even ears tiny. Paul Ashley even made a puppet which was ALL one feature. (E)

Attack the design of the head the same way you did the body the loose ovals the many lines, thinking the while of what is the chief personality characteristic; then pick out and emphasize those lines that seem most to describe the character. It is well to make a front and a side view, lined up with horizontal lines - gives you more of a chance to do your dreaming and mind-stretching before you start freezing it into the solid material. As you throw the lines at the shape of the head, feel your pencil moving around those shapes, as though they were physically there and you were "feeling" them with the pencil.

A pleasure of mine is to go through an entire copy of *TIME* Magazine, making a cartoon of every face in the issue! It's great fun, it teaches me to see, and to emphasize outstanding features. You might enjoy it, too!

Session 10 **Crafting the Head** (Part I)

If you are handy at carving, the quickest way I know to make a handpuppet head is with a hunk of balsa wood. You can carve it with a razor blade in jig time, slap some showcard color on it, and have it on the puppet right now! But in lots of places balsa is hard to get and frightfully expensive, so get a big hunk of spun glass (Florists use it for decoration.) It carves with a pocket knife, and when finished is lighter'n anything! Like balsa, it won't take any banging around, but nothing beats it for speed, in a shaped head. Of course any form, from a sock-darner to a salad spoon will serve for a puppet head by simply attaching the features to it cut out of felt, plastic, foam rubber, cardboard, and glued, tacked or stapled on.

Cloth Heads

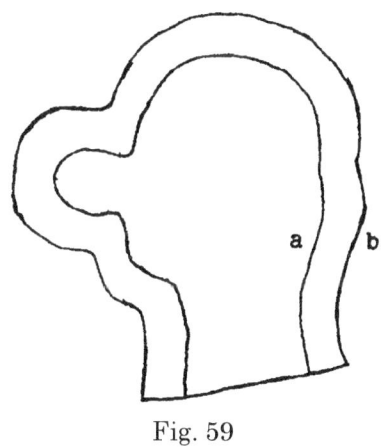

Fig. 59

Cloth heads I like. Wonderful things can be done with a needle and thread and some playful experimenting. After you have drawn the side view of your head a, trace it on a piece of cloth. However stuffing it will make it smaller, so draw another line b around it, at least 3/4" away. This may or may not be enough for your head, so if it isn't you have only to make another – at this point you have no great investment of time or money. You'll soon learn approximately how much bigger the cloth needs to be.

You know how cloth stretches when you pull it on the bias. That stretchability of cloth is what we depend on here. Try different cloths; a low-thread-count muslin, cotton stocking, knit rayon jersey. Old, worn-out material may not stand up to the pushing and prodding you're going to give it, so be sure it has some strength.

Sew your outline preferably on a sewing machine, turn it inside out, and start stuffing cotton into it. Cotton batting is fine – no need for surgical cotton. Poke it in through the neck, packing the nose tightly, and making the head solid and hard with cotton. But here's where the modeling starts: as you pack the cotton in, keep looking at your picture of the head, and with your other hand, press the outside of the head – the temples, eyes, mouth, chin – toward the shape you have in mind. Thus when you have filled the head, you won't have just a lumpy sack of cotton, but an approximation of the shape of the head.

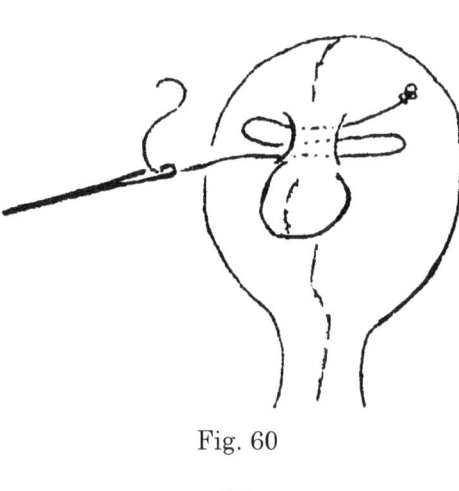

Fig. 60

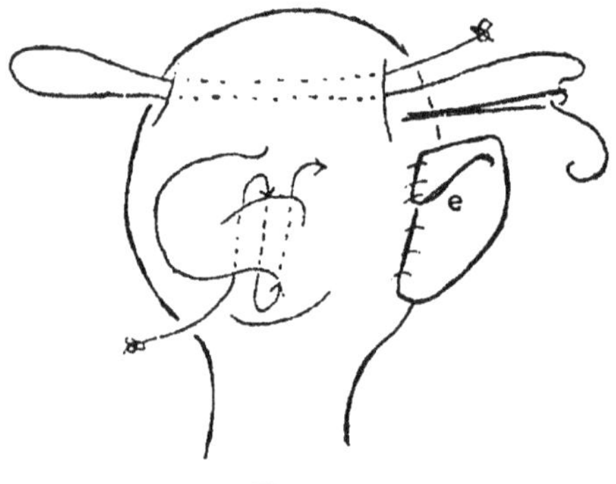

Fig. 61

Now with a long needle and some thread, start sewing the details. Need more of a bridge to the nose between the eyes? Decide just where the indentation should be, and sew back and forth, pulling the material into itself. Only you can decide how tight to pull it to get the effect you want. And it takes a little getting acquainted with, just as carving did if you hadn't done it before. Narrow the temples the same way, or shape the flaring nostrils. Having packed the cotton in tightly, it now supplies rolls of shape under the binding of your stitches. Experiment with dimples, snarls, frowns. Sometimes you will go clear through the head from front to back to get the cloth pulled in where you want it. If this similarly dimples the back of the head,

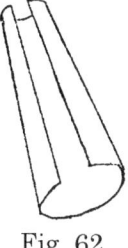

Fig. 62

don't be alarmed: you'll be putting a hat or hair back there anyway.

A thick piece of felt makes a very respectable ear e, eyebrow, eyelash, all sorts of things. Play with it. A cone of cardboard of a size to fit your finger is sewed or glued together (absolutely smooth on the inside; a little roughness here can be most irritating!) and inserted in the neck. The cloth at the bottom of the neck is brought around and fastened to the bottom of the cone (sew or glue, but keep it smooth.)

I have mentioned Duco Household Cement, but do you also know about Elmer's Glue? If not, you have great pleasure coming. It sticks ANYthing together, and I use it all the time, as in fastening the cloth around the bottom of the cone – gluing on felt features instead of sewing them – and in costuming, gluing the parts together instead of sewing them whenever possible, which is often.

Makeup

You can paint heads with almost anything: rubber base paint, casein, (showcard color is usually too perishable for a long run) but I prefer oil, for both cloth and wood heads. I get it at the hardware store, and instead of "Artist's" colors, I get quarter pound cans of housepainters' "color ground in oil." More for your money and quite as good. White lead for body, and eyeballs, teeth, et cet. Raw Sienna (with white lead makes a good skin color), Cobalt Blue, Burnt Sienna, Burnt Umber, Black, Cadmium Yellow (medium), Chrome Green (Medium), and a good hot Red (there are so many reds, you'll just have to look at the chart to see what you'll like for lips and cheeks.) Turpentine. The oil already in the paint will supply enough binder, and you use turpentine for thinner and to wash your brushes.

Three soft brushes will do 3/4", 1/4", and a "liner." Wash your brushes AFTER EACH USE, several times in turpentine until it is clear, then in warm water and soap. Rinse them thoroughly and "shape" them with your fingers so they won't be all squidgy when you are ready to use them again. Do this, and your brushes will last for years!

Save Tin Cans!

It's mighty nice to have enough things to mix paint in! And to be able to throw them away when you're done.

There's nothing to mixing paint that you can't pick up. Put a gob of white lead in a can, add some color, mix it, add enough turpentine to make it work well in your brush, and slap it on! You don't know what it should look like? Look around: you've a constant lesson in how to paint in the ads in the magazines – in color yet! Glamor gals? Look at the fashion ads. Cartoons? Breakfast foods, desserts, cleansers. Realism? More ads, and color photographs. If you're not in the commercial art business, you probably don't realize how many of those realistic pictures are drawn and painted instead of photographed, but a close scrutiny will tell you. And you can learn from their styles. Look in the dress shops at the faces of the manikins. The displays in the Drug Store. There's a complete art course right there in front of you, and it's ALL FREE!

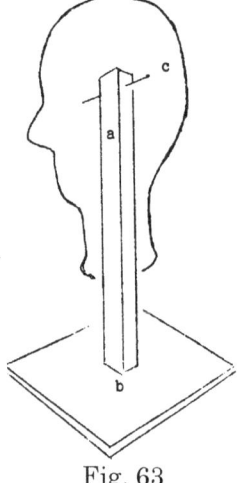
Fig. 63

Cast Heads

Let's look at another kind of head. Many people adore Celastic, and others can't abide it (maybe because they're unfamiliar with it.) Papier mache, home made wood pulp, and heads carved directly in wood are all good and to those who use them satisfying methods. However, here we will consider only the commercial product called Plastic Wood. It is reasonably priced, easy to work, allows you to experiment in advance on the clay, and to correct any mistakes you make after it is cast. Light, durable, and capable of producing any surface you desire from the slickest to the most textured. Saw it, sand it, nail it, put machinery in its hollow inside. And once you have the hang of it, it's easy as pie. [Note: Various brands of plastic wood behave differently: Something else – Plastic Wood brand, DAP, Mend-All, etc.]

Make an armature – that is, nail a stick a to a board b and a nail through the top of the stick to keep it from sliding up through the clay head. Model the head, keeping it in the size you drew on your sketch. When is the model of a head or any other work of art - done? When you can't think of anything else to do to it. Now check it for undercutting.

Fig. 64

You're going to pour plaster onto this clay model and when it is set, take it off. Plaster when it is set is hard, and doesn't give. So look over your model thoroughly for places such as indicated in Figure 64 where, in this case, there is a little space behind the ear around which the plaster will set and won't pull away. To avoid this, don't slice off the ear; simply fill in the undercut clay, and after the head is cast, you can carve it out of the wooden head.

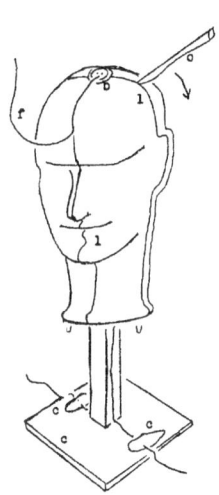

Fig. 65

Now we prepare to make a plaster mold. Score a small trench 1 around both sides of the head at the widest part (which usually includes the ears) and another straight down over the forehead, nose, et cet. I use the slicing edge of an orange stick, which I use to model with, but anything – a pencil – will do. This will be a three-piece mold. Now lay a piece of strong fishline in the trench around the side of the head, underneath at u, down the sides of the stick, and out across the top of the board to c and c, where they are fastened down by a little glop of clay. Smooth over the trench, burying the string just below the surface. Tie a button on the end of another piece of fishline, and bury it in the top of the head at b. Run it down the front trench, and fasten it off with its glop of clay.

"Plasteline" – sometimes "Plasticene"– a nonhardening clay with which we have been modeling, requires no greasing or other preparation to receive the plaster.

Plaster

You can use Plaster of Paris from the drug store, but the best is a building material called Molding Plaster – available at a true builders' supply. Remember that name – and don't let the lumberyardman tell you patching plaster is the same thing. It isn't. Molding plaster (interior decorators used to mold cupids on the ceiling with it) comes in hundred pound sacks. Sometimes you can find an open sack – but the cost of it is so much less than Plaster of Paris as to be silly, and if you're making any number of puppets, a hundred pounds goes awfully fast. You'll also need a pan, newspapers (to protect the table and floor), a big spoon, table knife, and tack hammer.

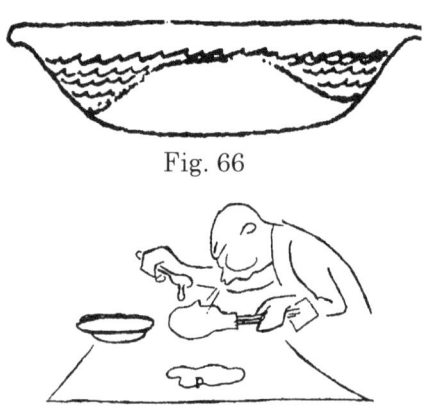

Fig. 66

Fig. 67

Put water in the pan. You must guess at how much you think it will take – but when you have guessed, add some more. It's embarrassing to come up with too little. Now pour plaster into the water. Let it settle, and continuing until you see it rising like a small mountain to just beneath the surface. Now stir it gently with your big spoon underneath the water. Pick up the pan and bump it gently on the table now and then to make the bubbles rise to the surface. We don't want bubbles.

When the plaster is like thick cream, put a puddle of it at p Figure 67 to let it get a start on setting up. Now spoon out plaster on the model's upturned face – pour it in his eye. Here bubbles can form too, so blow into his eye and any other recessed places – up his nose, corners of his mouth – until he is covered with a layer of plaster. Plaster is setting up all this time, so stand the model on his head in the puddle, being sure there is at least 3/4" between his clay head and the table. Hold him there with one hand, while you pile plaster up around him with the other. Finally he'll stand alone. When all the plaster is on him with no place less than 3/4" from the surface, you have time to smooth up the outside with the table knife, and with a stick or something score his name in the outside of the mold. This is mighty handy months from now when you wonder who THAT is a cast of.

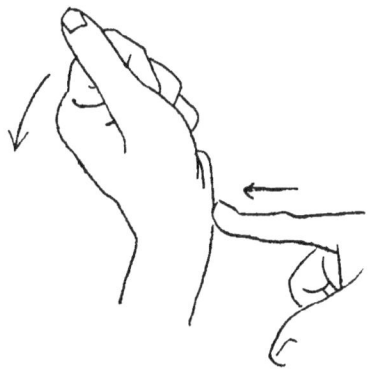

Fig. 68

Let someone wash out the pan while you stay with the mold. You're looking for a precise moment at which to pull the parting strings. Bend back your fist (Figure 68) and press your index finger at that point indicated. Notice it gives a little but not too much. Press your finger against the cast frequently, and when it feels like your taut wrist did, it's time to pull the string. Set the head up on its base, pull both ends of the side string at once, then at once pull the front string. This then has "parted" the mold, and there's nothing to do now but wait till it gets hot, then cold and hard, and it's ready to take apart.

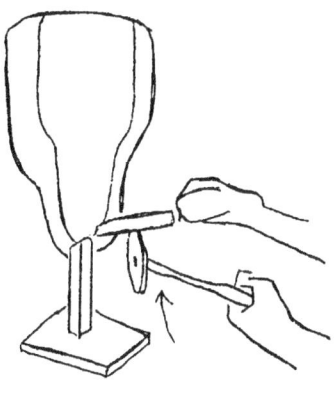

Fig. 69

Give it fifteen minutes. Insert the blade of the table knife in one of the parting marks and tap it gently with a hammer, which will force it apart. Do the same with another mark, and remove the clay from the mold. Fasten the two front halves of the mold together with big rubbers bands (cut from inner tubes maybe) and immerse the whole thing in a bucket of water for at least fifteen minutes. We want it soaked, for this will keep the Plastic Wood from sticking to it.

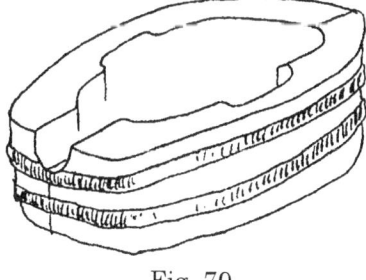

Fig. 70

- 81 -

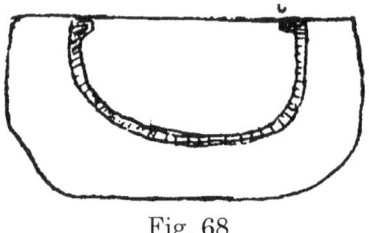

Fig. 68

Remove the back half of the cast from the water and line it with Plastic Wood. Dipping your fingers regularly in water will help keep the PW from piling up on them. Pack the PW tightly against the mold. At the top edge t make a little lip of PW. It's very handy in removing the cast from the mold when the time comes.

Most beginners make the PW unnecessarily thick. Particularly with handpuppet heads this is unfortunate, for every extra gram of weight on your finger tires you that much quicker. A stringpuppet head can stand as much as a 1/4" of thickness, but my handpuppet heads are no more than 1/8". And some of them I've been using for years and years.

When you have finished lining the back half, put it back in the bucket of water. Do the same with the front half. Leave them there twenty-four hours. Remove the PW casts from the plaster molds and set them aside to dry for another twenty-four hours. [Note: After removing the head from the mold, some people put it back in the water for another twenty-four hours before the air drying.]

The reason for immersing the PW in water for twenty-four hours is that it usually "sets" without shrinking under water. However in some areas, the water has some chemicals in it that STILL allow the PW to shrink somewhat, in which case you allow for that shrinkage in making your next clay model.

Don't be impatient. Let the cast dry in the air the full twenty-four hours. You can't "work" the material if it's wet on the inside. And don't set it on the gas heater to speed it up: PW does amazing things under such circumstances.

Addenda

In the final version of the Course, Steve substituted the following texts when discussing painting scenery and puppets.

Now what are you going to paint it with. Well sir, (or madam, as the case may be) as far as I'm concerned, there is only one medium to consider, and that is

ACRYLIC!

We use it for everything: puppets, scenery, properties, the proscenium – even the stage. Mixes with water, paints on anything, and once it's dry it's there forever. I paint our scenery on unbleached muslin, stapled to a frame made of 1"x 3" boards nailed into a rectangle the size of the backdrop I want. I don't prepare the cloth with "size" or filler, just lay out the scene with charcoal and start right in painting. Because I want the utmost flexibility for folding and packing, I use the acrylic just like painting with watercolor.

WARNING: If you use acrylic medium or gel with the paint, it'll make the scenery thick and stiff. If, on the other hand, you use the paint too watery, it will "bleed" into the surrounding cloth. Experiment a little. I'll bet you'll LOVE it.

Needless to say, you'll want to stretch the cloth tight when you staple it onto the frame. If you set up the frame so it tilts toward you at the top, it will help keep the drips from falling on the scene below.

Painting with acrylic-as-watercolor is much like painting with dye (as mentioned in a previous version of this Course) but it's infinitely superior. When it's done and dry, if details need sharpening it can be done by mixing some thicker acrylic and using it like opaque paint, which it then is. Just don't overdo it.

Acrylic is a plastic, much like Elmer's Glue, and if you let it dry in your brush, you're out a brush. Keep a bucket of water at hand, and when you're not painting, keep the brush in the water. Wear old clothes. Acrylic won't come out. Don't say I didn't warn you. Practically every stitch I own has acrylic on it, but you might not like it that way.

Most of my scenery is painted with one 1/2" house painter's brush and one 1/2" artist's bristle brush. I keep washing them as I go from one color to another. And of course when I'm finished, I wash them very thoroughly with warmish water and Lava soap.

Makeup

Heads can be painted with almost anything: showcard color (which is too perishable for a long run), oil, casein, rubber base paint, or our favorite – acrylics.

Acrylic is the only really new thing that has happened in the paint world in hundreds of years. It's really a resin suspended in water into which is mixed color. When the water evaporates, it forms a colored plastic, which is permanent, insoluble, and perfect for everything about a puppet show, including drying with a dull finish. White, Yellow Oxide, Cadmium Red Light, Ultramarine Blue, Burnt Umber, and Black should do about everything for you.

SAVE TIN CANS! They're mighty handy to mix colors in. Squeeze a little color out in a can, add a little water and stir. Thin or thicken until it works well for you.

WARNING WARNING WARNING!

Keep a bucket of water at hand and as soon as you stop using a brush, put it in the water? If this plastic paint dries on your brush, you can throw that brush away. If, however, you keep the brush wet while you're using it, and when you're done wash it thoroughly in warmish water and Lava soap until not a trace of color remains, your brushes will last for years. After washing thoroughly, shake out the water, and with your fingers shape the brush to its original form and stand it in a jar or something bristle-end up to dry.

There's nothing to mixing paint that you can't do. Experiment. Three soft round brushes will do: one as big around as your little finger, one half that big, and a quite small one. Medium grade and price. Cheapest just won't work. Now mix up some color.

Session 11 **Crafting the Head** (Part II)

You now have a head cast in Plastic Wood, lying there in two halves. Putting them together you will find inequalities of surface, which you shave off with your newly resharpened knife, until the halves fit well together. Some folk stick the halves together with Household Cement. I take some PW, softened with a little Plastic Wood Solvent, and lay a light layer of it all around the edge of one half. Then I pour a LITTLE solvent all around the edge of the other half, and press the two halves together, tightly. This squdges some of the newly added PW out the sides, and with some solvent on my finger I smooth this down, pressing it back into the cracks if any, put a coupla rubber bands around the head, and set it away to dry. This – happily won't take twenty-four hours. Before you put it away, check it over for any air bubbles, or inequalities you don't want. A little soupy PW and solvent rubbed into these will smooth them over.

Fig. 72

For stringpuppetheads (whee!, what a word!) insert a dowel in the hole of the neck, fastening it with more plastic wood.

For handpuppets, some – notably Mr. Alfred Wallace – like to line the neck hole with sheepskin! I've never done this, but Mr. W. used it successfully for years as a way of making any puppet fit any operator's finger. As I haven't that problem, I just make it fit my finger and I do it with PW.

Fig. 73

Packing PW into the neck hole with my wet little finger until there is no longer room to go in and out, I wet my index finger and insert it gently into the PW packing, to just before the second joint. When the hole is at the right angle and snug around my finger, I carefully remove my finger and let the PW dry. This gives me a perfect fit, which will always hold the puppet at precisely the point I wish.

Sharpen the details, cut out the undercutting if any, add bulk here or there with plastic wood if you wish, and you're ready to paint.

Do you go for a slick surface, like a china doll? Then sand the head smooth, give it a coat of showcard paint and let it dry, then sand that! The oftener you do this, the slicker it will get. When it's where you want it, paint it with oil as described heretofore. (Who, me? Lord no – I hate slick heads. But I'm queer.) Paul McPharlin used to tell of a girl who showed him heads painted with enamel! Quoth the great man, "Doesn't that make them a bit shiny?" "Oh yes," she replied blithely, "but we powder them well before each performance." The paint set-up I outlined to you comes up with a dull surface. If, however, there should be more oil in your particular mix than expected, and they should come out shiny when you don't want it, there is a very interesting thing called "dull varnish" which will not only dull the surface, but also protect the paint. Don't bother with it unless you have to.

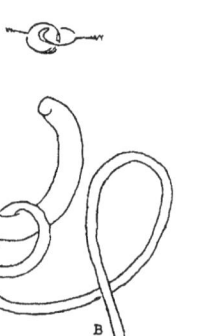

Fig. 74

A pair of 1/2" screweyes will do nicely for a stringpuppet neckjoint. Only trouble is, they rattle. So to get rid of the rattle, open one of them (using two pairs of pliers) and with a piece of ordinary grocer's twine [Note: Or braided nylon fishline] lay loops one after another all the way 'round the "eye" as shown greatly enlarged in Figure 74. When done, hook the other screw-eye over this covered one, close the latter, and tie the stringends A & B together. It's quick, inexpensive, and silent. Paint the hands – paint the feet, and it does seem there is nothing left to do to this stringpuppet but to dress him! Well!

In designing a scene, the wardrobe of the puppets is a part of the design. In a puppet stage, we are designing for a great distance. And if we know anything about color, we should use it to help us in overcoming the problem of distance, and in evoking emotion.

Colors are emotional things. The cold ones are just that; the blues, grays, gray-greens, are receding, rejecting, lacking in muscle and drive. Reds, yellows, oranges have fire and spunk – enthusiasm, forward-movingness.

Consider a scene. What is the prevailing tone – emotion of the action. Try to select a color which most suggests this to you and design your set with that in mind. I suggest you get a package of "construction paper" – that stuff kids use in their arts-crafts classes in school of all different colors. Select a piece of it to be your background. Now figure the emotional impact of each of your characters – who feels like red – like apple green like a livid violet or a sulking purple. Who's dolorous like brown, or brittle-bright like lemon yellow. When you have decided these things, cut little figures out of the respective papers, and put them on the color of your background. There, in its simplest form, is a statement about the emotional "tone" of your scene.

Who disappears into the background? Who sticks out too prominently? Who can afford to have a little more of this or a little less of that color in his mixture? You are determining, but on the basis of the relationship between the various parts and their surroundings. So your "stage picture" will be a whole, and each part will help the other. Perhaps your play is such that you can actually dress the characters as simply as that solidly in the colors you have chosen for them. If not you can make the major part of their costume follow that line. And this way the "bit parts" won't outshine the "leading roles."

Whenever possible, make as much of the costume "on" the puppet as possible. Shoes, of course, are carved instead of feet. Gloves if needed on hands. Hat's on heads, if they are never to come off. (Model the crown of the hat as a continuation of the skull, and when it comes to dressing, you have only to add a brim.) Does his suit require padded shoulders? That's pretty tough to do on suits as small as puppets', but if you carve the "padding" right on his shoulders, you have only to lay the suit cloth over it, and here it is!

Remember that a puppet on a scale of 4" to the foot is, at 2' tall, a third the height of a man, but only a NINTH the cubic content. So in choosing your materials for dressing him, figure this difference in the weight of the cloth. I have actually seen puppets who were supposed to be dressed in corduroy – dressed in human-sized corduroy! Of course they couldn't move – the weight of the material wouldn't let them – so all the construction time and skill was wasted. Never sew a thing together if you can paste it together (Elmer's Clue again.) Figure on tacking or stapling parts of the clothes to the wooden body underneath. Build the clothes right on the body; you're not having to change them between scenes anyhow. If you need a change of wardrobe, you make another puppet. (I had seven different Cleopatras in her show!) In *"Joan of Arc"*, the warriors didn't have any clothes on: their bodies were carved like armor. There is of course some sewing you can't get out of, but if you start thinking in the above terms, there's much you can avoid, to the betterment of your puppet.

Fig. 75

Handpuppets are something else again. With a stringpuppet you have something to work to, but handpuppets have no proper bodies to fit, and it's just "cut and fit" all the way. The hand which is the puppet's body isn't even the same on both sides, and so compensation has to be arranged for if you want more than the simplest little shirt. Understand, the simplest little shirt is fine – many great artistes never use anything more. But sometimes one wants an additional hump here, or tummy there.

Make a "foundation garment" of a good stout muslin or suchlike. Remember this has to support whatever you sew on it, but also it has to stand the strain of your own hand becoming a fist, stretching, bending, sweating (it gets hot in there!) and it has to be loose enough so you can slip an and out of it with ease, and strong enough not to tear against the pull of struggling into it. Fasten it to the head, sew the hands into it, and then you're ready to dress it.

One of the important actions of a handpuppet is that he can pick things up with his hands. Anything that inhibits this action, or calls attention to what is doing it rather than what is being done, is undesireable. Having used every kind of hand, I cast my vote for the simple felt mitten, so sewn into the puppet that my finger- and thumb-tip are at the palm of the mitten. This means putting on the shirt, putting on the mittens, and then sewing them onto the shirt sleeves at those points. Allowing for enough material around the back of the shirt for me to put the hands together, or to fold the arms, or whatever reach I may be capable of. This may require several repinnings, but when it's done, I have a workable placement, and one that allows the puppet to pick things up with his hands, rather than with his forearms.

Mostly I get a shade of felt somewhere near the face skin tone and let it go at that. If I want to be really fussy, I paint them with the face paint.

There are variations, of course – the felt hands can be long and thin, short and fat, even have separate fingers with little tiny lead weights in them so they can wiggle when moved.

Somehow, wooden hands on a handpuppet are more wooden than they are on a stringpuppet. I don't say don't use 'em I just say I don't.

Rubber balls are handy things. My "Mr. Biggers" is a tubby little guy, who has half a big rubber ball sewn on his front for a tummy, and half a smaller one sewn on his behind. That takes care of his side profile all right, but from the front or back that big space between thumb and forefinger doesn't feel right for a man so fat in other places, so some padding is sewn in there, and a bit less on the other side, so they'll match up.

As I say, it's "cut and fit" all the way, and the only practical suggestion I can give you is to have a friend with a comparably sized hand "model" the puppet for you while you look all around at it, and pin things on as they occur to you.

You can afford to – indeed you should – use sturdier material for dressing handpuppets than stringpuppets. You haven't the same problem of the cloth binding the delicate movement of the stringpuppet and you subject handpuppets to much harder wear. My handpuppets right now are all frayed – particularly around the sleeves.

A word here about "style" – not as it applies to clothes, but as it applies to your puppets and your show. "Style" isn't something you set out to get: it's something you get when you "set out." We create out of what we are. Kids of 12 create out of being kids of 12. In this course, you are being invited to ways of increasing your capacity so you will have more out of which to create, and your choices in how you increase your capacity are what determine your "style." So go forward gaily with this business of design; you can no more fail to express your own "style" than you can escape your own thumbprint. And your style will alter and "firm up" the more choices you make.

We create out of our minds and when we have our minds on something, contributing facets flow into it from everywhere. If you are really thinking about your new puppet Mrs. Blimpbottom, every time you see a feather or a belt or a fancy purse or a silly shoe, you'll consider how it, or an exaggeration of it, would look on her. The criterion of the validity of any idea you have in regard to Mrs. Blimpbottom is; does it make YOU giggle? Are YOU Interested? Amused? Some of my most successful shows were those that "knocked me out" as I was writing them!

By all means exercise your playfulness in considering materials. Is Mrs. B. the kind who would wear a Chore Boy for a feather boa? I have seen puppets dressed in so-soft leather, in rubber sheeting, in cellophane. You are in a position to make these decisions OUT OF THE CHARACTER OF THE PUPPET because from the beginning you have been seeing and understanding this character. Now you will not add anything to it that will weaken or distract it, but such things as will reinforce it, so that you and the observer will say, "Wouldn't you KNOW Mrs. B. would do – say – wear something like that?" This also saves you a lot of unnecessary work: if Mrs. B. isn't the kind to wear a whatchacallit – even though everyone else is wearing one this season – don't go to the bother of making one for her!

While you're making these decisions about Mrs. B., are you thinking about her voice? By now you have pretty good control of yours and you should have practiced enough so you're over the initial bother of thinking of "how to" every time you want to make a sound. Apply it to Mrs. B. Make yourself into her. Is she big – fat? Make yourself that in your mind. Sit down like her. Get up like her. Walk across the room like her. Now remember her emotional drive, remember a situation in her play and SOUND like her! ....

You DID?!! Why bless you, Honey, that's the way the Big Boys do – and that is creative art.

Session 12 **Stringing and Manipulation**

Okey, Boys –"string 'im up!" Now we come to that good time when we attach nerve-ends to the body and see if it'll twitch. If you've followed the instructions so far, you can look forward with calm assurance that all will be not only well but delightful. First the control.

Paddle Control

Fig. 76

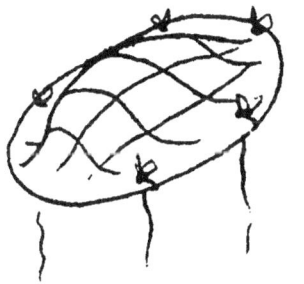

Fig. 77

On my first show I used the familiar "airplane" control shown in all the books, and that was all right, but my second show was a monster, with fourteen puppets on the stage at one time, and there just wasn't room above the acting area for that many controls! So I started digging in the archives. First I dredged up Figure 76, an ancient Chinese (I think) control made of a piece of bamboo. Next came Figure 77, which was nothing more nor less than the top half of a turtle's shell. Both these were small enough to fit above my stage, but when I made them in plywood and tried them out, they were awkward to handle. Taking off a little here and a little there, I eventually came up with (Fanfare goes here!) Figure 78! I offer you this because of its many virtues, and suggest that you try it out. Old timers who are used to another type of control curse it (patch!) but young timers, even little kids, pick it up and work well with it immediately. Maybe you will too.

- 95 -

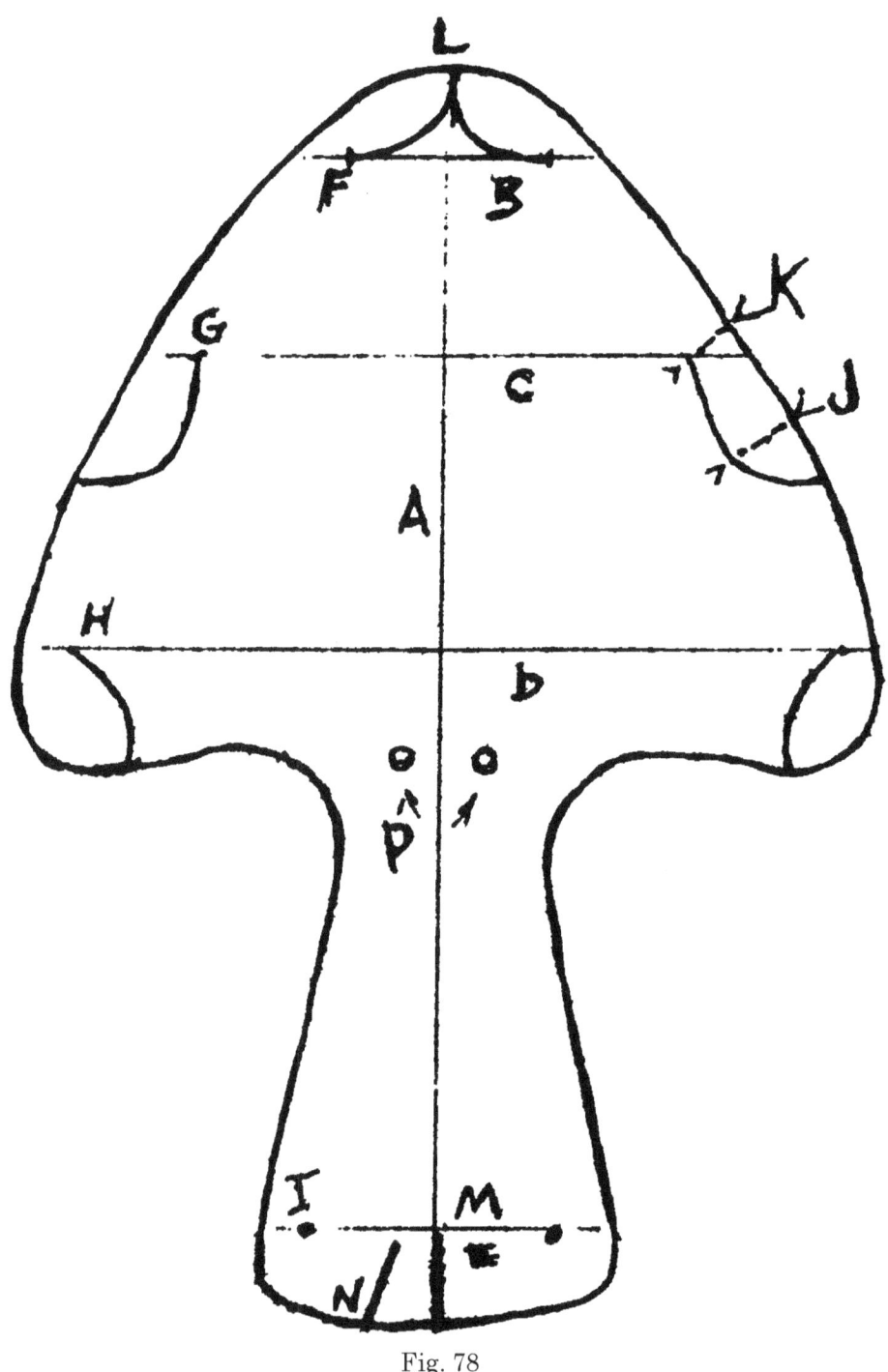

Fig. 78

Figure 78 is the actual size. Cut it out of 1/4" plywood. As we have been so precise in lining up all the parts of our acting-machine – the stringpuppet – let us be equally precise here. The line A exactly down the center. The lines B, C, D, & E at right angles to A. The points F, G, H, & I are the same distance from the center as their sister points on the opposite side, and are the points from which the strings will descend. The curved lines originating at those points and going out to the edge of the control are saw cuts (made with a coping saw using the smallest blade) for the admission of the string. Notice that the distance across J is greater than the distance across K. This is because the string is attached merely by bringing it up through the slot to the proper tension and wrapping it around several times – and that's all! The wideness at J keeps it from unwinding. The two front slots which have their points at P have a common opening at L and are to accommodate the leg strings. For this dreamboat of a control has no leg bar!

Let us look at some of the virtues of this control. It is so small that puppets can work closer together than with the common type. It is perfectly smooth around all its edges so nearby puppets won't get fouled up on it. You can't drop the legbar. Adjustments of string tension are immediate and simple, and readjustments or replacements are equally simple as there are no knots to tie or untie. When strung and balanced, it allows amazing latitude of action by the puppet while supported by a hanger on the stage! It's easier to wind the strings around, and takes less packing space.

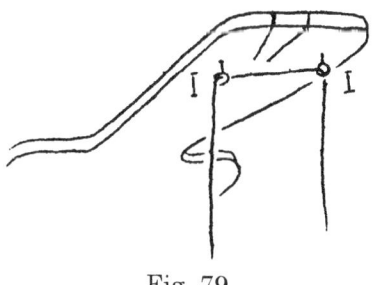

Fig. 79

Having sawed the six curved slots, saw M, which is for the back string (thus keeping the string point dead center) and N, which is the tie-off slot. The two points I are for the very smallest screweyes, through which an endless shoulder-string will run.

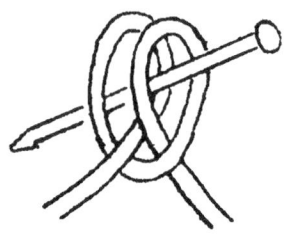

Fig. 80

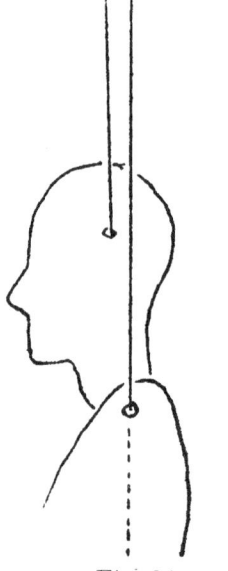

Fig. 81

You already have the nails in the body ready for stringing. Determine the height of the control from the floor, and run a string from one shoulder up through these two screweyes, down to the other shoulder and tie it off. The best knot in the world for this is the clove hitch, shown in Figure 80. This beautiful knot can be tied to the precise fraction of an inch of where you want it, and when drawn tight will hold anything forever (circuses tie their tent ropes with it) yet if you loosen one strand of it with a pin, the whole thing falls easily apart. What could be sweeter?

Next connect your head strings, and run them up to H & H on the control. When tieing them off, be sure the control is held perfectly horizontal. Just bring the string up through the slot, wrap it around four times, and you're in business. Notice Figure 81: the little nails placed in the head are just back of the center of the weight of the head, but when the strings are fastened to the control, the nails are slightly ahead of the shoulder strings. Thus the slightest tip forward of the control will cause the head to fall forward.

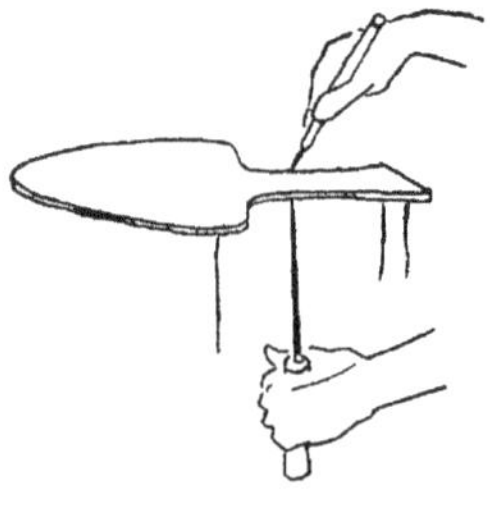

With the head and shoulder strings on, and the control level, place a pointed thing (ice pick?) under the control somewhere near as indicated In Figure 82 to find the point where the control, with the puppet on it, balances. Touch the front of the control to see that it makes the puppet nod his head easily, but not wobbily. Mark this point with a pencil. Now you have the point at which to drill two holes (P in Figure 78) through which to run some of that string you put his body together with. This now

Fig. 82

Fig. 83

Fig. 84

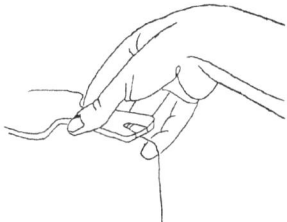

Fig. 85

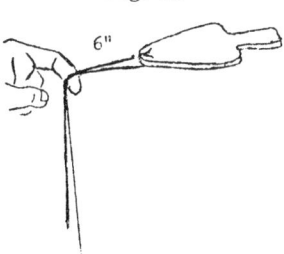

Fig. 86

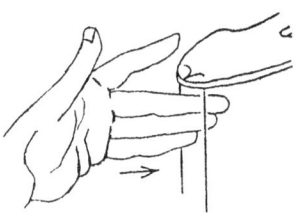

Fig. 87

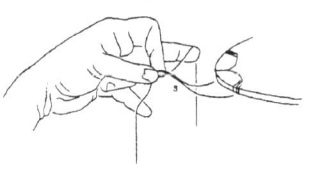

Fig. 88

becomes not only the string you hang him up with offstage, but onstage a way of partially animating him while he is not being hand-held.

My leaning rail has holes bored in its top edge every 6", and by bending a 1/4" rod in the shape indicated in Figure 84 and inserting it in the hole, and hanging the control on it, I can – while the puppet is hanging, get all his head and hand action, and in addition, walk him in any part of half of a 2' circle!

Back to our stringing: Attach his hand strings, at G, making them just taut enough so that when you tilt the control to move his head, his hands will move slightly, too! Helps "keep him alive." Attach the backstring, leaving it just a little slack so he doesn't bend over every time you nod his head. But by slipping your little finger under the backstring you have personal immediate control of such bending as he need do to bow, kneel, or bend forward when he sits or rises.

Attach the leg strings with enough slack so you can hold about 6" straight out in front of the control before they turn downward to the knees, while the legs are straight.

In order to make a legbar of your hand, insert your last three fingers between the two leg strings as in Figure 87, and then with the thumb and index finger, pinch the two legstrings together about 5" below the control. Now spread your second and little fingers with the legstrings over the tips of them as in Figure 88. Bring the leg strings up until they are taut against the knees, which will cause slack on the strings between your hand and the control, (at S) which has the effect of making the leg strings independent of the control.

By rocking your hand, you produce the same action on the legs that a legbar would do, but with the additional benefit of being in immediate contact with the strings instead of separated from them by a piece of wood.

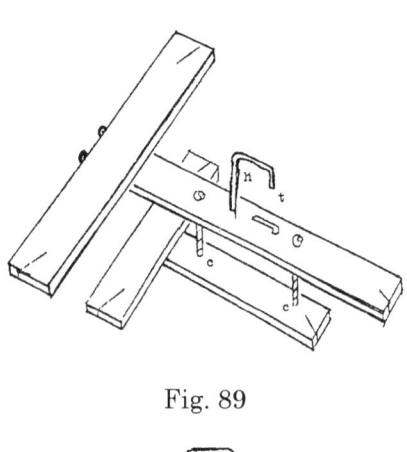

Fig. 89

With this means of control, one can do anything that can be done with a legbar, and manipulation is simplified as one never has to put the now non-existent legbar back! I have gone to some length to explain in detail a process which, once you have tried it, becomes quick as a wink.

One-handed Walker Control

Could you use another hand? This will give it to you; it's a one-handed walker. Instead of lifting off the walking beam to work it, this walking beam is attached to the part of the control that supports the puppet by two cords (C & C) which allows the walking beam to be tilted sidewise while the body of the control remains horizontal.

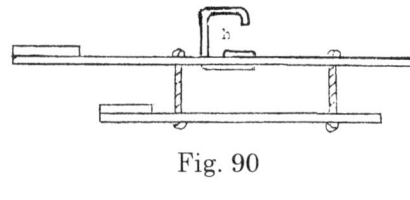

Fig. 90

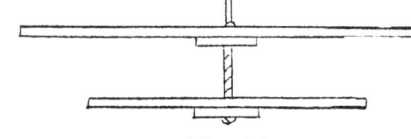

Fig. 91

Fig. 92

Fig 90 is a side view and Fig 91 is a front view. The hook h is coat hanger wire, and is used to hang the puppet backstage, and to hang it on specially constructed hangers onstage. The control must hang level (horizontal) when supported by the tip of the hook t. The space between should be an inch, so you can get your fingers in it if you wish.

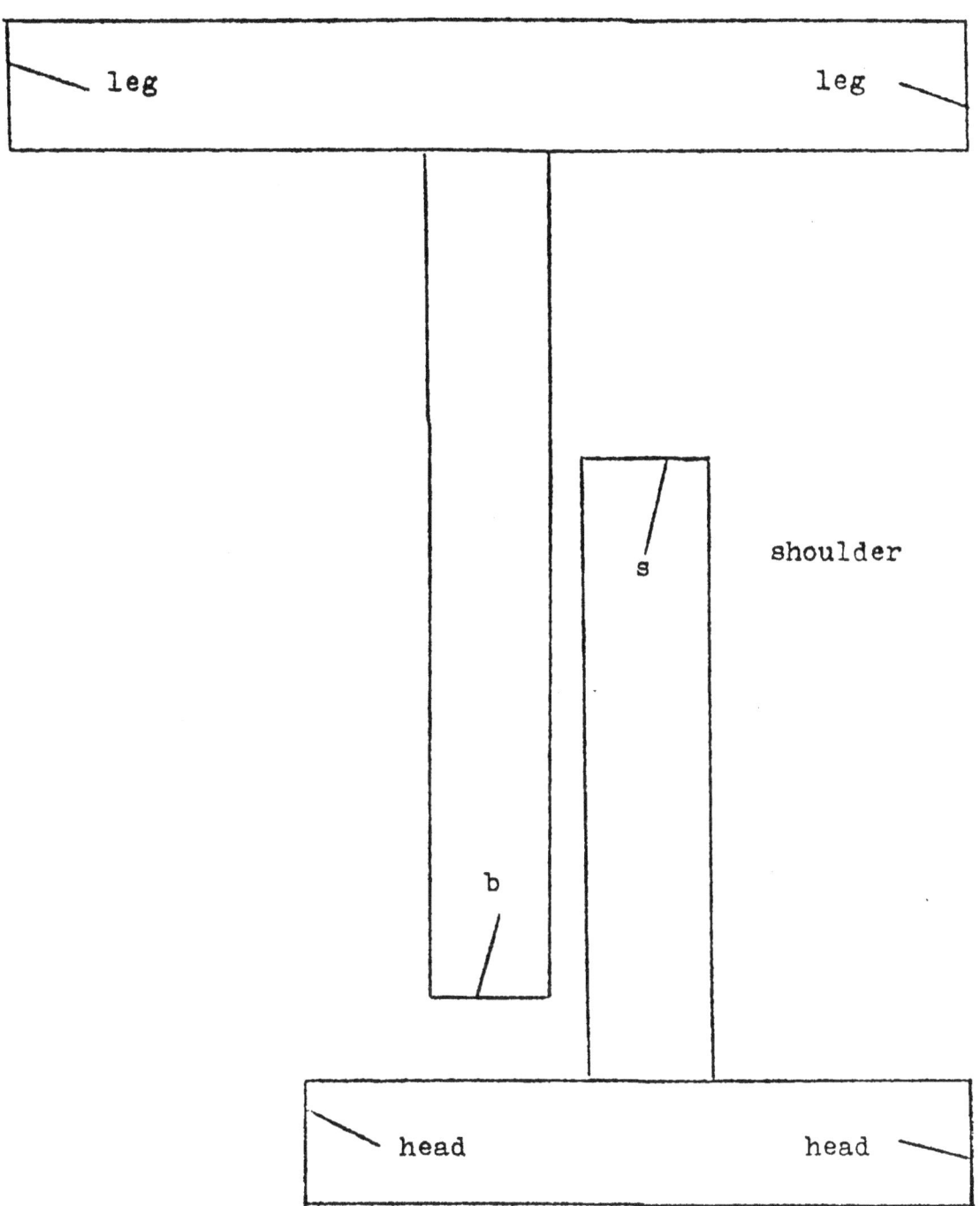
Fig. 93

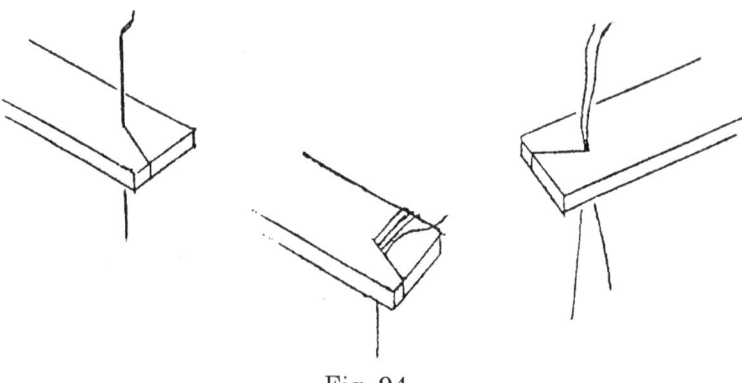

Fig. 94

Figure 93 is the actual size of the control sticks. They are 1/4" to 3/8" thick, of soft wood, nailed together to form the T. I have used it successfully on puppets from 6" to 30" tall.

The slots into which the strings are placed are cut before the control is assembled, with a "coping saw" – an inexpensive little tool you can get at the dime store. Its small blade is just right for the slot to accommodate the string.

You notice that the string slots are cut diagonally, and this is why: a well-controlled puppet has very precise tension on his strings – the leg strings for instance must be exactly the same length. Tying knots in string at exactly the same fraction of an inch and later untying them to make adjustments is much too difficult for me, so – draw the string up through the slot to precisely the tension desired, wrap it around the stick three times, bringing it up through the slot, and there you are. Because the area of the stick is wider at the end than where the string comes up through, it doesn't slip off and unwind. [Note: Steve then wrapped masking tape around the bar ends – either to keep the strings from slipping or to prevent the wood from splitting.]

Put the two shoulder strings together and bring them up through the same slot (indicated on lower control stick above)

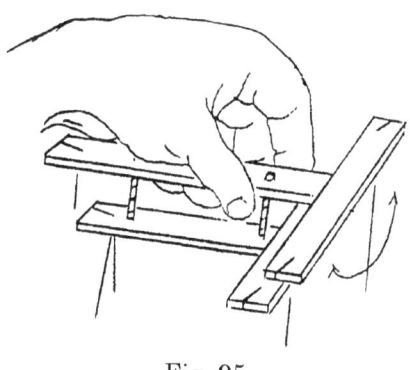

Fig. 95

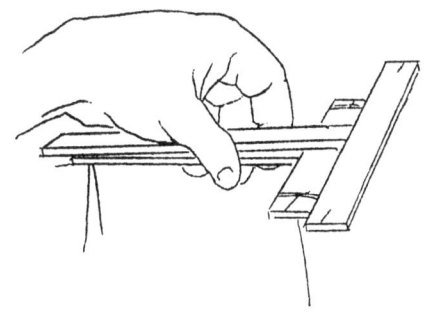

Fig. 96

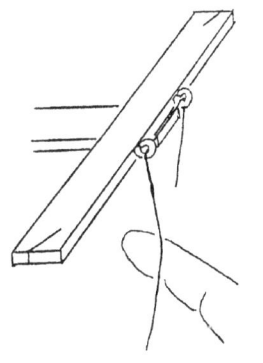

Fig. 95

adjust them until shoulders of puppet hang level, then treat both strings as one, and wrap them around for the tie-off.

The head and shoulder strings are the only ones attached to the lower part of the control. Attach the back string, and fasten it to the back of the top half of the control, leaving it just a little slack so he doesn't bend over every time you nod his head. Your little finger under it will tense it when he needs to bow, kneel, sit, or rise.

Attach the leg strings to the walking beam so that when the beam is level, the strings have no slack in them, but are not so taut that they lift either or both knees away from their normal hang.

To make the legs move, grasp the top part of the control as illustrated in Figure 95 and, holding that part level, rock the cross stick.

Puppets don't actually turn their heads as people do, but by dropping the head slightly forward and lifting one side, they appear to. To work the head, grasp the lower part of the control as illustrated here. Ignore the upper half – it will just lie there 'til you need it – and because the leg and back strings are now slack, nothing will happen to them.

For hands, run a string from one hand up through small screweyes on the front of the walking beam and down to the other hand. Same tension as the leg strings. Now, by hooking a finger under one side, you can move one or both hands! Use the smallest screweyes you can get.

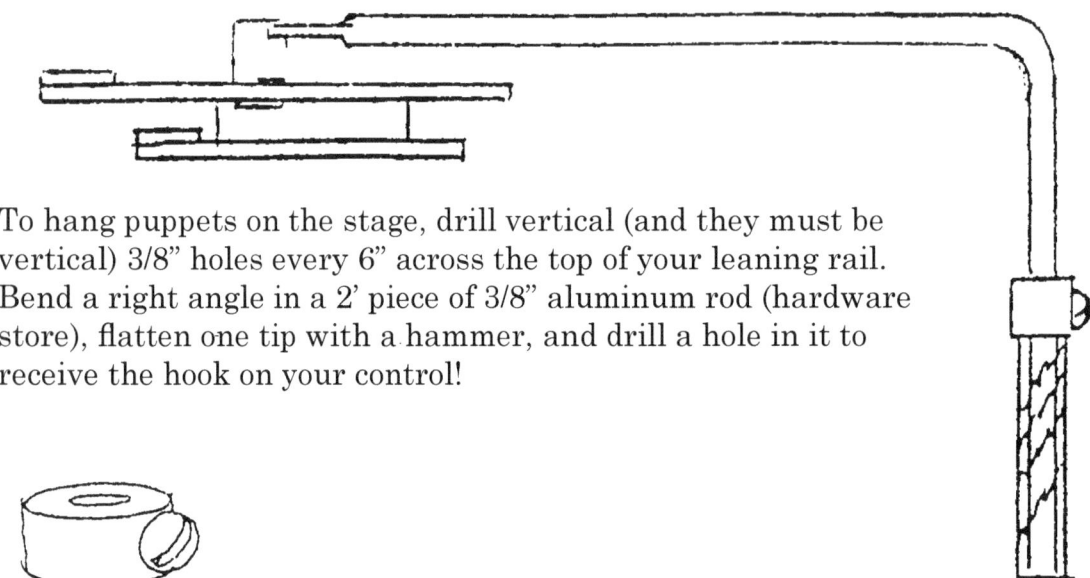

To hang puppets on the stage, drill vertical (and they must be vertical) 3/8" holes every 6" across the top of your leaning rail. Bend a right angle in a 2' piece of 3/8" aluminum rod (hardware store), flatten one tip with a hammer, and drill a hole in it to receive the hook on your control!

Fig. 99

Because hanging puppets mustn't sag or float, I have a machinist make a metal collar (Figure 99) with a bolt in a threaded hole to hold the hanger at the right height. You can see that ALL THE PUPPETS must be strung with the same distance from that hook to the floor, and ALL THE HANGERS must be the same height above the leaning rail for them to work interchangeably. You cannot be too precise about this; it is distressing to have a puppet hang perfectly on one hook, and flop or dangle on another.

How Do You Do?

Fig. 100

As we are all strung, let's manipulate. Let it be understood at this point that I am not advocating "realistic" movement in puppets. Puppets on strings do not move from inside as do people, but from outside, between the pull of the strings and the pull of gravity. Puppets do not walk as well as people do, and they certainly don't dance as people do. So it is necessary in manipulating them to make such compromises, exaggerations and distortions as best express the character, emotion, and

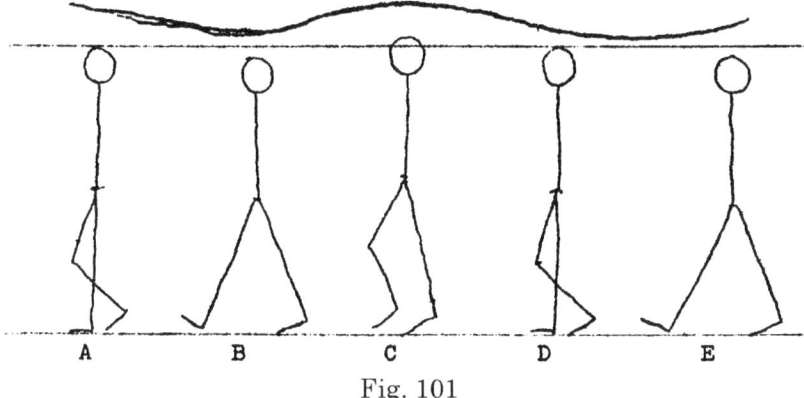

Fig. 101

situation the puppet is involved in. But here, as in designing the puppet – exaggeration of what? It isn't enough to let him jerk and flop haphazardly and then take a bow for parody: oh no. Let's look at some people walking, and see what goes on. This little guy is not – precisely – walking. He, and a million of his fellows get about this way – a sort of sitting- downskedaddle. Sometimes he does it because his operator thinks "that's the way puppets walk." Sometimes the operator theorizes, "Puppets aren't people, so why try for anything." That's like saying, "A flat canvas cannot be made really three-dimensional, so why try to paint dimension into it."

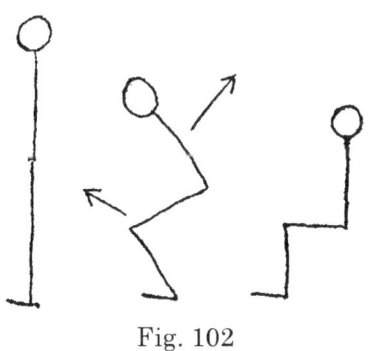

Fig. 102

Go out and look at people walking along the street. Line up the tops of their heads with a horizontal line on a building and see how they move vertically – in relation to it. You'll notice that, as in Figure 101, they go up and down, as well as forward. This is what you will learn to do in your manipulation. At first it's sort of like patting your head with one hand while you rub a circle on your tummy with the other, but you'll get it. The hand holding the control raises the puppet a little in the middle of each step, lowers him a little as the foot is set down. You develop a nice little rhythm. Walk your puppet in a circle around you (you'll get dizzy and fall over, but what the heck!). The goal is to get that rhythm into a habit you'll use whenever the puppet starts walking. While you're doing this, please remember B and E in Figure 101: when one leg is out in front, the other leg is equally that far out in back! You can do this easily by just giving it some attention, and leaving that lag-leg string slack while lifting the advancing one.

Equally as remarkable as their walking is the way some puppets manage to get themselves into chairs by maneuvering themselves over in front of the chair and then just flumping backwards into it. Notice how you do it, when you're not just "Falling down dead." There is the matter of maintaining your balance as you lower yourself into position (Figure 102). "Break" the puppet's knees, and as you draw them slightly forward, tighten the backstring (Figures 85 & 95) and lower him back into the chair. We have to make it appear that he is doing things because he wants to, and not because some big lug upstairs is demanding that he do it.

After you have learned these basic things you can start altering, magnifying, caricaturing them, and this puppet is responsive – dependably. The endless shoulder string lets him tilt his chest, his jointed middle makes contracting, twisting, bending possible. His beautiful shoulder joint gives him immense latitude of arm movement. And his built-in "stops" at elbows, knees, and ankles keeps him from doing the impossible unless the impossible is what you want.

All of the above instruction in seeing anatomical behavior applies equally to handpuppet manipulation, for the problem is the same; only the means are different. They are somewhat simpler in execution, for "you are there" onstage being it – but the process of knowing what you are being is the same. Neither puppet swings his arms in walking, as all humans do. Handpuppets haven't the rough task of how to make legs behave – but must nevertheless communicate to the audience the idea of humanlike movement, which surely indicates that the puppeteer must know what human-like movement is! In the great Burr Tillstrom's show we have seen the dragon, Ollie, who is a balletomaine, leap in the air and do "beats" with his feet – and **he hasn't any feet!** We've seen Ollie shrug – and he hasn't any shoulders! Over and over again we are confronted with the fact that Charlie McCarthy doesn't do the show; Edgar Bergen does it. Ollie the Dragon doesn't do the show; Burr Tillstrom does it. And your puppets don't do the show; you do it. And whereas in this Course there is considerable material about the tools, the primary objective is you, and your development of your knowing and seeing, and ability to project what you have dreamed up. THIS is where your show lies – this is what the sponsor buys and this is what you take a bow for! And money for. So if you have read quickly through those parts of the Course having to do with seeing, hearing, comprehending areas of experience you may heretofore have overlooked, this would be a real good time to go back over them and give them a whirl. All I ask of you is that you should do the best puppet show the world has ever seen!

In all this talk about stringing, I haven't mentioned the kind of string! The famous Tattermans used to use carpet thread. When I began, somebody said "20 pound test Japan silk woven fishline" and I went on with it for years. It doesn't have to be that heavy. Use the lightest weight that will stand up in your use. Black seems to be best. Some people use a plastic fishline called Monofilament, especially for TV work, but it stretches and on a stage it picks up light. [Note: Braided, black dacron or nylon fishline is now available.] Try things out. Be bold. Then LOOK at it!

Session 13 Creating the Handpuppet Stage

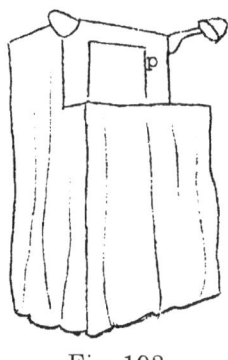

Fig. 103

"All the World's a Stage" — but we still have to build one to do a puppet show. All you string people sit back now, 'cause we're going to start with a handpuppet stage.

This is the one I use and it's about as simple as you can get — takes little time to set up and tear down, packs complete with puppets, sound system, extra speaker in the trunk compartment of any average car (not a Jaguar or an Isetta) and no one piece is too heavy to handle. All the acting is done on the area before the proscenium p which eliminates the problem of sight lines which often plague the puppet show. Lights can be replaced at the Drug Store. Only fastenings are four 20-penny spikes, and the rest is held together by gravity! The booth itself is composed of two collapsible frames a & b, four legs, and four battens.

Here's How

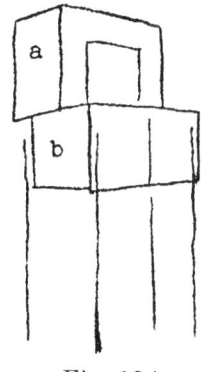

Fig. 104

Make 6 frames (of 1" x 2" planed stock) measuring 2' by 2½' outside. [Note: To assemble the frames, use half-lap joints reinforced with glue and screws.] Hinge four of these together as in Figure 105, to make frame b in Figure 104. They hinge on their 2' sides. When folded the frames should rest on each other, which means you should countersink the hinges. When extended, the frame will look like Figure 106.

Get a piece of 3/8" plywood, and cut an opening in it as indicated in Figure 107. [Note: Cut the proscenium from

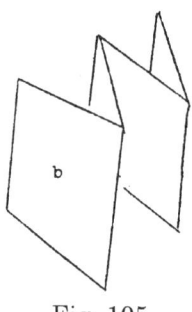

Fig. 105

Miranti plywood, the layers of which are thoroughly patched and solid. Cheaper plywood is finished on the outside only: its interior has knot holes and flaws which become exposed when the plywood is cut to shape, thus weakening the unit.] This is your proscenium. Now very precisely cut it in half at h precisely, that is, on a right angle, for now you are to hinge it together with what is called a "piano hinge." [Note: To assure a neat joint, cover the proscenium's piano hinge with a "dutchman": a strip of muslin thoroughly saturated with glue. Once painted, the joint will be virtually invisible to the audience.] Hinge the two remaining frames on either side, and you have a in Figure 104. [Note: In order to allow the light arms to attach to the Stage properly, the top hinges connecting the proscenium to the side frames must be at least six inches from the top. Cover the gaps between the proscenium and its side frames with dutchmen.]

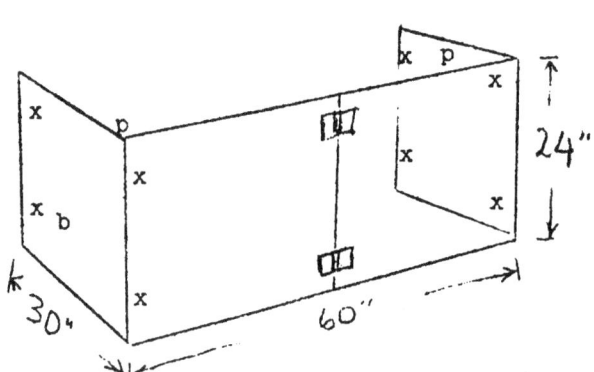

Fig. 106

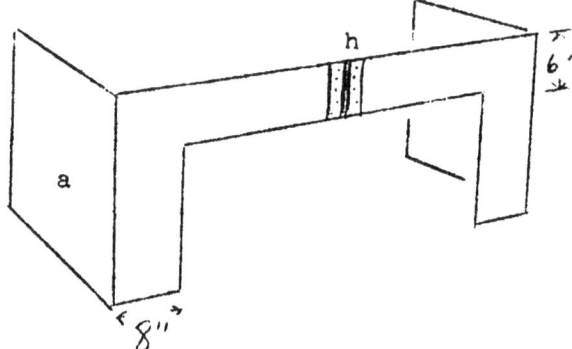

Fig. 107

Make a playboard of 1" x 4" stock, snugly in the space 'p–p', Figure 106. Screw on to it three angle irons where indicated in Figure 108, gauging the distance they project from the edges (approximately 3/4") to slip down over the outside of the frame. [Note: The playboard will be more stable if not one but two angle irons are attached to Its front edge, approximately 30" apart, dividing it

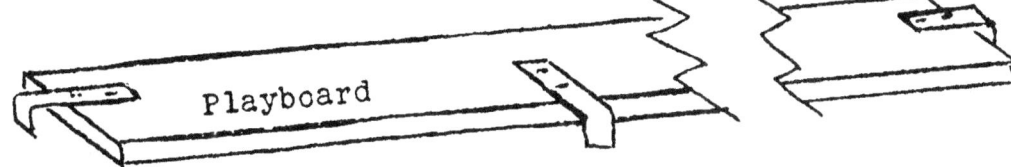

Fig. 108

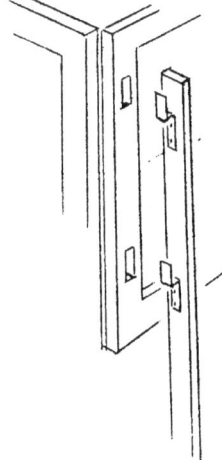

Fig. 109

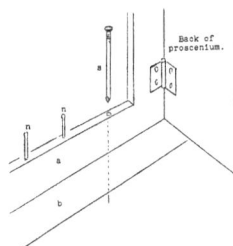

Fig. 110

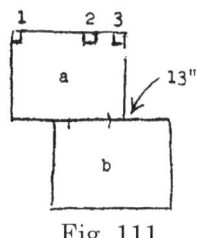

Fig. 111

into thirds.] This not ONLY provides you with a playing surface, but also stiffens the hinged center piece, and holds the sides at the right angle. When in position, it is to be flush with the top of the frame.

The four legs are equipped with angle irons (which you bend into shape with a hammer and a vise) screwed into place to match holes in the b frame, as indicated at x. Make a template of where the holes go, and use it also to match up the angle irons, thus making the legs interchangeable, so you don't have to stop and figure out which one goes where! You can make these rectangular holes by starting with a small hole made by your drill, and then sawing the rectangle with the coping saw you used for the slots in the control.

This view is from inside the booth looking toward the left corner. p is the playboard. The bottom of frame a is resting on the top of frame b. n–n are medium-sized finishing nails on which to hang puppets. They do NOT fasten the two frames together. This is done by the two spikes on each side s–s. Place a on b at a point where its front is 13" back from the front of b. Holding the two frames firmly together, drill holes on each side to accommodate the spikes. Then when you're, ready to assemble it, you just drop the spikes in place, and that's it.

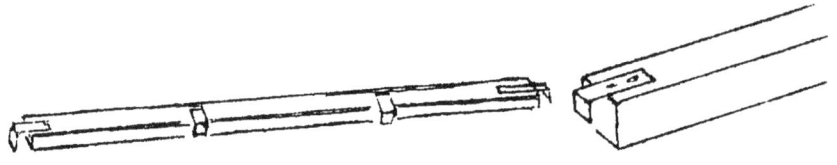

Fig. 112

Fig. 113

Make three battens 1" x 1" and as long as the inside width of frame a. Put angle irons on each end of them as you did on the playboard. They go at (Figure 111) 1 to brace the top of the frame, (and support the masking cloth when we come to it,) and at 2 to support the backdrop, or scene, before which the puppets perform. The third one, which goes at 3 has two extra angle irons on one side of it. These go over the front of the proscenium and stiffen it, as the playboard stiffened frame b. [Note: As with the playboard, an extra angle brace on batten #3 will Stiffen the hinged proscenium.] In addition, on this batten is hung the front curtain. (Everything in this equipment "doubles in brass.")

I am aware that so far I have given no measurements of height other than the height of the frames a & b. Only you can determine the height of your playboard from the floor. Because it's the easiest, I like to stand when I manipulate, and work with my face right behind the puppets, looking at them through the scenery. The point where the bottom of your puppet comes (Figure 113) determines the length of the legs.

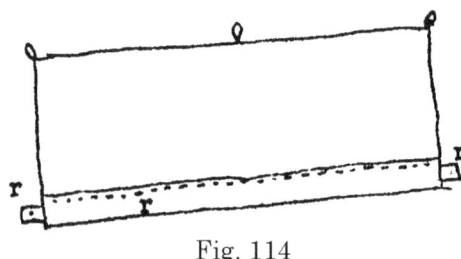

Fig. 114

Well! We've about got this little stage built, except for the "property" shelf And as my handpuppets handle about a million "props", it has to be a big one. So I took a piece of blue denim (because I happened to have it; canvas is equally good) and made a 3' x 5' thing to wrap the legs and battens in when "trouping." But why not use it for the shelf, too! Sew shoe string loops on one edge (find out where by putting it in place) and a pocket on the other. In this pocket slip a batten (which lives there from now

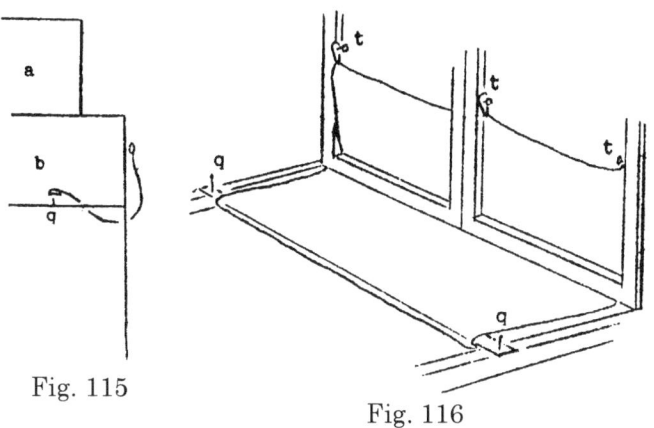

Fig. 115

Fig. 116

on, r) about 1/2" by 1-1/4" by the outside width of the booth (Figure 114).

Drive a finishing nail in the bottom batten of each side frame of b about 14" from the front q, drill corresponding holes in the ends of r, and slip them down over the nails. Bring the cloth down and under the bottom of the front of frame b and slip the shoestring loops over round-headed screws placed at t,t,t to stretch it taut. You now have a BIG shelf, which will catch almost everything that falls, and hold props for an entire show, but also "wraps up the show."

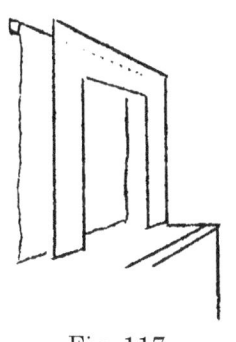

Fig. 117

From batten '2' (Figure 111) hang the "backdrop." Although I've been using this kind of material for years, I can't give you a name to ask for. [Note: Steve used alpaca for the scrim.] The point is, when you look through it toward the light, you can see the puppets in front of it, but when the audience looks toward its lighted side, they can't see you. I always use black, but not everyone does: I've seen all sorts of colors, and with suggestions of scenes painted on them too! The weave is so open that in painting it, the paint only hits the threads, and doesn't fill the spaces between. This is another opportunity to exercise your creative choice: when you find something you like – try it out and see if it works!

Batten '2' in Figure 117, is from 4" to 6" back of the proscenium, which allows your puppets to make entrances from the side if you wish, rather than having always to pop up from below.

Sometimes it is necessary to play in daylight and the light behind the booth would expose your presence through the

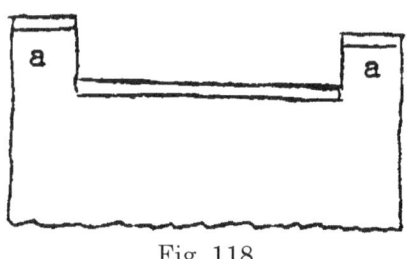

Fig. 118

backdrop. A piece of black cotton sateen as wide as the booth, running from 2 back over 1 (Figure 111) and thence to the floor takes care of that.

Draperies to "dress" the booth can be anything you wish, of course, but I prefer the cheapest kind of unbleached muslin, sewn up all in one piece to fit the booth, a & a fitting the top sides of the a frame, and the space between them fitting around the projecting sides of the b frame. [Note: A muslin masking is too thin to hide the puppeteers during the show – the stage lights shining down renders the material translucent. A heavier material is advisable.] I like lots of fullness, and sew it into webbing around the top. Don't skimp on material – make it a little fuller and a little longer than it should be to "fit" snugly – there is shrinkage when dying – and one can cut a little off better than one can add.

I select a color, and then do an intentionally sloppy dying job: wadding the cloth up, I dump it in the dye bath and instead of the constant movement and "evening out" process recommended, I let it come out all mottled – that is, some parts of the cloth get the full strength of the color, and some – where it was squdged over on itself – is much lighter. Seen from the audience, this gives "depth" and richness to the cloth that is not inherent in it and I get the effect of "crushed plush" for the price of muslin, and in addition have the benefit of it not taking up the great packing space that crushed plush would require. To further this effect, I pack it without folding – just dump it into the space and wad it down. When it comes out, it has a myriad little wrinkles, and these catch the light and further the illusion of richness, as well as avoiding the creased appearance of the tablecloth in DaVinci's "Last Supper."

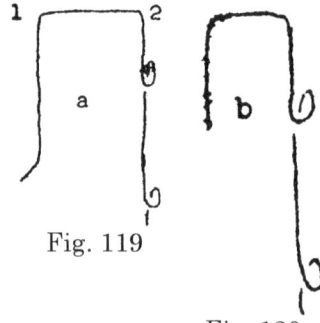

Fig. 119

Fig. 120

The "puppeteer's friend," coathanger wire, now gets its inning. Figure 119 is a pattern for the hooks to be made to attach the drape to the booth. These are

- 114 -

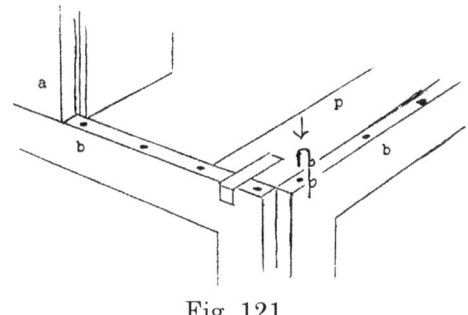

Fig. 121

actual size, and the two angles, 1 & 2 are taken directly from the battens which make the frames a. The loops bent into the wire are, of course, for sewing the hooks onto the webbing. Again you will need two pairs of pliers to make these bends, and one of them must be big enough with a good cutter for all the cutting you must do.

Figure 120 is the shape of the hook to be used on the b frame. It can't go all the way over the frame because it would interfere with placing the playboard. So drill holes at 6" intervals all around the top of the projecting part of the b frame, and sew the Figure 120 hooks to the webbing to correspond with the holes. Use fishline, or something equally stout for sewing on these hooks: they come loose with astonishing ease! [Note: While coathanger hooks are fine, most puppeteers will use Velcro to attach the masking to the stage.]

Y'know something? We've about got this little show wrapped up. Have to light it yet, and that's about it. So – lights!

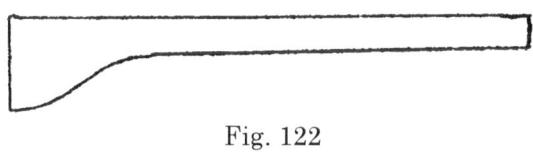

Fig. 122

So far we've managed to avoid any fastenings like bolts and butterfly nuts, so let's keep it that way by continuing to let gravity hold things in place for us where it will. First a word about light itself.

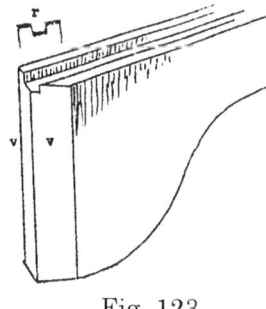

Fig. 123

If a light is turned straight on something, it flattens it out (look at your flash snapshots) but if a light comes from either side, it makes some shadows here and there, and makes it easier to see. So (Figure 103) we'll put a single light on either side of the stage, and if it has power enough, that will do nicely. As light intensity decreases by the square of the distance from its object,

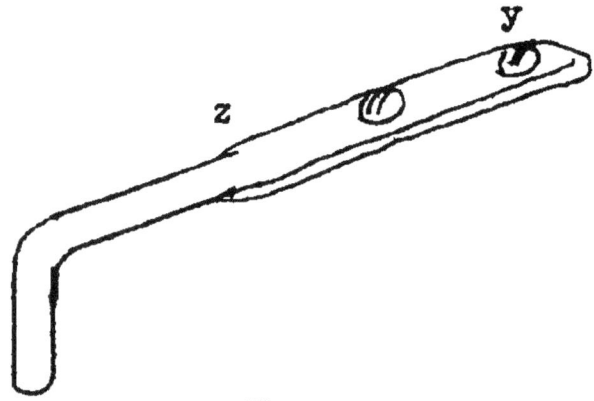

Fig. 124

we want these lights close in.

Take a 6" board, and cut this shape about 2' long. The next step is "nice" but not vital: rabbet a groove a 1/4" wide down the center of the top edge (r in Figure 123 is a rabbet) in which to countersink both the electric cord and the angle iron in Figure 1243. Bevel the wide end of the board v–v into a right angle.

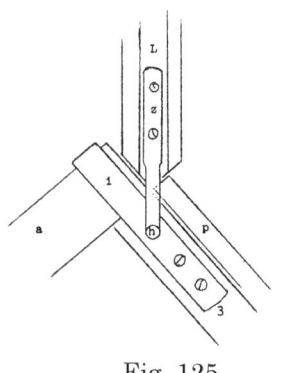

Fig. 125

Now we do a little more metal work: bend a 1/4" iron rod at right angles (hammer and vise) as pictured actual size in Figure 124. Holding the angle end with a pair of pliers, hammer the area from z to y flat, so it's about half the thickness it was when it was round. In this flattened area, drill two holes, to accommodate two round headed screws.

Figure 125 is a top view of the left front corner of the a frame. p is the top edge of the proscenium, a is the side section of the a frame, I is the angle iron on the end of the #3 batten which supports the curtain, L is this light bracket you're making, z is the top view of this iron angle you've just hammered out.

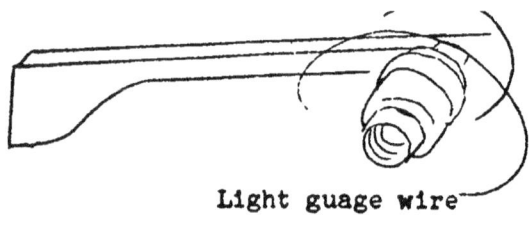

Fig. 126

h is a hole you are to drill in the angle iron i to accommodate the insertion of z. Hold L in place, lay z in the rabbet to locate where to drill the hole h. When that is done, insert z in h and, holding L in place, mark through the two holes where the screws are to go. Screw z onto L, insert the angle of z into h, and there's how you put up your lights!

What lights? Ah yes – "Birdseyes" at the Drug Store. [Note: "Birdseye spots" are actually 50 watt R-40 interior floods, available in any hardware Store. PAR-38 floods, which look something like automobile headlights, are unnecessarily heavy.] Get two ordinary sockets, (no switches) and enough rubber light-cord – say 50'. [Note: It is difficult to find light sockets without switches. Try electrical wholesalers or large hardware stores. Suitable substitutes are the inexpensive clamp-on lights found in hardware stores. Remove the clamp assemblies and attach the sockets to the light arms as Steve directs.] Wire the sockets. Get two aluminum shades – just big enough to cover the birdseyes – the kind that screw onto the ends of the sockets. [Note: Do not, however, use the thin aluminum shades which come with the clamp-on lights. They are not meant to handle the heat generated by the floods. The aluminum shades Steve shows are six-inch photographic shades, available from better photo supply houses, and are intended to be used with the floods.]

Now with L in position and a bulb in the socket and plugged in, aim the light at the center of the stage. Whittle the end of L to make a notch for the socket to rest in at that angle! Wire it to L, then wrap the socket and the end of L with "rubber tape" from the electric shop. (It stretches in application, and never lets go later.) Run the wire from the socket up over the booth and down the center of the back about 2'. Do the same with the other light. Here plug their "male" plugs into a two-way receptacle on the end of your extension cord – which is the remainder of that 50' you bought, and you're lit! If, later, you feel like being more elaborate with lighting, that's fine – but try this now, and see if you need more. Paint your proscenium, put up your curtain, and you have a THEATRE!

Session 14 **Creating the Marionette Stage**

On the following page is a marionette stage. It is also a stretching exercise. If you have a bent for construction you will take this all in at a glance. If you have done nothing like it in your WHOLE LIFE, don't be frightened. Just look at it for a bit and comprehend it. The stage and bridge are accounted for. lr is the leaning rail. cr is the batten on which to hang the front curtain, lights, proscenium arch. t & g is a " tongue & grooved" piece that slides up and down in the wider one below it to make it easier to hang the front top drapes and then slide them up in the air. Sm–Sm are the only two pieces of strap metal on the thing, to provide additional bracing. [Note: Four strap metal braces are used: two at the front and two at the back] The support for the sound system not only holds the turntable or tape machine up where it can be operated from the bridge, but gives additional support to the hanging rail hr which in turn helps support the front uprights supporting the masking, but provides places for puppets to hang on the sides ready for their entrances and places to mount spots for side lighting. kr is a "kick rail" to keep your feet from bumping the scenery, which hangs from the leaning rail lr. The bridge hinges in the center, the ladders, legs, and the three plywood stage supports fold into it. Wherever possible, "piano hinges" have been used (I was surprised when I first learned one didn't have to take piano hinges off a piano!)

Dimensions are whatever you want them to be, but you might like some of these as "taking off places" for your own decisions. Both stage and bridge were 2' x 8' in area. Stage 2' off floor, bridge 4'. Proscenium opening was 4' x 6', which is comparable to the proportion of a TV screen or the old fashioned (not wide wide screen) movies. If I were doing it again, I would undertake to make the stage floor even higher than 2' – what good is the show if it can't be seen? And there are some remarkably low theatre and school stages around the country. You have to make up for a lack of the architect's foresight by your own.

By a judicious use of hinges – regular, piano, and "loose butt," this stage went together with only seven "loose butt" pins and eleven wing-nuts. See if you can figure out where they went.

VIP!

If you're building your first stage, be sure all your bolts, nuts, pins for pin-hinges are the same size, so they can be used interchangeably. Setting up and tearing down is hard boring work and there's no need to complicate it unnecessarily. And when you build, build durably. This doesn't mean building out of two by fours and steel girders, it just means that if you know nothing whatever about carpentry, make friends real quick with a carpenter who will teach you, or at least get a book on how to put a nail and a screw in a piece of wood. It's not really complex – just unfamiliar to a lot of us who, as soon as we're acquainted with it, do it without another thought, and profit thereby.

Drapes

Unlike our handpuppet booth, there are lights backstage in a stringpuppet show, and they can't be allowed to show through, which means the drapes must be opaque. Best thing I ever used was the "crushed plush" I mentioned in Session 13. It costs somewhat more than the flimsiest muslin, but it lasts forever and ever, it looks as elegant as anything, it doesn't show dirt (and ALL backstages are dirty – it's a law or something!) and because it's already "crushed" when you get it, it can be used wadded up to stuff in around breakable parts of your equipment.

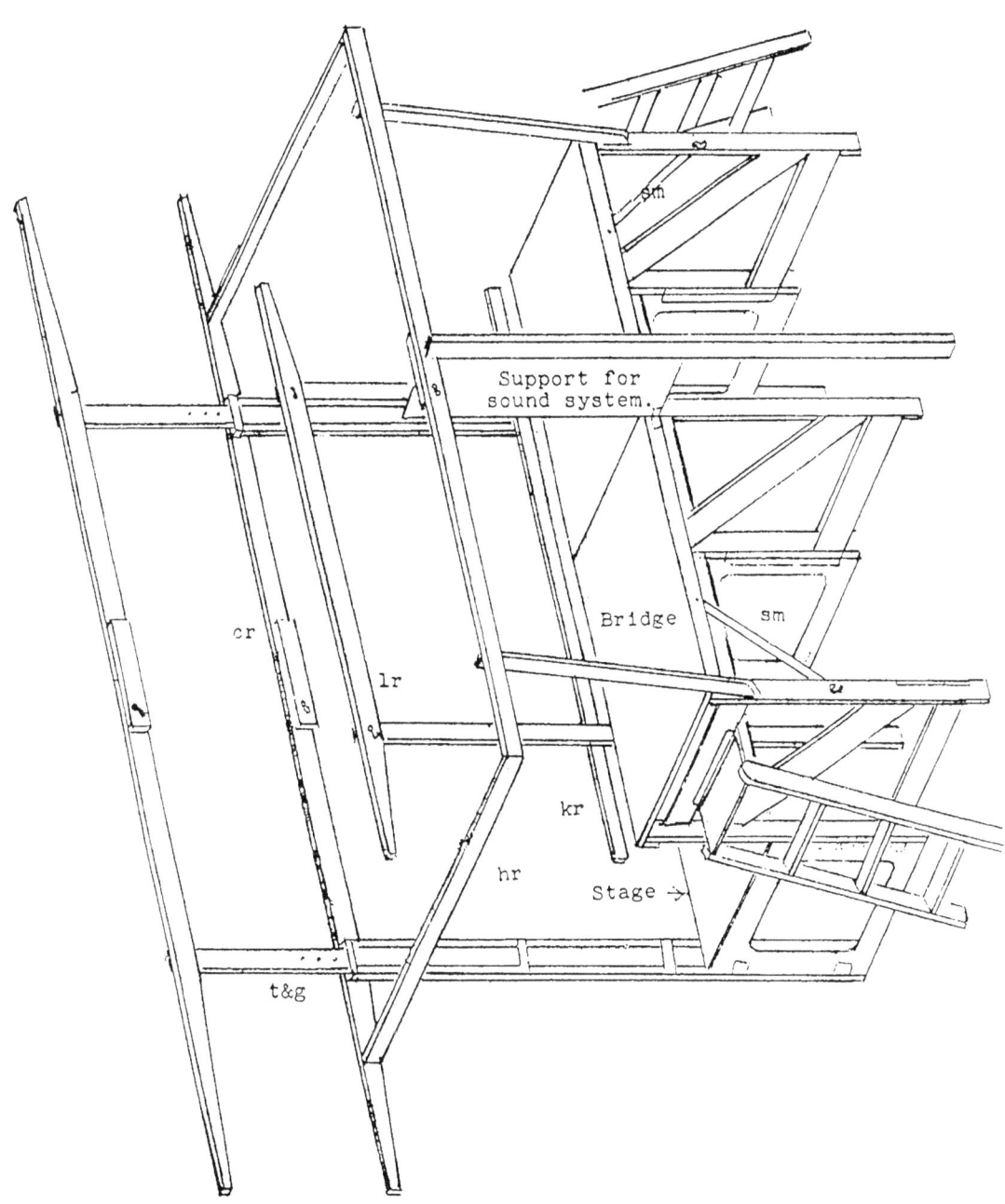

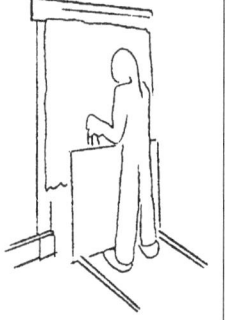

Fig. 128

First show I ever did with the old familiar doorway, with a sheet for masking and a card table on its side for a backing. Crayon on wrapping paper for scenery. Floorlamps in the next room for lights. Ah – simplicity.

More complex was a show with a cast of seventy PUPPETEERS! (Boy's School) about evenly divided between hand- and stringpuppets, and all of whom had to perform.

A three-sided screen 12' high, with a proscenium opening cut in about the middle of it, and lit from the front made the playing area. Hand-people stood on the floor, but for string people we

Fig. 129

built a platform at the level of the floor of the opening. This was 2' back of the opening when hand-puppets were working, so they could use the same scene support. When time came for the string-people, the platform was shoved up against the opening, and the puppeteers climbed aboard via 6' step ladder. It solved the problem just fine but it was hardly a "traveling" equipment.

Simplest string stage I EVER saw being used professionally (that means, taking money for it) had no bridge at all! The operator just stood on an ordinary little wooden bench and leaned over the bankdrop! The stage was built like a short fat bedstead, with the head and foot being the proscenium and

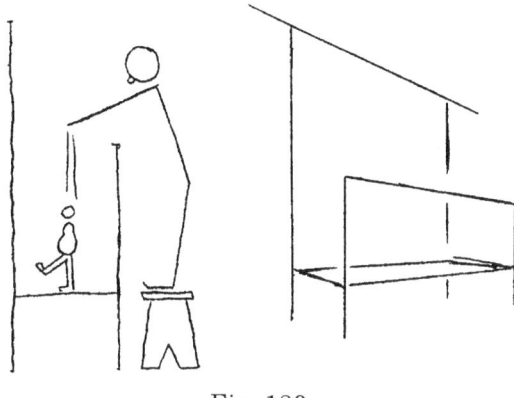

Fig. 130

scenery supports. If I remember, the puppets offstage were just hung on the back of the scenery. This was a one puppeteer operation, and I can imagine situations where it might be quite satisfactory.

You may have noticed that practically all of my stuff is built of wood; I just got started out that way, I'm familiar with it. But if you happen to "feel" for metal, by all means use it. The Tatterman's *"Peer Gynt"* stage was aluminum. The Bil Bairds' have a dream of a huge metal stage. (I'm beginning to long for the handpuppet "fit-up" Walter Wilkinson trundled about the British moors on a barrow!)

Get Up Off the Floor!

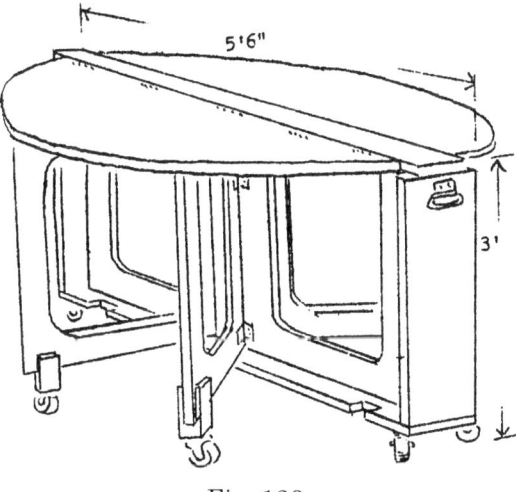

Fig. 128

This advice applies not only to nightclub patrons, but to club puppeteers. You can't dance around on most tables, so you must somehow take a tablestage with you. Fig. 131 is how Bob Longfield solved the problem. The two castored supports on either side fold into the central portion, and the whole thing goes in the car. A consideration for club stages is that they often must go quickly through standard-sized doors, wheel out into the acting area, and be set up ready to go in less time than it took you to read it.

The "drop leaves" on most club stages make that possible, and of course the puppets

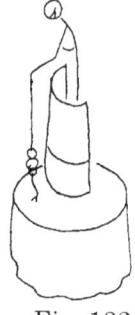

Fig. 132

come out with the set. I'd like to see a stage made like a big silk hat. Real elegant. Puppets as well as puppeteer would go in the crown. Hey – turn it over and let the puppeteer come out as a magician's rabbit, and do handpuppets and magic! THAT would get it up off the floor where the customers could see it!

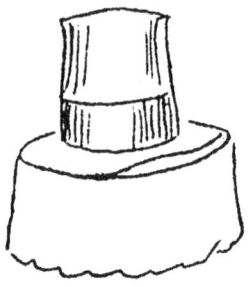

Fig. 133

Perennial problem in any stringpuppet stage is how to help them walk predictably and without sounding like horses going over a wooden bridge. Stretch a "ground cloth" over the stage. It must have enough body to at least muffle the patter of little feet, and have a texture that will help hold the foot where you set it down, without being so tenacious it trips him up when he's walking. I used a rubber mat with good effect. Canvas is hard and tends to get slick. Duvetyn works, but picks up lint. One company used a sheet of Celotex, but I don't know how they transported it. Black is better than white, but maybe you want to be fancy and have a different one for each set. This would be beautiful for the guests in the balcony, but remember that everything you do during a scene change takes time.

Whatever way you build your equipment, save it from a rainy day. There will inevitably come SOME day when it's so far from the car to the stage door that something's going to get wet. If you're the kind that packs everything in trunks and rucksacks, be sure they're waterproof. If you're the kind that likes to dump things loose in the car, be sure they're not water soluble, either as to material or decoration. If you have crushables, arrange for crushproof containers, for someday someone may drop it down a flight of stairs. It might even be you. I have.

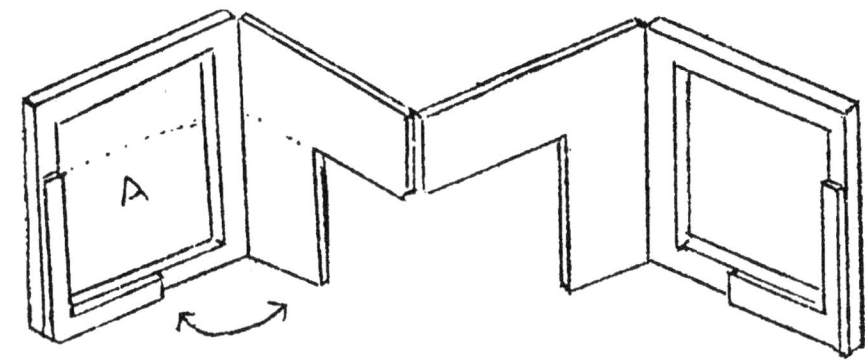

Fig. 134

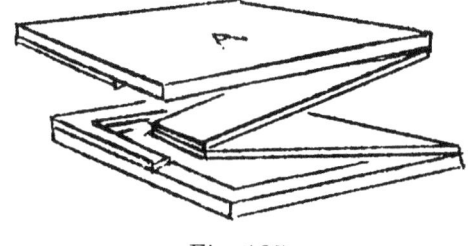

Fig. 135

While speaking of packing, let's go back to A of that handpuppet stage, Figure 104. If we were to fold A up, and lay it down on a folded B, we'd have a box with no top and bottom, and a hole around one corner where the stuff we cut away to make the stage opening is missing. Cut a batten-width strip of the scrap of the plywood you made the proscenium of, and fasten it (screws) on the inside of the two outside frames as in Figure 134. Now when you fold it again, as in Figure 135, you see that the new pieces have filled up the holes. Screw a piece of "trunk fiber" on the outside of A and your new box has a top. Screw a similar piece of trunk fibre on the opposite outside of B frame, stack them together, and you have a case in which you can carry the lights, extension cord, drapes, and a couple other odds and ends. A webbing strap around it two ways holds it together and makes a handle. (Now if you can just get someone to carry it!)

Caution! Slippery Roads

Don't let your first professional engagement slip up on you without having thoroughly packed, unpacked, and repacked your show completely. Some very serious people have done this, and when the time came to get to the show they: a) couldn't get it all in the vehicle they had provided, b) lost some of it along the road (really!) and/or c) found when they got to the theatre they'd left some one vital thing at home. When home is more miles and hours away than you have before showtime, this is rough.

When you're all organized with what goes in what, look at it there in a heap and see if it looks like you knew what you were doing. You might take a tip from the old time drummers as well as show people, and paint everything the same color. This not only looks "professional," but it makes everything easier to find when you're moving out of that strange auditorium.

If you can possibly do it, make up no one piece that requires more than one man to carry it. In the first place most people don't like to carry stuff, even when it's supposed to be their job, and in the second place, you'll have to lug it around yourself on more than one occasion, even if – like me – it says in your contract that there is to be help there to carry it in AND OUT! Whenever I can, I put nice big casters on things. Even when it goes bumpity bumipity across the cracks in the pavement, it saves an awful lot of lifting.

You now have all the really pertinent details for the simplest and most complex of stages; anything further should come out of your personal inclination and your shows requirement. Here's your chance to stretch your faculties, and create something for the benefit of YOUR show, and the wonder of the rest of us!

Session 15 Creating Scenery and Props

And then there is the matter of

Scenery

Happens I am a nut on scenery, having been painting it since I was BAby! (in the "legitimate theatre," that is.) But it also happens I spent 25 years "on the road" with a puppet theatre, and my enthusiasm for magnificence of effect is tempered by my awareness of the demands of transportation and setting up. So I'll tell you what I think about scenery for the puppet stage:

Audiences don't come to the puppet show to see how good a painter you are. They come to the show to involve themselves emotionally in the despairs and successes of the hero. (All right - the "heroine," you Suffragette!) That is what the show is about, and the puppet, the props, the scenery, the lighting, the music, your voice, your manipulation - EVERYthing is subservient to that. Everything is only to put that across. And when the "set" draws attention to itself, you have not done well - you have done poorly!

Consider the shows that have been touring around (and I don't care what your age; they've been in every generation) where the actors used no scenery at all! Just used a bare stage - sat on stools in today's clothes and involved you in the problems of the characters they were reading. Made magnificent entertainment! And that's what you're delivering - or should be!

Now don't decide that Stevens doesn't like scenery; I LOVE scenery! But I don't want you to swallow up your show in facade, when it should consist principally of heart.

Let's go back to your original dreaming of what your show was like. It may be that you were (properly) so concentrating on what the hero wanted and how the villain opposed him that you had only the feeling of the circumstance and not the details of where it was taking place. If so, may I congratulate you. That's very good: things - feelings inside the character at a given moment are what color the surroundings. Everyone lives in the very same world, and yet what different worlds we live in - due to our emotions. See what is indicated by the words we use to describe these various worlds and think of a "set" that would go along with them: "I feel blue." "We'll have a hot time." "I'm sitting on top of the world!" "What a dark brown taste of despair." "What is so rare as a day in June!" "There's a rainbow 'round my shoulder." And so on; you see? The words themselves suggest a simple allover color tone for the scene. So just as we thought of the most expressive allover color for the puppet's costume, so we think of the all-over tone for the scene. This is the "kick-off" for your scene design.

Having determined that, go next to "line." Vertical lines are hopeful, uplifting, moral. Think of tall forests, cathedrals, straight men. Horizontal lines are placid, restful. They're not "going somewhere." Diagonals have muscles in them - action - opposition to the restful horizontal or the virtuous vertical. Criss-cross lines are full of conflict - opposed to each other -confused - undecided - talky and choppy. Excited!

All these interpretations are important to your choice of using them in your scene - and here - as in our early learning about what a man is like, you use them knowing what they are and what they do not by accident.

How do you use them. Get out another piece of wrapping paper, and make a line on it. If there were one line that would best express the feeling of this scene, what would it be? On that line, build the rest of the scene. Is it sheltering like a home, a mother's arms, a womb? Is it brusk, adventuresome, like a cliff, a knight in armor, a ship's prow? Is it threatening, like a gallows, a saber thrust, a tiger's mouth? Again the wonderful creative question: what is it like? This one line - this one direction, is the important thing - for everything you add to it will be colored by it. And when the audience sees it, they will know instantly what you meant, and can turn their attention away from it and to the course of their hero's fortunes. It is sad but true: scenery that is "seen" is a failure. But the beauty of this attack on the problem is that if you have this original "line" or feeling, you can dispense with infinite detail, which saves not only your adding it, but your puppets combating it.

Draw the setting. Sure - you know how to draw; the way you drew a puppet is the same way you draw a house, the witch's oven, the giant's castle, anything else. But you haven't had enough experience, enough instruction? Let me direct you to the Saturday *Evening* Post, or any other magazine you happen to have about: here is the most wonderful gallery of art the world has ever seen! Not only do these wonderful magazines regularly run color reproductions of the masterpieces of the past and the present, but their ads have the best of current drawing, for you to study, to take apart and look at. Painting? They have MASTERS doing it, and if you are really interested, you can learn everything you need to know simply by looking at them, seeing where they put this stroke, how they shaded that part, how they imparted the idea of foliage, stone, or distance. All-over color scheme? It's in every drawing. Interior decoration? Natch. Landscape? Outer space? Fantasy? Natch! It's all in your house right now. All you have to do is LOOK at it. You have available the best instruction there is!

Now - how you gonna paint it? Well sir, there are two ways which I will recommend. One is Romain Proctor's way; and it's a "gooder." First, get a set of old fashioned curtain stretchers - the things your (great-grand) mama used to dry her lace curtains on. Then, get some unbleached muslin (good of cheap thin stuff). sew it to the size of your backdrop, and stretch it on the stretchers. Stand it up and fasten it to something at the top so it leans a little bit forward (when your brush drips, it will fall on the drip cloth underneath, and not on the painting). Use the same house-painter's "color ground in oil" that I recommended for painting the heads, but this time, the thing you use to thin it with is gasoline! You can immediately see that this is hazardous! DO NOT SMOKE! DO NOT USE NEAR FIRE OR FLAME! as the saying goes. Check your insurance! For any juniors taking this course - TALK IT OVER WITH YOUR PARENTS! If they say "no" - go on to the next method! Y'hear?

Now you mix the color with gasoline, and paint it as you would transparent watercolor. The value of this method is that once painted, it is impervious to that one time in a thousand when the show gets caught out in the rain: the scenery won't be ruined.

The other method - and one which I have used with invariable success, is to paint with dye. Proceed as above, but instead of paint, just go down to the drugstore and get as many colors of ordinary package dye as you think you'll need. Simply mix it with water, and go ahead and paint. You'll find it takes a bit of scrubbing to get it started on the raw cloth, but it makes good clean color, and you have no fear of explosion. True, if it gets caught out in the rain, you're out a set of scenery, but I have scenery which has been "trouping" since 1933 and it hasn't had an accident yet, so

Happily we are not "Artists" of the type bound by prohibitions against mixing media: we can put anything with ANYthing if it gets the effect we intended. So when you've painted with your dye until you can't think of what to do to get that particular effect -maybe you can sharpen it up with crayon! Maybe a little highlight would snap it up? No reason you shouldn't add it with opaque paint. Mostly you won't need it, but if it occurs to you, anything at all - DO it. It's your scenery.

There's only one restriction! Your setting is a "background": keep it there. Most scenery is painted in a "high key" - quite light - and the light that is put on the stage bounces off the scenery more than it does off the puppets, making the puppets look as though they were in the dark on a well lit stage! There are several ways to combat this. For one thing, you can keep a puppet handy to compare with, and don't paint anything on the drop lighter than the puppet's face. As an extreme of this, I have painted scenery on black velvet, working from dark to light. And boy - with all that black around, my most brilliant highlights were 'way down in tone.

If you covered your stage floor with hundreds of boxes, door-knobs, and rocking chairs, your puppet would have a tought time moving through it. So if your backdrop is full of contrasty shapes and colors, the audience's eye will have a hard time following the puppet. Give everybody a break; keep it low in key, and keep it simple.

Want to look at examples of scenery? Encyclopoedia Britannica is as good a place as any. You don't have to read the text - looking at the pictures will do you more good. The backgrounds in advertising illustrations are stage sets for the product or the message; look at them as settings, and see how they are held down.

Remember always: what the audience sees is the composite of the setting AND the puppets. The color of the puppets' costumes is part of the scene. Use the color of the set to emphasize the puppet, not to swallow him up.

Caution: for years I rejoiced in a yellow-gold front curtain. It was elegant! Yum! Only I didn't look at it in relation to what immediately followed it. The lights on it - so close to it - made it glisten and sparkle, and when I opened it the audience looked in on what looked like The Black Hole of Calcutta by contrast! Yeeps! Don't you do it.

Properties

If you took a tape recording of everything that was said by your family over a given period, you would not have a scene of a play; a lot of stuff would have to be taken out, if only to attempt to maintain continuity. Same thing with props; don't put everything you can think of on the stage. Use the fewest props possible. If you're doing stringpuppets, one of the things they don't do well is handle things, so when I am writing the script, I write it so they don't have to. Handpuppets - that's a different matter, but except for Joan of Arc drawing and brandishing her sword (which I had to have two mechanical geniuses named McElroy figure out for me!), I don't recall any of my stringpuppets being required to do anything more complex than pushing open a gate or playing a flute.

More man-hours have been wasted going through the stores trying to find a prop the right size than have been spent in making them. Maybe one can stumble on something the right size now and then, but mostly it's better just to go ahead and make it in the first place. As such props are as much fun to make as the puppets themselves, it isn't such a chore. I have stood in sheer delight before a puppet sized tack hammer I have made!

Lighting

There's a lot of fuss made about lighting, but it's pretty simple, really. You've already seen what I consider adequate for a hand puppet show, and that principle of cross-lighting holds

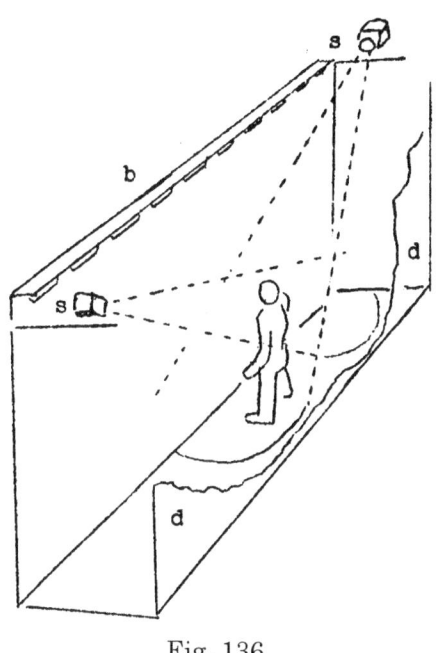

Fig. 136

with marionettes. Have you ever taken any pictures with a flashbulb? Then you know that if the flash is on the camera, the picture you get of Aunt Maud is flat - and so is the background, and everything else. When you read further down in the "how to" instructions, you are offered extension cords which will get the flash off to one side, or auxiliary flashes so the subject can be lit from both sides, or even the rear. This is because lighting from the sides allows some shadows to appear on the front of the face. (Has it occurred to you that the only way we can see anything is because of the shadows that tell us what shape it is? If you could pour an even amount of light all over your stage and around every puppet and prop, they'd be practically invisible! So! First of all - forget footlights. Why? They throw a light up under the shaded side of the object which is unnatural, and when it's strong enough it eliminates the molding shadow. (In horror pictures they always light the monster or the demon from below, for the very reason that it IS eerie and unnatural.) The only real problem in lighting a marionette stage is that the backdrop is so close to the actors it's hard to separate them. So if you will run a "border light" of medium intensity right across the width of your stage opening b made of many bulbs (I prefer the long narrow bulbs, 40W, used in stores for counter displays) it will give an evenly distributed soft light over the acting area and the backdrop d and because it is many bulbs, it won't make shadows. Then the spot lights S across the acting area, without spilling over on the backdrop! That's the trick, for it puts a hard, sharp light on the actors - picking them out from the softly-lit backdrop, and modeling their form with light from either side. How much light - how many spots - you determine by looking at it, from as far back as you can get. (If you're not building it in a theatre, go across the street and look at it through a window!)

Many people use the Birdseye spots I recommended for the hand puppet stage, masking off the "spill" to keep the light off the places it's not wanted.

There are "gelatins" which will put colored light on your stage, but I have found that except in rare instances, if I paint the color I want in the set, I can use ordinary white light for the whole shebang, and have day, night, whatever, by having the painting say it is so. If you get a good lighting setup, stick with it.

If you're handy with wiring, you can rig a switchboard sufficient for the job. Resistance dimmers can sometimes be bought from Army surplus big enough for a puppet light. But on all of this I advise you to do what I do -have an electrician do it! I don't know an ohm from a watt! Fancy professional dimmers - even whole switchboards are available from theatrical supply houses.

All right - you're built, you're painted, and you're lit. NOW what are you going to do?

Session 16 **Music, Rehearsals, & Performing**

Wanna go to jail? Wanna be a lawbreaker? Practically all puppeteers are lawbreakers, an' y'know why? They use music in their shows. And except for the ones who have special music written for them, mostly they use records. What else can they do? Yet right there on the label it says this record is to be played only in the home for personal and private enjoyment, an' you go doing a public performance of it for a fee and boy we gonna put you UNDER the jail!

The only reason I can see that there aren't more puppeteers UNDER the jail is that the average puppeteers' income is relatively "peanuts" and it isn't worth fiddlin' with him.

Now, as your mentor, I certainly am not going to admit that I ever broke the law this way, and I certainly am not going to suggest that you break the law this way. However, if a person WERE going to illegally use records in his show.

The best way is just to go listen to records, to find what sounds most fitting. How to find the record you want is sometimes easy, sometimes not. I have gone to record shops when they weren't busy, and after finding a sympathetic clerk, said "I want something that sounds like three awkward newly-hatched baby ostriches dancing," and by golly she just reached into the stock and came up with a perfect thing! Another time a Doctor of Music went to some pains to get me the actual tunes and instruments undoubtedly heard by Cleopatra (for my show of the same name) and it was utterly worthless to me. It didn't sound like what a modern audience thinks music for Cleo should sound like. So lists of selections aren't much good to me: I suggest you listen until you find what sounds most fitting to you.

The good machine for puppet shows these days is the tape recorder. When you have your selection of records (new ones, please, with no scratches) you can transfer such parts of them as you intend to use to the tape, in the sequence and for the duration that you require, and then one hand runs the music for the show! It's wonderful. In Figure 116 the thing labelled "Support for sound system" indicates a way to get it up there where you are, so you can run a puppet with one hand and the music with the other.

Recorders come all prices and sizes: Marge Kelly has one that weighs seven pounds – mine weighs about 25. Get as good fidelity as your purse can afford. I have an external speaker for mine, which plugs into the machine, but gets the sound out into the audience better.

The question of whether to put a show on tape is a frequent one – that is, the dialog as well as the music. When I can, I do a show "live" for the response of each audience is different, and so the "timing" has to be different – the speed with which you read speeches – the time you allow to elapse between them. An audience soon learns whether you're going to wait for it to laugh, or go ahead without them, and – not wanting to miss the next line they don't laugh! That's why we so seldom hear laughter in movies. But a professional actor waits for the laugh, humors it along if he can, and starts the next line just as the laugh starts to subside so he can try to get another one rolling before the audience gets out of the habit! Movies obviously can't do this, so when they have what they expect to be a laugh line, they follow it with one that doesn't matter if it gets lost. So we get a lot of "nothing" lines, which doesn't help the laughter much.

Sometimes – a store show – a fair – where there are to be many shows a day, a taped dialog show is the only logical thing to do.

That's when the foot pedal comes in handy! Strangely enough, a footpedal on a tape machine can stop the sound in the middle of a word – and when it starts up again, it is at normal speed; doesn't sound distorted or anything, and by using it judiciously you can get practically the same effect of timing out of a taped show that you can "live"! Great age we're living in! Also it's a boon when something goes wrong in manipulation; the dialog doesn't go merrily on while our hero, instead of slaying the dragon, has his sword-arm stuck behind his back!

`Nother thing the tape machine is wonderful for is learning your lines! Read the show onto the tape, and then play it back over and over while you are painting the scenery or building a prop. (Notice how everything in this course is good for at least two things?)

Well – what are we waiting for? Let's rehearse! Some of us can't start rehearsing with the puppet until we have the lines of the play learned "letter perfect." Some feel it's better to learn the lines with the puppet in hand. Some elect to personally assume the character, and "walk through it" as though they were going to be bodily on the stage themselves. There is much to be said for this – you learn how the character feels and behaves through your muscles as well as through your mind. The business of watching the marionette through the mirror is much vaunted, but however much value it may have, it is soon over, and you are "doing" it straight down the strings instead of caroming off a piece of glass over there.

There is one pitfall to avoid, however: it's important that the manipulator should "feel" how the character feels, but there have been some who were so busy "feeling" (and even putting "body English" into it) up on the bridge, that it never got down through the strings, and the poor dopey puppet just stood there, conveying nothing to the audience. To paraphrase a cigarette slogan; "If it hasn't got it out front, it hasn't got it."

When you get the lines learned so you're quite comfortable with them, it's a good thing to run through the show just whispering the lines, and trying to do as much communicating to the audience as you can with the action of the puppet! Give him no words to lean on at all! Just try acting with him. Some wonderful things can be discovered that way.

Doing a puppetshow is more complicated than playing a harp – it often makes me think of an organist, who makes music with his feet as well as with his hands on several keyboards – and a person simply **can't think** of all the things that must be done: he has to learn the show so thoroughly that he can reach for the next puppet or the music switch or the curtain or the light switch **without thinking!** `Cause why? `Cause he has to have his mind and his attention free for the business of acting – of creating the emotion for the character he's running down there on the stage. Puppets live only by that part of your life you put into them, and the instant you take your attention and intention off them, they're dead as mackerel. If anyone in the world can make a puppet live, it's Burr Tillstrom, yet on the occasions when they handed him a list of kids' names or sponsor's products to read, the person on his fist who had been a sentient being an instant before turned into a piece of cloth.

During every rehearsal you must do everything that is to be done on the night of the show – and that means every music cue, light cue, scene change, prop movement, and all the timing. Sure there will come up times when you simply have to stop to fix something, but a real show is your goal, and you do a real show only by doing a real show. Let it not be with you as it was reported to be with a Famous Name in this business, who said as a matter of fact; "No puppet show is any good **the first** two weeks it's on the road anyway. It takes that long to break it in." I have no record that the Famous Name did that first two weeks for a "rehearsal" or "no good" fee. As a consequence, every season two weeks of audiences saw a rehearsal and thought they were seeing a performance. Let's not you do that, huh?

I fasten a little ledge in front of me on the back of the proscenium to hold the script during rehearsals, so if we get stuck I can refer to it without getting down off the bridge. Alongside it is a pad and pencil, so when the puppet won't do something, I can make a note to fix it – AFTER the rehearsal – not during it, when I'm trying to establish habits of timing.

If you don't have a "director" telling you what to do, and there are two or more of you working, take turns going out in front to see what the other is doing. (When you criticize the other guy, he may not do what you tell him to, but I bet YOU won't be guilty of the flaw you saw in him!)

As you get more and more comfortable in the show, it will tighten up, and you may find that the music is now too long or too short. With tape – you can fix it. It's so easy to splice tape: get the man from whom you buy the machine to show you how – and NOTE: carry a little pair of scissors and some Scotch tape along with the machine. "Save your life" some time.

Of course you will rehearse the intermissions. Whether you are playing for little kids or big. ones or their great grandparents, a wait is a wait is a wait. Having decided how much time to allow for an intermission, rehearse everything you have to do during that intermission every time you rehearse the show. Hard work? You bet. But as a matter of fact, in rehearsing the show you are training a bunch of muscles as well as reflexes, and unless you're fortunate enough to have someone else to do all that jumping up and down and running back and forth for you, you're going to need this actual physical stamina. It's a beautiful thing to watch professional puppeteers backstage at a complex and well rehearsed show. It looks so calm and relaxed and effortless! And this is the work YOU are doing in these rehearsals.

To Kid or Not To Kid

In my first show (string) I endeavored to cut down the scene-change-time wait by having a handpuppet appear above the stage to be both Master of Ceremonies and Program. That was back in '33. In Bil Baird's latest appearance in a Broadway theatre, he had a little stage on either side of his BIG stage, and individual booths up and down both sides of the proscenium opening! There were no intermissions for scene changes; the action just moved from the big stage to the little stages, and kept right on going! As it was a two hour show they broke it in the middle for sanitary reasons, of course, but the rest of the time it was non-stop.

Many puppets have talked to kiddy audience, and invited them to talk back. This is a legitimate device if that's the type of show you're doing, and you don't let it get "out of hand." Little kids at a puppet show are learning social group behavior – many of them have never attended a "live" show and, not knowing what is expected of them, take their cue from how they behave at home in front of the TV set, or at the endless "movie short" programs with which various organizations baby-sit them en masse, and where whooping and racing about doesn't bother anyone, because everyone's doing it. Or these lovely little angels will do what the kid in the next row is doing; talk back to the puppets, or just make funny noises, or tease the girls, or whatever.

When a puppet invites the kids to talk to him, he's taking a chance of a mass response of innocent, irresponsible noise. I've played places where the minute a puppet appeared, the whole audience ROARED at him – they were taught to do that by my predecessor! That's the point: kids are willing, and will do what is expected of them if they understand what it is. If the puppet is going to have an exchange with the kids, he must be perfectly sure of himself and of them, and be explicit in what he expects. If they start getting out of hand, he can stop everything and explain it to them. Then everyone has a better time, being on sure ground.

If you let it get completely out of hand, you may be able to salvage it by a personal appearance before the stage. Here again, your attitude must be one of understanding authority. You're not bawling them out; you're explaining the rules by which people play this game called attending a show, and you want to help them have the very best time at it. You can't fool them; whatever words you say, they'll know if you're one to be listened to or ignored. Your heart shows through, and if you go out there to do battle with them (and I have seen such!) you've already lost.

But with one season of experience, you'll be able to "feel" the audience, and gauge your puppets' ad libs to fit the circumstance.

Make It Easy on Yourself

As you are rehearsing, including setting up and tearing down, it is obvious that you will put props where they will be ready to hand, arrange hooks, eyelets, snaps, et cetera here and there for your convenience. Perhaps you will find you can do without this or that particular brace or holder, or that if you had made this a little differently, it all would have been much simpler to operate. I know you've done a lot of work to get it this far, but do go ahead and change it. Now is the time, and you'll feel so good every time you use the altered thing thereafter. Don't be like one of my friends who, when he has the show built, never never never changes or alters anything, but suffers along with it for years. He just has a "block" against re-doing something. However, you and I have been erasing and re-arranging ever since this Course started. As Oscar Wilde said, "I have the simplest tastes. I am always satisfied with the best."

Out-of-Town Tryouts

There is no substitute for rehearsal. So you rehearse until you have it as smooth as grease, and you can't think of another thing to make it better. Now do what the big boys do; have a dress rehearsal. Have an audience of people you know. But don't listen to what they say after the performance. Listen to how they act DURING it. This is a vital part of your equipment as a showman: the ability to do a performance, and at the same time have all your antenna out to catch the response you're getting from the audience. That's why you have to rehearse the show until the gestures are automatic, because here's yet another thing your mind has to be doing while you're performing! What didn't they respond to? See if you can figure out why. Now take it "out of town": give it to some organization – free. (An organization that wouldn't ordinarily buy it?) Here's a final piece of advice, reported in Time magazine:

> "Rogers and Hammerstein ruthlessly cut their favorite songs or scenes if they detect that alarming rustle of inattention among spectators. "What I like about R. & H.," says General Stage Manager Jimmy Hammerstein, Oscar's #2 son, "is that they're conditioned to what works. If it works, they keep it in: if it doesn't, they scrap it. They listen with real objective ears."

Go thou and do likewise!

Session 17 **Animated Faces**

Having, I trust, sufficiently directed your attention to what I consider of greatest importance – the performance – we'll now go back to construction and pick up a few oddments. Sooner or later a person wants to animate a face, with blinking eyes, flapping eyebrows, and a moving mouth. I dislike doing it so much that I avoid it whenever I can, but sometimes even I can't get out of it. So let's start with the eyes.

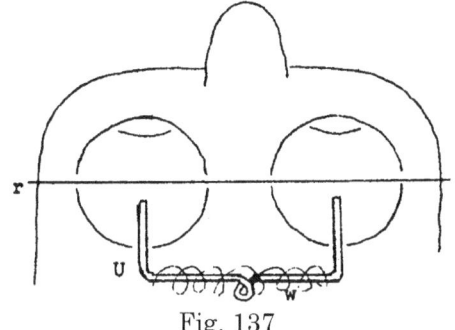
Fig. 137

Simplest is the way "sleepy dolls" are made: a rod r runs through the head from temple to temple, through the eyeballs. As it's almost impossible to drill a hole straight through a wooden ball, most of us get wooden balls or "beads" which have the holes already in them. String them on the rod, place them in the sockets, and that shows where the rod is to be fastened inside the head. Coat-hanger wire bent in a U is inserted in the backs of the eyeballs and makes the eyes work together, as well as providing a place for the weight which opens them by gravity after you've pulled them shut.

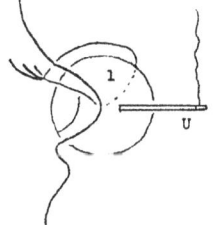
Fig. 138

Simplest weight w is "spool solder" (hardware store) applied by wrapping it around the U until it's heavy enough to open the eyes. Figure 137 is looking down on the assembly from above. Figure 138 is looking at it from the side. Eyelids can be painted on that part of the ball that is exposed when the eye is shut, or a lid of plastic wood can be placed on the ball to give added thickness 1. You may want a

Fig. 139

bearing at r – and at other places as we go along – and Figure 139 shows the simplest way to make them: a little piece of thin brass, copper, even tin, is punctured with an ice pick. Being graduated in size, the pick will make any size hole required, and the "burr" of metal it forces out on the other side makes an even deeper bearing. To apply, scoop out a little declivity in the plastic wood, set the bearing in place, and seal it over with a smidgin of plastic wood.

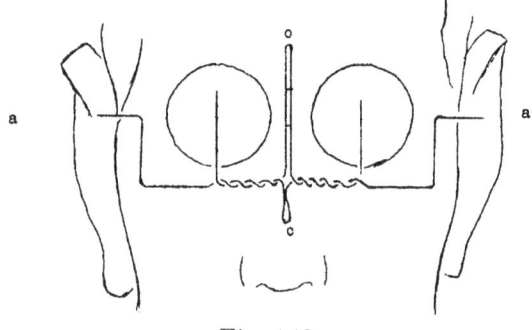

Fig. 140

Maybe you're not satisfied with eyes that just close and open; maybe you like them also to look from side to side! Then Figure 140 is for you. This is the eye action Rufus Rose used in the television show *"The Blue Fairy."*

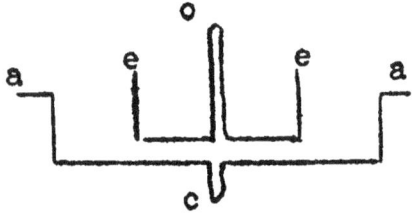

Fig. 141

Figure 141 shows the components; two pieces of good of coathangerwire. Bend the loops o & e, turn up, at the center of the eyeballs. When you get out to a & a, they line up to be the axis on which the eyes close and open.

On the back of the eyeball attach a small screweye S.

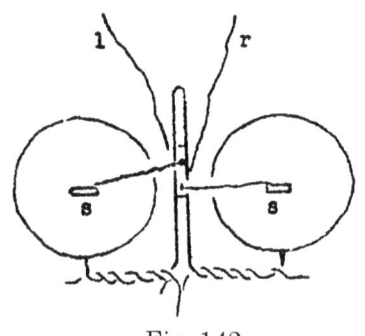

Fig. 142

In the tall wire loop o drop a little solder and in it drill two small holes. String from the screweyes, through the holes in the solder and out the top of the head will make the eyes look right and left. String from O will open eyes, string from C will close them. Notice that O in Figure 143 is bent a little forward, °and C a little backward, to make a more effective pull on the string. If the

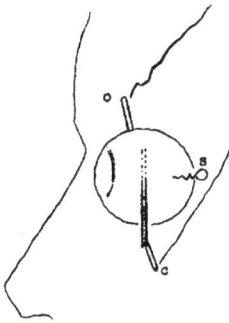
Fig. 143

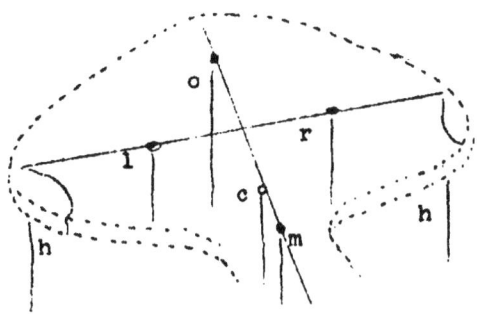
Fig. 144

strings are attached to the control as indicated in Figure 144, tilting the control will make his eyes look right and left: pulling C will close his eyes. C is attached right before the mouth string m. l & r on a line with the head strings h.

Hand puppets are animated in the same way, with the strings coming down under the sleeve, and operated by the other hand.

Eyelashes are made of leather as often as not, and pasted onto the flat face of the lid. Make yourself a little paper pattern first, and save miscutting the leather.

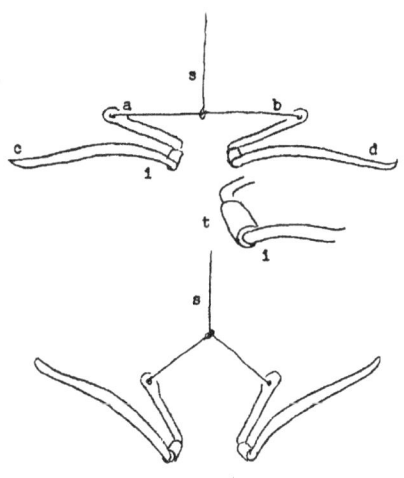
Fig. 145

For eyebrows, a slightly-softer-than coathangerwire would be good, and a bit of brass tubing for it to run through. With a hammer, flatten out enough length to be the brow. At the inside end 1 bend it at right angles, slip the bit of tubing over it, and put the wire through a hole in the forehead, and seat the tubing in place with plastic wood. When set, bend the wire now inside the head back toward the brow, but angling a little up, as indicated. A string fastened from a to b will keep the outside points c & d from going any lower than you want them. If you pull up on string S, the outside ends of his eyebrows will go up. The same thing can be applied to

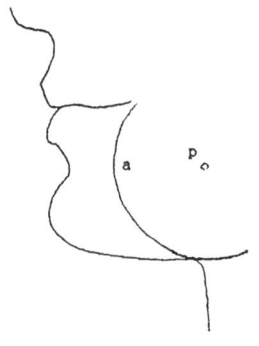

Fig. 146

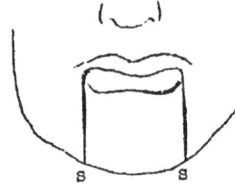

Fig. 147

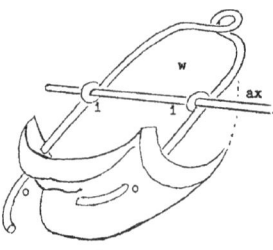

Fig. 148

Fig. 149

mustaches. If you put the pivot point on the outside end of the brow, the center will go up and down.

Having flattened the piece of wire that is the base for the brow, you can glue felt, fur, or whatever you like to it for the desired texture.

Here's the simplest way to make a mouth work. You start with the modeling: locate a point on the cheek p which will be the center of an arc a around which the lower lip and chin will slide. In modeling the face, this arc is present so that after the face is cast in plastic wood, the two vertical sawcuts (S in Figure 147) are right on that arc.

When sawing out the chin, the two cuts must be absolutely parallel! and at precise right angle to the axis rod (ax in Figure 148) to which the chin is fastened. (Like everything else, if you saw it crooked, you can fix it, but if you are very careful you can do it right the first time, which is a comfort.)

Now with the chin sawed out, and before you have put the two halves of the head together, place the axis rod in the cheeks at the points p being sure its horizontal position is at precisely right angle to the vertical sawcuts S. Make a wishbone w of wire, wrap it once around the axis rod at I & I. Then through the chin from the inside to the outside at o & o. Make a trench for the wire to lie in, and, bury the wire with plastic wood after fitting the chin into place. The slots, S & S are sanded perfectly smooth. It is possible to make the slots nearly invisible with a good fit. I use a coping saw to cut the slots with, for as fine a cut as possible. If when you get it sanded the slots are still too wide, insert a slip of waxed paper in one slot to protect one side, and press moist plastic wood into the other, to fill it up. Being moist, it will stick to the unprotected side, and as it dries in the air it will shrink enough to leave clearance for the action.

A spool solder weight wrapped around the curve of the wishbone (Figure 148) will close the mouth – a string will open it.

Handy

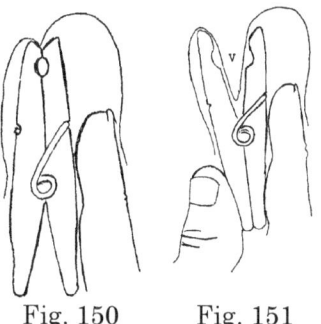

Fig. 150   Fig. 151

When a puppet (hand, that is) simply must pick up a club or something with one hand, a spring clothespin built into the mitten will do the trick. I made these mitts of chamois so they would "give" better and grip tighter at v. The thumb of course is wearing a plain mitten. Carve the handle of whatever is to be held to best fit the clip.

Ball and Socket Joints

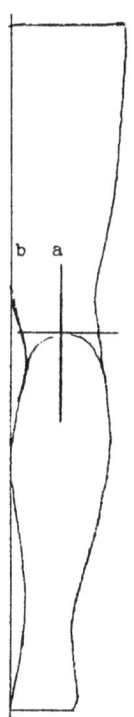

Fig. 152

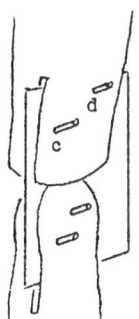

Fig. 153

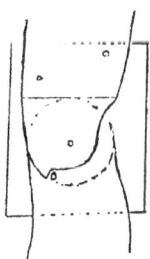

Fig. 154

Ball and socket joints can be simple and easy. At the knee make a vertical line in the middle of the thickness of the wood a parallel with the inside vertical line of the leg b. Duplicate it on the back. Saw the leg in two. On the sawed surface of each half, connect the front and back lines. Saw a slot in each STAYING ON THOSE VERTICAL LINES. Saw-slot of a thickness to let a piece of trunk-fibre fit snugly into it. Insert fibre, put leg together.

To make a perfectly fitting hole for a fine finishing nail, clip the head from the nail, insert nail in drill, and drill into the wood. Using this technique, fasten trunk fibre in the upper leg with small finishing nails C & d. (Ball is not yet made on lower leg.)

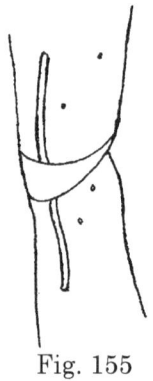

Fig. 155

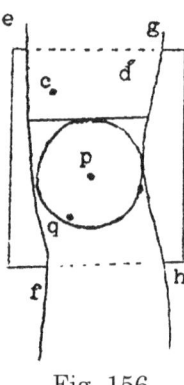

Fig. 156

With a compass, locate the point p (Figure 156) so the circle touches the front, top, and back of the leg. Just inside the edge of the circle locate q which will be the "stop". Drill nails into each of these. With a pencil outline the leg on the fibre from e to f and g to h. Remove nails from p and q. Remove lower leg from fibre and carve top into half a ball. Make it as near a circle as possible, particularly from front to back. To finish it off, put a piece of sandpaper in your palm, and grind the ball into it, rotating it back and forth like winding a watch: it'll come out smooth and round. Figure 154 shows the shape of the finished fibre. You now have the holes at p & q, and leaving the fibre in the upper leg, you cut away all but what is indicated here. Widen the slot in the lower leg by folding sandpaper and "sawing" it back and forth in the slot until the slot slips over the fibre with ease. Don't go whole hog now and make it sloppy – make a real precision fit, which will rotate but not wobble. NOW put in the q nail and the p nail, and the mechanics are finished – the leg will hang as you designed it originally.

The socket is even simpler: Figure 155. Wet the ball, and keep it wet while you apply plastic wood to the bottom face of the upper leg, molding it into a "cap" or socket. It will start "setting up" at once, and as you pat it into shape, occasionally flex the knee, which will shape the inside of the socket, and make a perfect fit. Make the cap a little fatter than you want it, for it will shrink a little. When dry, carve it to just the shape you want, sand it, and there you are!

Same process for elbows. Pie, huh?

A word about moderation. You don't have to build everything you know into every puppet you make. Some puppets have very little to do: make them so they can do it and STOP. Puppets that don't have to bend or sit, I make with solid torsos. Puppets that don't have to sit or kneel, I make with knee joints that can only walk. When a puppet has only to

Fig. 140

hail Caesar, I build him a stiff arm. If he didn't have to move his head, I'd give him a stiff neck. If his hands are tied behind him, carve torso and hands and arms all in one piece. This not only saves construction time, but it makes the puppet more efficient. When I first built *"The Last Supper," I* made thirteen completely articulated puppets, only four of whom worked anywhere else in the show. The miserable **hours** of my life I spent jockeying those other nine into place sitting behind that table, and aching because I was making the audience wait!!! Then one season I woke up; made a "three-gang" arrangement as in Figure 157, and cut my setting-up time by a third! They each had head action, which was all they ever used, and by fastening their chest pieces on a plywood easel, they not only took their positions more quickly and dependably, but they saved packing space.

I may say that nobody – not even the Saints – came marching in to complain. For we are not duplicating Life here – we are interpreting it. You are making your statement about how "being" seems to you, as an artist.

Ssession 18 **Finding the Audience**

I never quite got over my surprise when I drove my big DeSoto up to the University, or Woman's Club or whatever, and did a performance for a real top fee, and packed up to return to my Home in the Country, to have a person say to me, "But can you make a living at this?" Sometimes even, "But what do you do for a **living!?**"

Now I'm not saying this is the pot of gold at the end of the rainbow: you can starve to death doing this, just as you can doing anything else. But there are several people about who have made a good living doing puppets during the time other people were starving with them, and tearing the market down by doing bad to impossible shows. So what does this mean to you?

In the first place, it means that you must have something good; and good means good to the person who is going to buy (i.e., consume) it. A good kid show is worth nothing to a University audience. My "Passion Play" would go over like a lead balloon at a fairground. Charlie Kettering, the most successful inventor of his day, who changed a nation's way of life, said, "Remember that you and I get no place in the world except as we serve the fellow who pays for our dinner."

Now we've completed the circle we started at the beginning of this Course; we're back to your original dreaming. Remember, you were to picture what kind of show you would have the most fun doing. If you were at all honest with yourself, you moved toward that kind of "statement about being" that came most naturally to you, that best expressed your particular kind of fun. And the truer that kind of statement is, the quicker it will reach kindred souls. Years ago a very famous puppeteer said to me, "Let's not kid ourselves: we can never be that universal success that everyone in the world has simply GOT to see. Some people simply can't **stand** puppets. But we can be a success in that circumscribed area where a sufficient number of people know our work and agree with it, and have us back again and again and are glad." Well, that's the way it was with him, and that's the way it was with me. Let's take some others: Ellen and Romain Proctor made their statement and have been going on and on successfully for more years than I've been in the business, and it looks like they'll never stop. Ed Johnson felt like a one-man marionette show, and he turned out the most elaborate, most complex, and tremendously spectacular show, which has been bought for years and years. Burr Tillstrom felt a show shouldn't have a "message," but should be "entertainment" pure and simple, and his purity and simplicity made the biggest stir of puppets in the public consciousness that had ever been experienced! My forte was religious drama and it swallowed up all my other endeavors until the major part of my income was concentrated on Christmas and Easter. Rufus Rose had a feeling about *Pinocchio,* and he did it, and thought about it, and aimed toward an ever more satisfying expression of it until his TV show titled *"The Blue* Fairy" won the Peabody Award as the best TV Children's Show in America in 1958!

What do these several examples say to you? These people wanted it clearly enough to know that they wanted it. They wanted it enthusiastically enough that their minds gravitated to anything that would further it. This is the touchstone! This is how you will be it!

Let's see how people do it. Suppose you've been aiming at a school show. Do your rehearsals, do your "out of town tryouts," and then go out to sell some shows. "Case the joints" first – in your vicinity, how many puppet shows have they had in what length of time? How much did they pay them. Ask around, and know what the "going rate" is before you go in to sell your show. If you ask less than they've been paying, you're "probably not as good" – if you ask more – they don't know you, and they already have a resistance to you.

You'll very soon find out that while you can sell an occasional "spot booking," most of the assembly programs were set up for the year last summer – even last Spring! Independent self-booking puppeteers "make the rounds" in the same way and usually at the same times that agents do – building up that personal contact for entre and for repeat bookings that the Proctors and the Johnsons have. But in the words of the immortal salesman, "If you wanna get the business, you gotta make the calls."

Another way to do school shows is to contract with a School Assembly Circuit. There are four– five big ones, several smaller ones, and you can get their names from a copy of PROGRAM at 151 W. 51 st St., New York, NY 10019.

Write to them, tell them what you've got, and ask where they are going to preview talent for the coming season. Usually in the summer, the various agents get together, and the entertainment program is made up of people "trying out" for the coming season. If they take you on, they will "guarantee" you so many weeks of work, and there you are – in business!

What you get per performance is considerably less than what you would get if you were booking yourself, but you don't have the time, expense, and effort of selling, which makes a big difference – especially if you're a person who hates to "sell."

You should know that once you're "in business" in this way, you are going to WORK. Being on a school assembly circuit is no picnic; it's as hard a way to make a living as there is in all show-business. The hours are long, the "jumps" are hard, the money is small, the audiences are "innocent" and often need your help on how to behave, the schoolmen have other things to do than lay out the red carpet for you, and the janitors find you're just that much extra work for them. Because the kids can go to your show instead of attending classes, some performers have felt their only function was being an excuse for indolent kids not working. (Bet you never read this anywhere before!)

That's the bad part. The good part is that you "do by doing," and there's lots of doing in School Assembly. If you like kids (some people don't) you'll enjoy their applause, and you'll feel good about the opportunity of saying to them whatever your show says. Most important to you as a showman is that you have to do that show over and over and over. You can just turn it on at curtain time and let whatever happens happen – in which case you might as well sell shoes or punch holes. Or you can pay attention to what's going on between you and each audience, and remold it, and polish it, and tune yourself so fine that you know every breath that being taken in that audience and how to control it. Then every show can be exciting, and profitable in more than the fee, and you'll come out of a season in School Assembly knowing more about your art than when you went in.

A personal representative seems like a real good idea, but I was never able to find one. According to legend, there was one – count `em – one such person once, who was fabulous! She would take on one company, and do nothing but sell it. And how she could sell! And for her commission, she took half the fee! Yep – 50%. But when your half was $10,000 for the season, that eased the pain. But they're a seldom breed; most agents seem unable to sell puppets.

When Burr Tillstrom made his big splash in TV, a lot of the great Big Agencies figured "This is what TV is," and they sent representatives to every puppeteer they could find to sign them up for exclusive representation. Their big inducement was that this Agency handled all the "greats" and therefore you would benefit from prestigious association. Trouble was, and is – these behemoths are not interested in helping make you great – they're interested in selling what sponsors will buy, and selling means putting the list on the customer's desk and letting him take his pick. Their very magnitude is what makes them worthless to us, for when the customer sees BOB HOPE, RED SKELTON, JAMES MASON, DANILOVA, Stevens Puppets, DANNY KAY, ET CETERA, who they gonna buy?

Sol Hurok brought "The Piccoli" here in '32, and again a couple years later, and more recently someone sponsored a concert tour of the Salzburg Marionettes, but that's about all the activity puppets have had on the concert stage.

Once in a while someone starts up a puppet theatre, but with two exceptions it never lasts long. One of the exceptions is the puppet opera at the Kungsholm Restaurant in Chicago, which was the plaything of a rich man, and since his death is continued as a part o the restaurant's attraction. The other is the Turnabout Theatre in Los Angeles, which has names, novelty (puppets at one end of the auditorium, a "live" show at the other) and a constant turnover of tourists. A show aimed at adults recently opened in an off-Broadway theatre and closed before the week was over. A famous company with frequent TV appearances recently built the biggest show with the biggest cast with the biggest and best equipment in the whole world, I'm sure, intending to tour it at a rumoured fee of $1500 a performance. The tour was only a handful of performances, and they are now arranging one-shot dates.

What does this add up to? It would seem that in the public mind, puppets are for kids – and little kids at that, and that big kids and grown-ups just don't want to come in large numbers. It may be that producers simply don't produce things in puppets comparable in content and skill to what adults accept as ordinary standards.

With all this negative information, what has a puppet show got left to show to? The answer is:

The Captive Audience

Bless it – if it weren't for the captive audience, we'd all starve to death. This is the audience the organization hires the entertainment for – and when it sits down to be entertained, we do it. Fortunately, there are lots of such organizations. In addition to the schools, there are Fraternal Orders that have ladies' nights, Service Clubs, people interested in providing entertainment for orphanages, underprivileged and crippled kids, holiday shows, even birthday parties. Industries hire puppetshows for their Employees' Parties. Women's Clubs and Art Museums, and Universities too, hire puppetshows that are made especially for them. Churches will employ religious puppetshows once you get your foot in the door and convince them they won't be outraged. Business firms have special shows built to extol their products or services, and to give special messages or instruction to their own personnel. Community Chests, co-operatives, fund drives are all users of special puppetshows at one time or another. If you give it a think, you can recognize organizations in your community that could benefit from your services as a puppeteer. But it is primarily the organization that gets them there.

What you have to do is sell the organization, which largely means selling the one person who has charge of that particular department or function. When you look the situation over, get as much information about the purpose – the THING THEY WANT – as possible, and then sit back and dream up a presentation, a how-to, the way you dreamed up your own show at the beginning of this Course. Sit with it a while, put it away, and come back to it again. When you get it to where it makes you enthusiastic, make up an outline of it so you're real familiar with it. If you're real excited about it, make sketches – picture it – get it into as visible a form as you can, before you go see the

Person In Charge. If you have photos of previous work, add them to the presentation, and take along your favorite puppet – the one you know from experience intrigues people most.

When you go to see him, you are doing two things: you are rendering him a service, by offering him a new idea, a new tool, to help him do his job in getting them the THING THEY WANT, and you are also doing something for you; you want to do this show, and be paid for it. So this also must go into your presentation. Along with the idea of the show for the purpose, you must figure how long it will take you to make it, how much it will cost in time and money, and how much profit you'll be satisfied with. This is the second question he will ask, and you can't fumble around and dig your toe in the dirt and say you really don't know. Who else does know? And unless you're just being whole-heartedly charitable and can be happy with that, don't consider being underpaid: by the time you pile up all those work hours, and make changes in the script at their suggestion, and do all that rehearsing, if you feel underpaid you'll be unhappy, and the show will suffer, and the Cause will suffer. Better you should have stood in bed.

How much do puppets cost, supposing they want a special puppet built of their trademark say, or the incoming president or whatever. Puppets cost whatever you want to make them for: around here they cost anywhere from one hundred to one thousand dollars each. You have to determine the price – it's as little as you will be **content** with. The current practice is to make the puppet and rent it to them – with you manipulating it. It doesn't become their property. This keeps them from firing you and hiring someone else to manipulate it. Another thing – some people around here won't even make a puppet these days unless in addition to retaining ownership of it, they also get a share of the profit of any subsequent exploitation of the character (like Disney dolls, or Howdy Doody toys, for instance.)

Wanna work nightclubs? You'll need an agent for that. But first, do you know about nightclubs? Have you ever been in one? Well, this is just like anything else; find out WHAT THEY WANT before you build your show. See at first hand what the other acts do, and what nightclub puppet acts do, before you build yours. Each different outlet for puppets has its own patterns, its own requirements, its own style. And you must become thoroughly familiar with this style – this tempo, before you make something and offer it for sale. I think many people do puppets because they can pour their statement out through the figures while they remain out of sight, but a nightclub performer has to sell not only the puppet act but his appearance and his personality as well. If you have this kind of personality, by all means pursue it. just don't "go off half cocked."

According to one ex-nightclub performer, the low fees are very low, the distance and time between dates is **murder,** living expense on the road is more, one is confronted with withholding taxes et ceterra here as any where else, and the minimal 10% commission is frequently paid not only to one's own agent, but to a booker as well. One Very Top Act has literally gone around the world in the attempt to get enough work, and still has to take on other jobs than nightclubs to keep going.

Session 19 **Working in Television**

"How can I get on TV?"

"How can I get in the movies?"

Oh boy! Here we go. Well, first, let's look at puppetry again. When I discovered puppetry, I leaped into it with immense glee, for here was a form of theatre over every detail of which I would have the complete say. EVERYthing would be done as near my heart's desire as my abilities and the medium would allow. And it was so!

It is no longer so when you go into TV or movies. The money involved in these media is so great, and the mechanical processes are so complex, that there has to be a specialist on every one of them, and what every one of them does affects not only the character of your show but also the manner of doing your show, from the script through the quality of your voice to the **seconds** of length of performance. To enter either of these fields you must be prepared to stop being "the boss".

Straight from the mouth of one of the leading TV puppeteers comes this advice: go to a small independent station and do something simple. Starting off with something elaborate will "kill" you with this complex strangeness of production. Learn what TV production is about. Listen. Observe. You're investing in an education in this mode of your craft, just as you did in the early session when you studied your prospective sponsor to see what he wanted.

When you get to where you really have something to sell this medium, you'll have to join the Union. No Union, no job. AFTRA, the American Federation of Television and Radio Artists has an initiation fee, and dues graduated according to your income. Minimum for a network show is higher than for a local show. Additional fee for doing commercials. These are among the myriad details to be acquired as you are doing your stint for learning.

"We don't have any lack of puppet shows," one TV executive told me, "we have a lack of where to sell them – of sponsor interest." This is your cue: all through this Course – turn your mind on it, and dream up ways in which puppets can better say – display – a thing for a sponsor than anyone else could. In the *"Rough and Ready Show",* the parrot, the toucan, and the humanized ear of corn could not have been done as well by people. In March and April, 1959, two shows; *"Art Carney Meets Peter and the Wolf* and *"Art Carney Meets the Sorcerer's Apprentice"* had puppets as an integral part of the show. In Rufus Rose's *"The Young Sinbad,"* donkeys, dragons, goats, cats, rocks, birds could not have been done as well any other way.

Movies are something else again. Hollywood producers are like other people who once in a while "discover" puppets, and write them into a show, but by the time the film is finally edited the puppets wind up on the cutting room floor. "I *Am Susan"* had puppets as an integral part about a million years ago, and just a few years back "*Lili*" couldn't cut them out. George Pal uses stop-action puppets which are stiff jointed, will hold a pose they're put in, and shot one frame at a time to make the illusion of motion. He did years of *"Pal Puppetoons"* and created some magnificent short subjects. Now his use of puppets is largely in outer space pictures, and an occasional toy sequence as in the latest film of *"Tom Thumb."* Puppeteers are hired for stints such as this, and for stopaction commercials. To get such a job is a matter of getting known by people who sometimes do this, and being available when they need you. This cannot be considered "steady" employment.

The many people involved in "your" show mentioned on page one are multiplied in film work. In a studio, the designers' union must design the costumes, the wardrobe union must make them, the plaster-workers union must make the molds, et cetera. In one film, after all these strangers got through doing what they were supposed to do during the day, the puppeteers took the puppets home and did it all over again at night. So it would work!

Don't understand me to say nothing good can be done this way: the puppeteers learned much of value while doing it the studio's way. Just be prepared to be auxilliary rather than autonomous.

A more immediate way to do puppets on film is to contact movie makers who produce commercials, and institutional films. The film you see at your service club, or your child sees in school, on conservation of our national resources, or how an assembly line makes for better living – things like that are made by concerns one of which may be near you. Go to your local TV station and ask someone about those "public service" films and who made them. Then, with your publicity of past achievements, go to the studio and talk with the man there. Remember he knows about film but he in all probability doesn't know about puppets. Your job is to help him find a way in which puppets would help one of his sponsors get WHAT HE WANTS, in a way he couldn't get some otherhow.

In order not to walk in on the film producer "cold" (that is to say, completely ignorant) get and read at least one book on how a film is made. See what your local library has, and if there's nothing there exciting enough, have them get something from the BIG library they "take" from for you.

"Live" shows on TV have some correspondence with your own live performances, but shooting a movie is another process: it's shot in bits and, pieces and always out of sequence, and you must know the process and form of writing a movie shooting script, then breaking it down into a shooting sequence.

Do You Want It

My exposition of each of these several fields of activity has been merely to taste the flavor of the area, and the things that most immediately impress the newcomer, and beckon or repel him. I have emphasized the difficulties, the unpleasant features, not to shoo you away from tackling them, but to expose you to a few of the conditions which, if come upon unprepared, might discourage you at the outset.

The important thing is this: the only way in which you can succeed in any of these fields is to want it so much that you are willing to concentrate on it – to give it your whole mind, your whole enthusiasm. Confuscius say, "Man who try to sit on two stools at once fall on behind." You know the creative process – you know that while you are dreaming up a show or a character, it stops when you start thinking about the grocery list or that cute blonde. Whether it's a school show, a nightclub show, a TV show or a movie, there is so much to be known, to be created for and to be acted upon in each of them that you're doing yourself and the art less than justice if you water down your effort with a conflicting interest. Big Business recognizes this: when you apply for a job these days, Personnel asks, "Why do you want this job, why do you want to work for this company, what do you propose to work into or up to?" It is of the utmost importance to you that you ask yourself these questions, and answer them. How about right now? (Go ahead – I'll wait.)

Back to the (relatively) simple things in life: Here's an enthusiastic report from a Midwest puppeteer who has been successfully performing for years:

'We play mostly in large Public Elementary Schools. $60 for a single performance – $90 for two in the same place, same half day. $125 for three in the same place, in one day.

"In the beginning, the salesman should first have a good product" (You hear that, folks? M.S.) "Then play the percentages, that is, expect to make 10 or 15 calls to sell one show. Later it will be easier.

"The schools love the shows we do, and by now most of the Principals are old friends, and it is a pleasure to see them again and renew our friendship." (That's a bonus.)

Publicity

This is a very ephemeral subject: nobody – including Madison Avenue knows the exact value of publicity, yet everyone must do it. I have sent out tens of thousands of mailing pieces, and I can't attribute a single date to them. I've spent thousands of dollars in magazines that went to Program Chairmen, but I can't recall a single date that came from it. Personal contact, and word-of-mouth I know does it, but – ! Maybe it's mailed in publicity that nudges, and then personal contact that sells! "Oh yes, we got your folder," is a good thing to hear in an interview – at least you don't feel comPLETEly from Mars. Also, when he says there's nothing open now, you have something to leave with him. Sometimes he passes it on to someone else and I get a date that way!

How shall it be? If you're not a commercial artist, or feel timid about tackling it, I'd suggest having a professional do it, because it is you when you're not there, and all the other "flyers" the sponsor gets are as good as those other players can afford. It can be done several ways – one is with photos.

I never would have finished my stage puppets in such detail if it hadn't been for publicity photos, for while the audience can't see detail, dat of devil camera can, and it's through its eye the customer looks. Get good photos whether you take them yourself or have it done – not a snapshot on the lawn. If you have been interested in photography heretofore, go into it just a little deeper and you'll be able to take better puppet pictures than 'most any professional photographer for this reason: Photography shows up ALL the WORST features of the puppet. Puppets I have thought the most beautiful of my creations have glared their errors at me from a photo! So that I had to make them over. And, you know what you intended the puppet to look like – the professional photographer doesn't, and so can't spot the failing and forestall it. After a little practice you can.

Blurbs

The part of your folder that talks about your excellence is called a "blurb," and this may be the hardest part for you to write: it was for me. How can I sit there and brag about myself. But this is a false attitude: a piece of paper is impersonal – it is not you speaking, it is speaking about you. So don't be bashful; if you have merit, let the paper say so – not blatantly but frankly and gladly. They want you to be good – and you are. You needn't list everything you've ever done (one avid young man listed all the jobs he'd ever had – one woman announced she had been the broad-jump champ in nineteen-ought-something! Really!)

Comments from satisfied customers are standard inclusions, but sometimes the ones I wanted most to comment never got around to comment by mail – so I carried a large "autograph" book in the equipment, and when they came enthusiastically backstage and whooped about the show, I shoved a pen in their hand and asked them to say it for the book – and man! Get 'em while they're hot, and you've got the MOST.

Make a positive suggestion to them – have them get in touch with you for a date, more details, SOMEthing. Prices are not mentioned on publicity, but all other details are – how easy it is to have your show, what it's about, how long it runs, how glad the audience will be that you were brought there, you availability, your name and address (and phone number for sudden emergencies?) But in all your exposition of your excellence, be clear that it exists solely for one thing – WHAT THEY WANT!

For my publicity I used "photo-offset" a great deal; it allowed me to do a lot of my own composition on the piece. As you inquire into it you'll learn a whole flock of new things – and that's part of the fun. Lots of puppeteers being artistically inclined – make up their own mailing pieces. Some companies find a need for supplying the sponsor with posters. Only rarely in my career have I found any great need for them: Ofter I made a mailing piece which was a poster on one side, and vital statistics on the other. For captive audiences, they don't blanket the town with posters as a rule.

Where the sponsor is soliciting the public to attend, supply them with 8x10 glossy photos for news stories (or if a very small town, "matts" – if you don't know what this is, ask your printer) and news stories. The sponsor doesn't know how to do this, and the newspaper doesn't know about your show (and is only running it as a community service anyway) so you write up about four "blurbs", starting off with the blanks for the sponsor's name, the date, the place, the time – well here – I'll show you:

>"Laughter shouldn't be cruel," says Martin Stevens, whose puppet show, "The Fun House," will be presented
>
>(where)
>
>(when)
>
>(by whom)

> "We have plenty of traits in common which are laughable," says this showman, "and these can bring us closer together." The puppet characters Stevens uses are prototypes of ourselves and our neighbors ....et cetera.

and follow with the rest of the blurb. Notice the formula: first a "hook" of common interest, then what it is, and the vital statistics so that however much the paper has to cut off the bottom of the copy, the message has been delivered. A single double-spaced page usually sufces for one newpaper blurb. Contracts are necessary – not because they are binding, for if anyone wanted to break a contract he could find ways to – but because each of you has a record of what's expected. No need for a fancy one:

Stevens Puppets

Contract with

(Sponsor's name)_____

–

Address)_____

To present ____performances) at this address

_____

_____

On (day)_____, (date) _____, (hour)_____
(day)_____, (date) _____, (hour)_____

And to be paid at the time of the performance a fee of _____

The parties agree that if through unavoidable circumstances the performance(s cannot take place, this contract shall be considered null and void, and there shall be no claim for damages by either party.

In the witness whereof they have set their hands:

STEVENS PUPPETS

By:_____

_____(Sponsoring Organization)

By:_____

Date:_____

Please sign and return one copy.

———

This is enough, unless you want to add "The Sponsor agrees to funish two men to carry the equipment into the auditorium before the performance and out again afterward." A clause which I have found to be very very helpful.

A final word about relationship with sponsors. Schools are pretty used to shows coming in and out, but most other organizations – at least the person you will touch, the Program Chairman – are operating on a "first time" basis; the P.C. is elected for one year – mostly she never did this before – she wants everything to go off slick as grease, and you're an unknown quantity that could threaten the success of her day. She'll be worried about that, so when you know approximately when you will arrive to set up, let her know. It will soothe her, otherwise the poor dear will chew her nails off.

People ITCH to get backstage, and if you let them, you have to be nice to them. A moment before you were the guest – now you're the host. When they grab at the puppets don't hit them with the sound system – first be glad they're back there, and then explain why they mustn't touch.

When those jerky reporters ask those INSANELY obvious questions, answer them sweetly – they don't know any better, and when the news photographer wants to pose you in that ridiculous situation – so what? This is interest – this is news – this is noise – and if anyone should suffer from it (which is most unlikely) it'll be the sponsor, not you. Remember, a minute ago puppetry was abstract – it was dolls. Now it's concrete – it's alive – it's you! Do you love your art? Then represent it, charmingly, enthusiastically. I've met people who were still warm with pleasure because some puppeteer years ago was pleasant to them backstage. THIS is your "public relations" opportunity. You can even get dates out of it!

All right – we've had a nice tour of the terrain. I trust you have heard some things you wanted to know about, and that you have tried out at least those things that applied to your particular bent. Maybe you've even ventured into some new territory, and found it fascinating.

In closing the formal part of this Course, I should like to tell you my favorite story. It applies to all I have said about voice, drawing, dreaming up scripts, carving, selling shows, seeing, making a career – everything: It is the only formula for success in puppetry, your happiness, your self-awareness, your achievement:

A little old man with a rowboat ferries passengers across a river at $.10 a head. When asked, "How many times a day do you do this?" He replied, "As many times as I can, because the more I go the more I get. And if I don't go, I don't get!"

Go, man – GO!

Session 20 **Personalized Sessions**

Written for Rick Morse

5-12-71

Dear Mr. Morse:

Thank you for your applause for the Course, and with your permission I should like to use it in my advertising.

Glad you liked the mold method. Anything that makes making them easier helps. There's such a lot to making a show; I always come to a place in the process where I'm sure I haven't done anything yet, and will probably never get it done.

I think Margi has written you some real great stuff here, and I propose to incorporate it in the Course.

Much success to you, and let me know how you come out. I'd be glad to have a picture of some of your results.

Cordially,

(signed) Steve.

* * * * * * * * *

May 12, 1971

Dear Rick:

Steve has turned your letter over to me (Mrs.) since I've done more of that sort of thing than he has. He can sew too, but he's nice enough to make me feel needed!

Fig. 158

For marionette clothing, I follow Steve's original sketch – sometimes doing library research on the period involved if it is period costuming – and start by putting head strings only on the marionette. Then I hang it from the ceiling, overhead pipe, or (in our case) a costuming rack that Steve made years ago so that its feet touch the table top. I make a pattern to fit by cutting out what I think will work from man-sized Kleenex or paper dinner napkins. Then I bend and fold these on the marionette, using thumb tacks for extra hands to help hold things, until I get what looks like a fit. Certain basic forms for garments may be "learned" by experience or by getting simple sewing lesson books from the library to get the usual shape of a shirt or pants or coat or sleeve, etc. Many times I use soft old garments of ours instead of new material because their age causes them to drape more softly, giving better "outlines" from a distance than stiffer materials – and aiding in easier, more natural movements of the puppets. Never use stiff material over a moving joint. A solid sequin coat of arms may be glued right to the chest, but don't try to connect shoulder or neck joints with it, for instance. Sometimes when using old garments, it is possible to utilize the hems that have been pressed in for years and are therefore softer. For instance, the hood of a cloak might be made from the sleeve of an old T-shirt so that the part around the face uses the hem of the sleeve, making that nice looking even up close, but not bulky because it has been pressed many times in its original use.

I use nylon jersey as much as possible, with cotton jersey (such as T-shirts) as second choice and occasional very soft fabrics such as chiffon velvet, sheer cotton, and the finest chamois leather (sold to use for washing rags for cars). Have your relatives save old slips and nightgowns for you. Dip them in Rit for the needed colors. I once ran across a factory that makes these garments and bought oodles of "mill ends" in a dozen colors and we've used from that supply for years now. Avoid all stiff fabrics, no matter how appealing they may seem off the puppet!

When I've adjusted my pattern, I cut the fabric, allowing 1/4" for seams. I try to plan plenty of extra fabric so that I can throw away and do over the parts I made incorrectly. Then – and this is the important special method – DO NOT SEW PARTS TOGETHER AS THO [sic] YOU WERE MAKING DOLL CLOTHES! Many self-taught puppeteers make this mistake and the results are disasterous [sic]. For instance, sew bodice and put it on marionette. Then complete sleeves, but instead of sewing them to bodice, gather shoulder opening by running stitch all around opening, putting sleeve on puppet, and pulling gathering up so that it gathers around the string that holds the arm on. Then, with fingers, gently pull bodice sleeve opening over sleeve gathers. Sometimes you'll want to tack the two together AT THE TOP ONLY. This allows the arm full freedom of movement and from a distance of only a few feet, will look like a regular sewn garment. Be sure the sleeve is wide and loose enough at the elbow to allow a complete bend. Remember that the pull of a string is not as strong as your finger muscles, so you must make maximum ease of joint movement in every garment. Body strings are attached after garment is complete tho [sic] occasionally it means unfastening part of the sewing to attach the string. Usually the strings go right through the garment.

Press all seams with steam to make them as flat as possible because a normal seam on a tiny person is grossly out of proportion.

Now – that was for marionettes. Hand puppets are a bit easier in many respects. Easier to sew – but perhaps not as easy to make realistic. Their "figures" are never "normal" so we just do the best we can to create an illusion and leave the rest to the imagination of the viewers.

I start all hand puppet bodies by drawing loosely around the hand of the person who is going to use it – the particular hand that will most often be in it according to the already written script. I cut two of strong black cotton fabric – muslin that has NOT been treated for permanent press if I can find it. Permanent press fabrics do not wear as well with constant perspiration and rubbing that the inside of a puppet gets. I stitch these together leaving neck, hand and bottom openings, of course. Then I put a second row of stitches close to the first. I "clip" the turning points up to the second stitching to allow the curves to move freely. Do not turn this inside out. The finished seam is already "inside" on the hand, where it should be. Try on for fit and freedom of movement. Then, using your sketch, build any extra padding on top of this undergarment. In the case of Mr. Biggers, half of a rubber ball was fastened to his stomach and halves of a smaller ball were attached for his behind, and shirt and "pants" attached over these. A belt hides the joining of shirt and pants. Neck of shirt is firmly attached to head and hands are fitted OVER black undergarment and UNDER shirt sleeves. If I remember right, Mr. Biggers also had small shoulder pads (made just like real ones) to fatten up his shoulders and back and chest. These are attached at the top only, so they can bend and move around without undue stiffness. The outer garments are made just like I make marionettes clothes – but making a soft paper pattern first and sewing things right on the puppet instead of trying to make it off the puppet and then put it on – like doll clothes.

Wigs may be made of dozens of things – all of them fun! If you want a sure-fire success that will always remain in perfect condition, design it as part of the puppet, and carve it as part of the head. Paint it with dark color in the creases and folds and lighter colors on the high ridges and you are set for the life of the thing. This is what Steve does by preference and it certainly is by far the most practical solution. However, it is not as much fun and so he generously permits me to have fun whenever I request it – so here's how I do that:

I think the one you saw pictured [Maid Marian, all-picture issue of the *Puppetry Journal*, 1970] was a cutdown doll wig. You buy doll wigs at doll "hospitals" in cities. – also buy a supply of doll hair nets in various colors. These are needed to keep many "real" wigs under control and they wear out and must be replaced every 100 performances or so. Real wigs are a lot of trouble to keep up.

Other wigs may be made from women's stretch wigs, switches of artificial hair, chore boy pot cleaners in colors or metal (gold makes a dandy curly headed angel kid). Nylon hose raveled to tatters can be dyed and shaped into beautiful hair and is fairly easy to control. Feathers make some of the best hair ever: Look for good ones at the Salvation Army or such places where used clothing is sold. Buy the old hat for the feathers. Also party favor places and scout headquarters sell "fluffies" which are dyed chicken feathers. Other glamour girls can be made with ostrich maribou [sic] which can be bought at theatrical supply houses. While you are there, consider "chainette fringe" which makes some of the most beautiful hair in the world and can be bought in very long lengths at the theatrical supply houses or short lengths in drapery departments of department stores. Embroidery thread skeins can be attached on a strip of muslin (this seam becomes the "part" on the head) and this works especially well for braids on a little girl. This should be enough to stimulate you to "think hair" when you are designing a puppet and need ideas. (Oh, yes, some of the most delicate and beautiful wigs I've ever made were from angora goat "fur," glued right to the head and it is delicate enough to be brushed and arranged in many ways. The best "comic" hair for large marionettes or hand puppets is monkey fur – hard to get (from furriers). Other fur scraps make excellent short haircuts or "fright wigs.")

Thank you for the kind words about the course. I agreed with you and not just because I love the guy!

      Sincerely,

      (signed) Margi Stevens

Written for Ronnie Burkett

               8-29-71

Dear Ronnie,

Well, I'll tell you. You being so enthusiastic and all, here are the dimensions and stuff about the stage as printed in a narticle (y'know what a narticle is?) `way back in nineteen ought forty-seven. It should tell you everything you need to know – but I hope you'll not stop at it, but dream up a better one nearer your heart's desire. (don't tell any of the other students I sent this – I never sent them one.)

Animals. I draw a front, side, top, AND back view – to help me visualize what it's gonna look like. Usually the shape of the critter is what determines whether you use a side or top profile. Look at cartoons of animals to see what others have emphasized.

You can cut the animal's profile out of a single board, then cut 2 side pieces for rib or 'belly width and nail them in place. 'gives you good flat parallel surfaces for the insides of the legs to move against. As with humans, go LOOK at critters. See how they move.

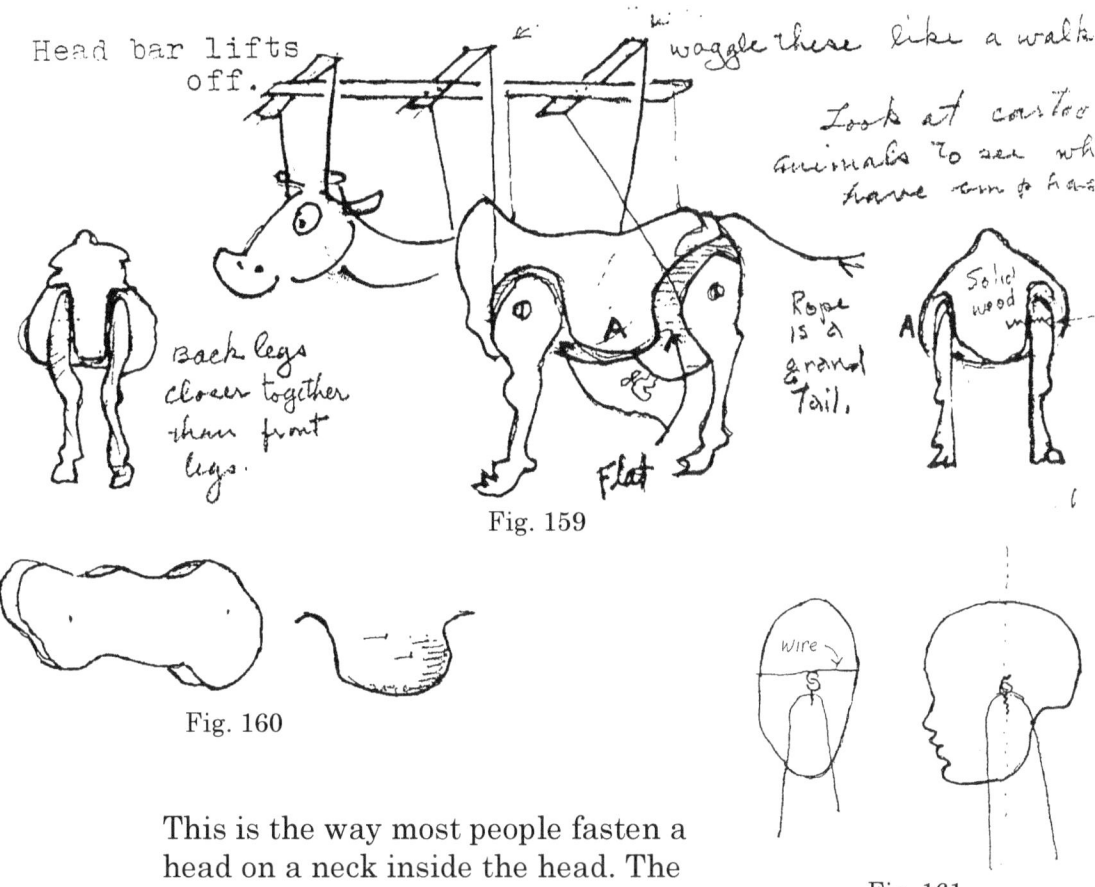

Fig. 159

Fig. 160

Fig. 161

This is the way most people fasten a head on a neck inside the head. The front half of the head should weigh more than the back half so the head will tilt forward when relaxed. "Yes" action is okey – "No" action is punk. Only dire straights make me use it. I put a lei of flowers or something around her neck at the collar bone and use a regular neck joint.

There is no problem in making a serious show interesting, exciting, or anything else. The problem is in getting an audience. Would you believe that people who had had glowing reports on *"The Passion Play"* engaged it, at considerable fees, and then sent their children while they went golfing, because "puppets are for children." With the best recommendations in the world in front of them, people showed me the door saying huffily, "We take our religion seriously; we don't want any Punch and Judy making fun of it." While we worked it up to where it was a major part of our income, I'm reasonably sure our dates came from one person telling another – and that all the money we spent on elegant brochures, booklets, advertising, mailing pieces, was quite wasted. Now here's a fella out in Carson, California who comes up with The Marionette Theatre of the Word. He's's writin' a book – and wants to encourage people like you to do what you want to do. Write him. Tell him I sent you, and ask how to go about getting audiences. I say, if you gotta do it go ahead, and you'll find ways to get it seen if your enthusiasm lasts long enough.

If you must have real-looking wigs, go to a doll-hospital and buy a wig for it. If there's none around, go to the toy department, with the size of the puppet head and buy a doll, whose hair pleases you. Did that just now, with a plastic doll, whose hair was crocheted right into the plastic. Couldn't take out each hair and replace it in the wood. So just cut off the top of the doll's head and stapled it – hair and all – to the puppet's head. Looks great. Most of the new plastics won't stick with any adhesive – hence the staples.

Alas – I haven't a single folder on any of the religious shows. Stopped doing them in the fifties, and since then all the material – including photos has disappeared. Sorry.

There, I guess that takes care of Session 20. It is a considerable pleasure to me to have someone as interested and enthusiastic as you take the Course, and I should be pleased to hear from you subsequently and hear what you've done with it all.

                                                Cordially yours,

                                                (signed) Martin Stevens

Written for Jim Menke

April 16, 1959

Dear Jim,

Here are the Sessions 15 through 19. Especially for you I included ball and socket joints, which I was going to leave out.

Yeah – of Sleeping Beauty is kind of a Poo, isn't she. Never done nothin, never wanted nothin. Poo. So you have to rig something for her. Does she look in a crystal ball and see her "one true love," and is told he isn't born yet? Then the 100 year sleep is a boon rather than a bane. Does she deliberately prick her pinky with the spindle so she can wait for the Prince to get born?

There must be lots of girls in court for the Prince if he wants 'em – so what's he go looking for SB for? Does he see an old painting of SB – a hundred years ago, and that sours him on all the local belles? I haven't seen Disney's SB yet, but I see he rung in a dragon to be overcome before the Prince could give SB a smack.

Just play with it – what's he like, what's she like. If they're not like anything, make them like something – then maybe out of that will grow the conflict.

What's the point of view? Is it his show or her show? Maybe attacking it that way will get you into it. Maybe he has some fault – some bad habit, that will hold him up.

Cheerio,

Steve

(undated)

Dear Jim

I'm afraid my reputation is larger than my performance. True, Joan (of Arc) did draw her sword and brandish it, but at that point we drew the curtain: she never put it back 'cause she couldn't!

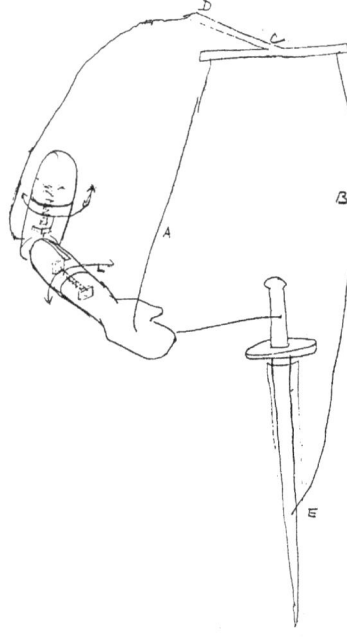

Fig. 162

In order for her to do that complex movement of reaching across her body and turning her hand over, we sawed her upper arm U and lower arm L in two, and inserted a bolt in two imbedded nuts in each half, so it could rotate. By pulling on string A the hand went to the sword and drew it out. When it was out, B lifted it into position. Both sword and scabbard were made of metal, so because of its weight and inertia, the sword wouldn't jump out to meet the hand. String B, of course, goes into the scabbard with the sword. C is a detachable bar on the control and D is an extension out at right angles, the string from which lifts the elbow on the movement across the body, to facilitate the gesture. So you lift elbow D and draw tight string A in one movement until the sword is out, then lift B to raise tip of sword. Point E is determined by trial and error.

These two strings on right arm are in addition to the regular hand string which I have not shown and which keeps the swivelly(sic) arm from turning round and round.

Marge says she bets she could make him put the sword back in the scabbard, but...

If I were a Prince, I'd have my sword in my hand when I entered, and after I had hacked through the thorns, I'd drop the damned thing and forget it.

Thank you for your congratulations. We're very happy. Marge does a lot of club work and is quite familiar with the "Morning Show for Kiddies." Seems like a good idea to me...

Glad you're "out on tour" and hope you have a triumphant season. When you're over this way, drop in.

       Cordially,

       Steve

     * * * * * * * * * *

          Labor Day plus one, 1979

Dear Jim:

Hot dog! Here we go – to try out the new Menkeneckjoint! Interesting coincidence that we're trying it out on Aladdin, too! Damn! I wish I coulda seen yours – right there at the fest and all! I was annoyed at the Fest, but the fact was that I had just had surgery on my left hand, and discovered it was inflamed, and my arm and shoulder were hurting, and I (and my darling Margi) figured I'd better hightail it back to the doctor. SO we did. Of course when we got here, the "doctor is away this month!" so a strange surgeon prescribed a medication, which promptly upset my stomach and had to be discontinued. Cripe! When the proper surgeon DID return, he shot cortisone into my shoulder, gave me some antiinflamatory medication and said to see him again in a month. My left hand still will not "make a fist" which does not please me, but I'm functioning otherwise, have Aladdin all designed, and am ready for your Big Invention!

The problem with a chase in Legend (of Sleepy Hollow) is lack of space. So we solved it with a movie technique of "pulling back" to include more area. In other words, we changed the scale for the chase scene. Make two little horses and riders – paint the set to their size. You still can't run miles over hill and brake, but you can chase back and forth in a figure eight, and you can get ahead of and confront, and you can get far enough apart so when he throws the pumpkin it can sail across the stage (on a coat hanger control) to knock Ichabod AND horse clear off the stage accompanied by a scream of terror for the tag. It works for

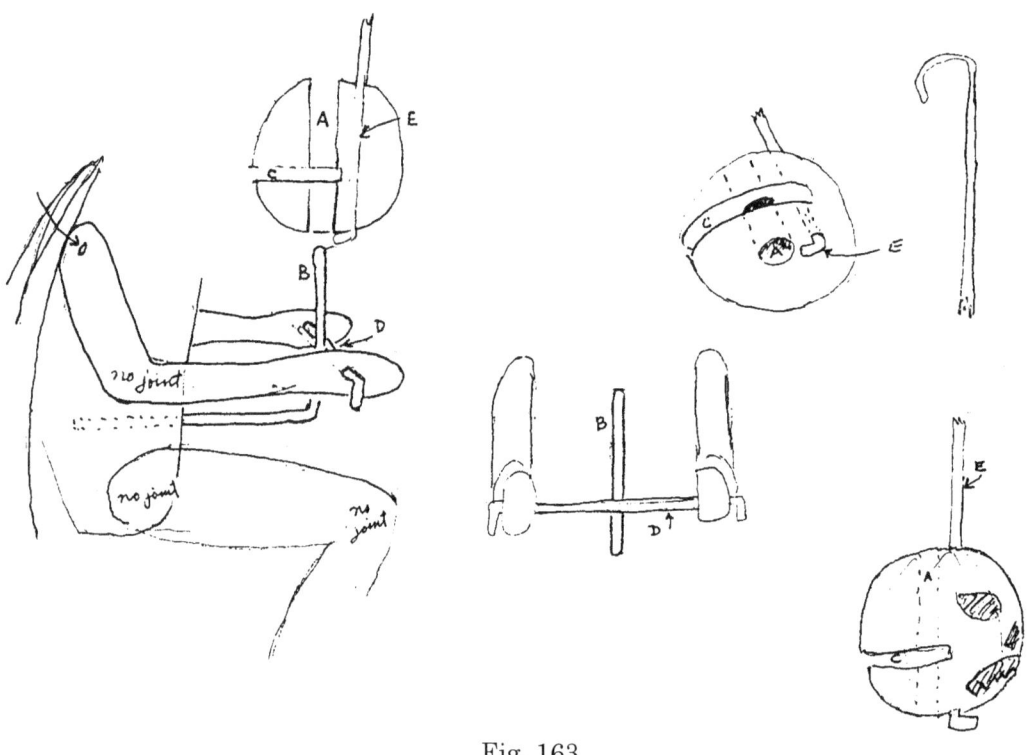

Fig. 163

us, and – like the burning of Joan of Arc – has never caused one comment about the change in scale. Try it...

The regular Ichabod is 24". The little one is 12". His horse, Gunpowder is only 12" from head to rump. Headless is black on a black elegant steed, black cloak, hold yellow pumpkin carved of wood, 1-1/2" diameter with verticle (sic) hold A, which slides down loosely over B, a coathanger wire fastened permantly into Headless' belly. Slot C in side of pumpkin slides toward Headless on coat hanger wire D, which goes through Headless' hands. E is coat hanger wire which goes vertically through pumpkin and up to control and IS the control for flying it across stage.

Shoulders of Headless' stiff arms are string-jointed. When you raise control wire E, it lifts pumpkin and hands up over Headless's no-head, when free of the restraint of B, it can sail across the stage and smack of Icky in his scared puss!

Headless is anchored permanently to his horse (he "has a good seat" as the horsey people say) but Icky is seated on a spring, which allows him to lurch as he gallops, and he has string hip joints so his stiff kneed legs dangle. Okey?

Snow White, eh? I did one for Rufus (Rose) a century ago, and confronted with seven dwarfs and the rest and only six hands, I wrote "Snow White and Three of the Seven Dwarfs." Worked out just as well. They sang: "We are three of the seven little dwarfs who go to work in the mountain."

Well – this isn't getting Aladdin's neck joints made. Here goes.

                                          Love and kisses

                                          Steve

Appendix A

LITTLE LIBRARY OF USEFUL INFORMATION

MARIONETTES

Complete Instructions for Staging Your Own
Marionette Show—How to Design and Carve
Puppets, How to Build Stage and Backdrops,
and How to Operate Marionettes

Number 113

Copyright 1947 — Popular Mechanics Co.
Printed in U.S.A.

POPULAR MECHANICS PRESS
CHICAGO 11

Puppets, says the dictionary, are small images in human form—but Martin and Olga Stevens, leading puppeteers, make them talk and act like living people. Here's how they do it

STAGE

PART I

By Kenneth Murray

A MARIONETTE show, skillfully handled, is real entertainment — with all the dramatic atmosphere, costuming and dialogue of the professional stage, and the character and individuality of adult performers. In fact, so realistic are the shows put on by the Stevens Marionette Team, top-ranking puppeteers, that children have asked to be introduced to the "actors" after the performance. Except for the controlling strings which, with the small size of the stage, are the only "give-aways" of the puppeteer, marionettes can be made to go through a complete dramatic performance with an illusion so perfect that the audience is hardly aware of it. And Martin and Olga Stevens, who make their own marionettes, have revealed the reason is that the figures are copied, to a rough but close scale, directly from human models. Movements of the models are studied carefully so that the marionettes may have the same limitations, balance and dissimilarities as the prototypes.

Preparing rough blanks. In making a puppet, front and side profile sketches are first made on a 15 by 24-in. sheet of brown wrapping paper pinned to a smooth surface. General dimensions of the professional-type marionette figure can be determined from Fig. 16. Many professional puppeteers choose a model from life, using a scale of 4 in. to 1 ft. And, as already mentioned, they include all variations from the normal to give the completed figure character and individuality. Be particular in meas-

YOUR OWN SHOW with these marionettes

uring and locating knee and other joints so that naturalness will be built directly into the figure and will not be entirely dependent on skill in handling the controller. The location of the center line, passing through shoulder, hip and knee joints, is important because the correct position, Figs. 15 and 16, assures natural balance. If you make the figure without proper balance, special strings will be necessary for control during performances. Correctly balanced, the figures will assume characteristic poses quite naturally when merely supported by the controller strings.

Cardboard templates are next made from each view of head, torso, arms, legs, hips and feet. Carefully mark the center line on each template, Figs. 1, 2, 3 and 16. Then square up the stock from which the parts are to be cut and mark center lines on the wood as a guide in locating templates. White pine of the grade and quality commonly known as sugar pine is the best material to use, with poplar or basswood a fairly good second choice. Front and side profiles are marked carefully from the templates on each piece. Saw out one profile, then the other, as in Fig. 6. In sawing the head, Fig. 9, notice that it is slightly heavy in front of the center line as in Fig. 16. This location of the center line allows the head to nod easily and without tipping inward when the figure is performing.

Hand carving. Carving the sawed blanks to the required contours may look difficult but actually it's quite simple once you get into it. With the exception of the head, the job is merely that of whittling off the sharp corners of the pieces and scraping and sanding the rounded surfaces to a smooth finish. Use regular carving tools or a sharp carving knife. Make the chipping cuts across the grain and control the tool by bracing it with the thumb of the left hand so that it cannot slip. On the head, Fig. 10, a little more patience is required to shape the features, and a photo of the model from which the profile drawings were made can

DECEMBER 1946

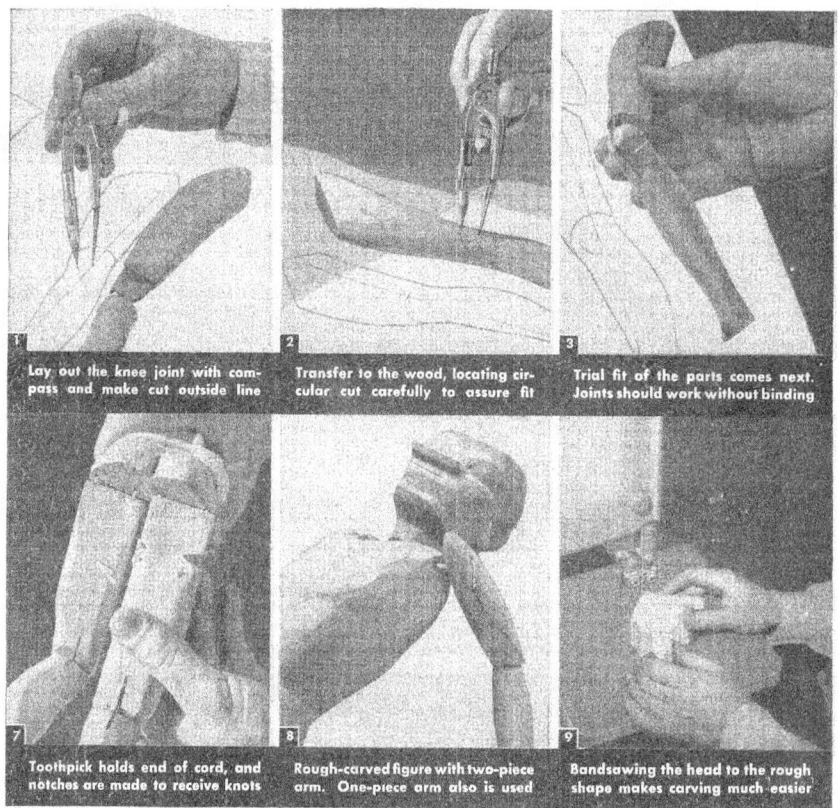

1. Lay out the knee joint with compass and make cut outside line
2. Transfer to the wood, locating circular cut carefully to assure fit
3. Trial fit of the parts comes next. Joints should work without binding
7. Toothpick holds end of cord, and notches are made to receive knots
8. Rough-carved figure with two-piece arm. One-piece arm also is used
9. Bandsawing the head to the rough shape makes carving much easier

be most helpful. Don't bother to include details that cannot be seen beyond the first row of the audience.

Joints. Various types of joints have been devised by puppeteers but the simple string-and-fiber-hinge joints are so completely satisfactory that many continue to use them. Position of strings in the hip joints is indicated in Fig. 16. Ordinary cotton chalk line is used. A notch is made in the leg to receive the knotted beginning end of the cord, which passes diagonally upward, through the lower part of the torso and back to pass out the side of the hip, Fig. 7. Round toothpicks are driven into the exit holes to secure ends of the cords and to permit later adjustment, as the legs must be of exactly the same length.

Use a compass to mark a circle equal to the diameter of the leg at the knee, Fig. 1. Draw a line across the leg immediately above the circle, and saw the leg into two parts. Slots for the hinge are cut as in Fig. 4, using a keyhole saw with a blade of the same thickness as the fiber from which the hinge pieces are cut. Holes for the hinge pins are made by using brads in a hand drill rather than hammering them into place. Note that the fiber is shaped to strike a stop pin, Fig. 17, so that the leg cannot double up in a forward position.

As the first step in forming a ball-and-socket knee joint, round off the upper end of the leg and, after wetting the ball portion so that wood putty will not adhere, shape the socket as in Fig. 5 by applying the wood putty to the adjoining part. The completed joint is shown in Figs. 3 and 12, the latter also showing finished ankle joints which are made in a similar manner but without the use of wood putty. The ankle hinge, which is self-stopping in both directions, is shown in Fig. 18. It is important to round the heels and toes so that the figure will walk in a natural manner.

Simplest way of making the shoulder

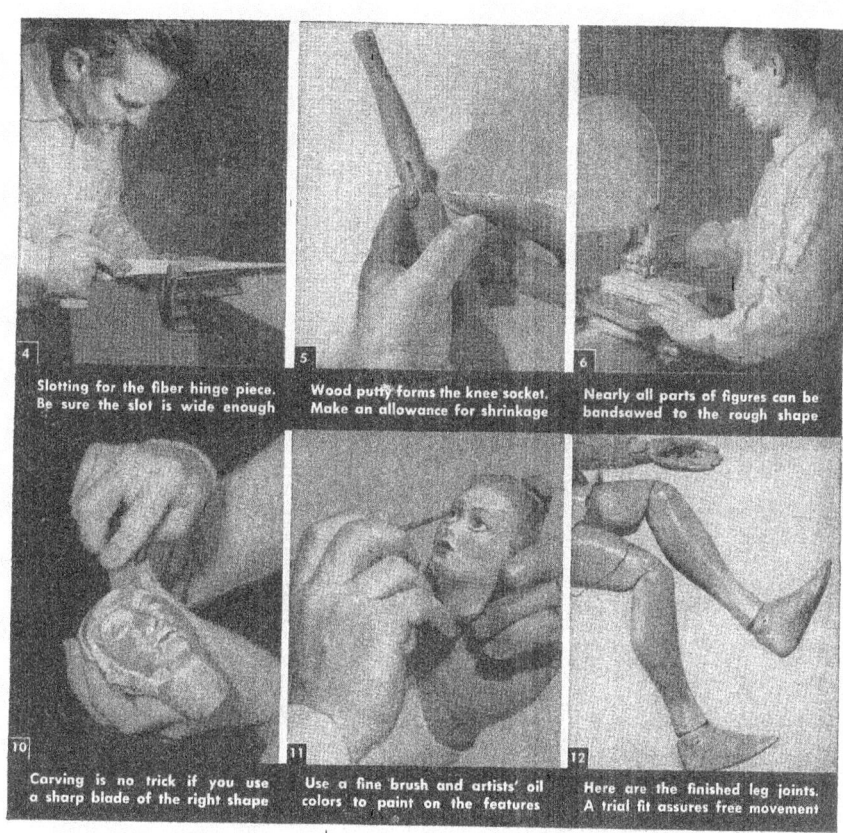

Slotting for the fiber hinge piece. Be sure the slot is wide enough.

Wood putty forms the knee socket. Make an allowance for shrinkage.

Nearly all parts of figures can be bandsawed to the rough shape.

Carving is no trick if you use a sharp blade of the right shape.

Use a fine brush and artists' oil colors to paint on the features.

Here are the finished leg joints. A trial fit assures free movement.

joint is with a chalk line, Fig. 8, the end of the cord being secured with a toothpick as in joining the hips. Despite its simplicity, this joint gives a perfectly natural action. It will be noticed that the elbow in Fig. 8 also is hinged. However, this requires additional control strings and is not necessary except in more detailed acts. Elbow and wrist joints may be added at any time.

Head movements. Ordinarily, puppeteers use the very practical screw-eye joint in which the neck extends into the shoulders, like a ball and socket. This simple head coupling, shown in Fig. 16, is recommended for both amateur and professional use. One of the screw eyes is wrapped with cord, in half-hitches, to eliminate operational noise. Slacking of the head-control strings permits the head to nod and turn in either direction.

Painting and clothing. Homemade wigs or ready-made doll wigs provide natural-appearing hair when the head is to be un-

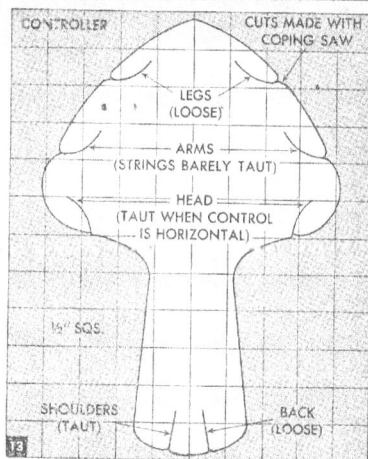

DECEMBER 1946

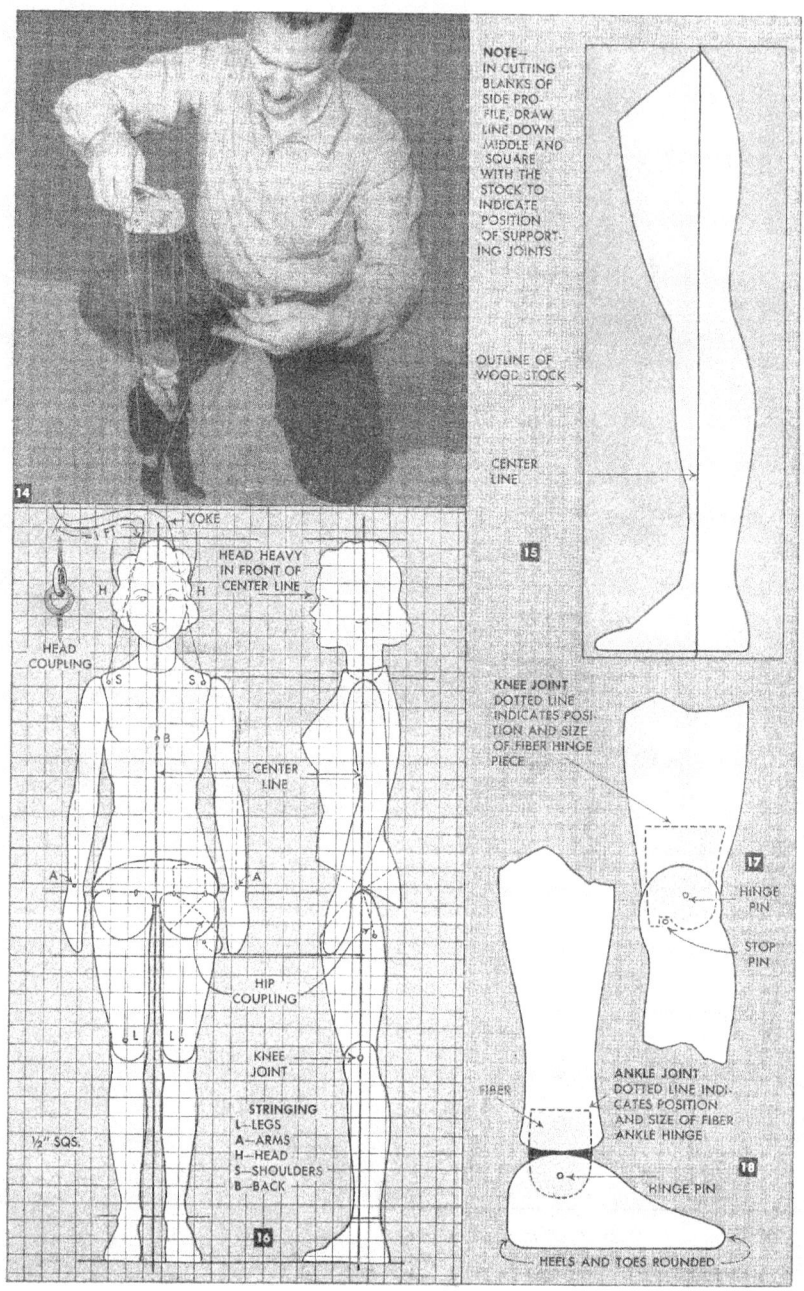

covered, but ordinarily hair simulated with paint will be adequate. Finishing of the head is done with artists' oil colors, Fig. 11, the features being painted in with a fine brush after the ground coat of flesh-colored paint has thoroughly dried. The latter also is used for the body. Characterization and personality, developed by the use of paints, are important for a professional performance. Costumes can be of your own design or reduced to scale from regular patterns. It is important to note that, for these small actors and actresses, clothing must be reduced in weight and texture by several times, as nothing could be more unnatural than to use cloth of standard weight which will not drape properly. As an example, to simulate the appearance of a velvet robe, use silk jersey; for a fur coat, use velvet. Clothing is attached with an adhesive or with very small tacks.

Stringing and controlling. Use fine black fishline for stringing the marionettes, attaching ends to parts of each figure with small tacks. Avoid loose string ends at the figure and replace broken strings rather than knot them together. The controller is convenient to handle and does not require separate controls as used with the customary airplane type. It is cut from ¼-in. plywood with coping-saw cuts for the strings as in Fig. 13. Surplus string ends are wound around the handle. Use of the controller is shown in Fig. 14, with the strings shortened to include the figure in the photograph. In this illustration Mr. Stevens is demonstrating how the loose leg strings are grasped in the left hand to control walking movements. Entire support of the figure is by the shoulder strings, which form a yoke ending 1 ft. above the head with a single string connecting the yoke with the controller. To maintain natural balance, it is important that the center of the yoke be exactly above the center line of the figure. Head strings are taut when the controller is horizontal. The head turns when controller is tilted to either side and with the controller tilted forward the head nods. The back string is loose to permit it to be caught with the little finger. This causes the figure to bow naturally.

Abrasive Strips for Puppet Work Can Be Made From Cellulose Tape

Handy and efficient abrasive strips for finishing or touching up model parts can be made by sifting emery on the adhesive side of a strip of cellulose tape. Cut off a suitable length and fold over the end for finger grips. If an old salt or pepper shaker is available, it can be used to apply the emery uniformly. An abrasive wheel for a small motor is made by turning a wooden wheel and attaching cellulose tape to it sticky side out. Abrasive then is sprinkled on the surface. The wheel should be turned from waterproof plywood, which has less tendency to warp than the regular type of plywood. A small floor flange will serve as a hub in most cases.

Electric Fan Mounted on Spotlight Housing Cools Lamp

Heat generated by a spotlight or a floodlight can be dissipated if a small fan is installed in the light housing to force cooling air over the bulb and thus increase the efficiency and safety of the lamp. The fan and motor from a car heater, with a few alterations, will adapt itself to this job if the proper power is available. A better solution, however, would be to use a motor that will run on standard current and fit it with a fan. The motor should be mounted on extension brackets so that it will not block the free flow of air into the housing by being too close to the vent holes. Small strips of flat iron can be bent and drilled to form brackets which attach to the motor and the light housing with self-tapping sheet-metal screws. It may be necessary

also to add an extension to the shaft since the standard for motors of this size is fairly short. As a safety precaution, to be sure that the fan is running when the light is on, wire the motor in parallel with the light switch. This cannot be done, of course, if there is a separate source of power for the fan. — Lyn Grover, Los Angeles, Calif.

Stage Your Own Show

PART II
SETTING UP THE STAGE
By Kenneth Murray

MARIONETTE stages designed for amateurs will give more satisfaction if the stage and accessories are modeled after those of the professional. This stage, which was designed for Martin and Olga Stevens of the Stevens Marionette Team, is compact and portable, and is equipped to handle complete dramatic productions. The area about the proscenium is masked with a grand drape, with an overhead drape and traveler drapes at each side, the whole arrangement being similar to valance and side drapes of a window. There also is a short drape underneath, and the drape support has a track for stage curtains. Then there is the stage for the marionettes, and back of it the puppeteer's bar, which also supports the backdrop or background. The bridge, with ladders at each end, is somewhat higher and has guard rails on three sides. The marionettes are controlled by operators standing on the bridge. Figs. 19, 20, 22 and 23 show how the stage and bridge are set up from a single folding unit.

Bridge. The top of ½-in. plywood and the ¾-in. wood rails or stiffeners, to which the top is screwed, form a packing case for other members of the bridge and stage when the unit is folded. End supports, Fig. 21, are merely braced frames, each hinged at the top with ⅜-in. tie rods which pass through the sides of the bridge, the ends of the rods being peened over. Braces are on the inside to allow the supports to fold into the bridge. A ladder is hinged to the top cross member of each end support, a piece of ½-in. plywood separating two sets of hinges on each, this arrangement permitting the ladders to fold inside. A 13-in. length of chain secures the center step of the ladder to the middle of the support cross brace. The center support is somewhat narrower and is attached with piano hinges. Flat-iron braces hold the supports in position while the bridge is in use. Lower ends of the braces are attached with bolts and wing nuts on the inside, while bolts securing the upper ends to the bridge are peened over.

The stage. Fig. 24 details construction. Most of the parts in Fig. 21 are shown by dotted lines in Fig. 24. Stage top is of ½-in. plywood 24 in. wide and in three sections so that the end sections can fold back on the center. Piano hinges are used for the top sections and two of the ½-in. plywood supports. These two are hinged to supports for the bridge. The center support is somewhat shorter so that it will fold inside. A piece of plywood to make up the difference in height is hinged to the underside of the

JANUARY 1947

Here's the bridge being unfolded. Unfolding begins with the "package" upside down. Notice that the puppet stage is attached to one support, or leg, of the bridge for folding

Bridge unfolded and right side up with the stage in place and the grand drape going up. Note extra piece of plywood attached to support under the center of the stage

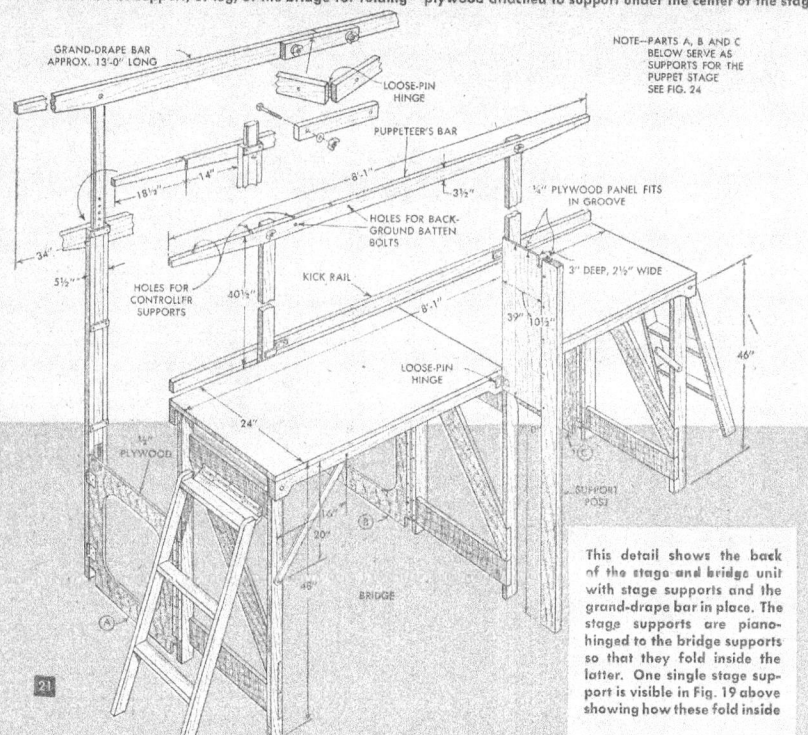

This detail shows the back of the stage and bridge unit with stage supports and the grand-drape bar in place. The stage supports are piano-hinged to the bridge supports so that they fold inside the latter. One single stage support is visible in Fig. 19 above showing how these fold inside

In just a few minutes more the stage-bridge unit will be ready for the show. Here the puppeteer's bar is being bolted in place. Setting up takes about 30 minutes

Guard rail comes last. This serves the dual purpose of preventing operators from accidentally stepping off the bridge and as a hanger bar for "actors" awaiting cues

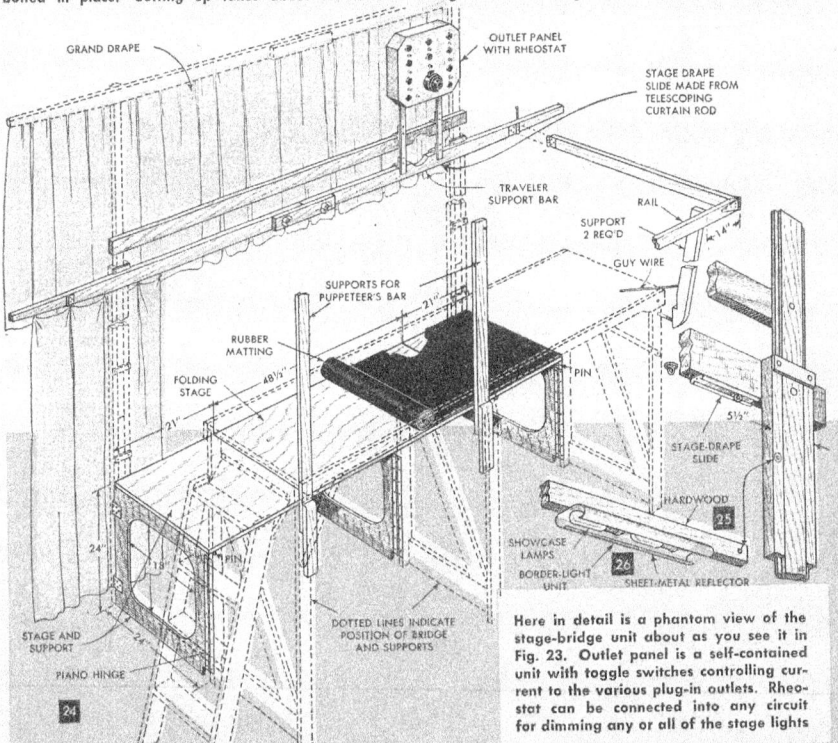

Here in detail is a phantom view of the stage-bridge unit about as you see it in Fig. 23. Outlet panel is a self-contained unit with toggle switches controlling current to the various plug-in outlets. Rheostat can be connected into any circuit for dimming any or all of the stage lights

JANUARY 1947

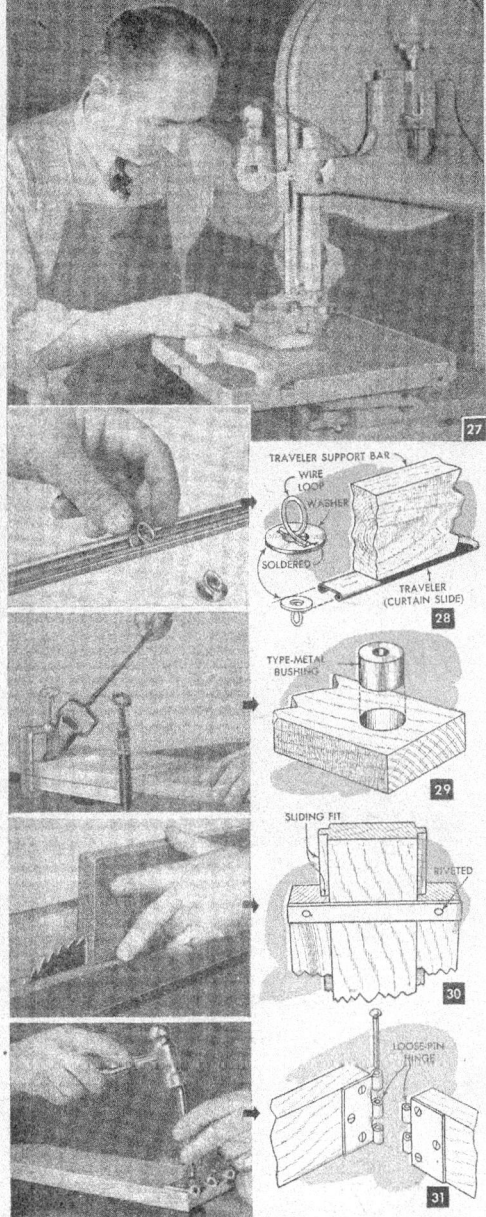

stage, and in turn is pin-hinged with loose-pin butts to the center support when the stage is set up. This part will be seen in place in Fig. 20. Each end support is pinned by means of loose-pin hinges to those on the traveler support uprights, Figs. 21 and 24. The puppeteer's bar, Fig. 21, is bolted to the front of the bridge and fits between it and the stage. Uprights supporting the bar are lap-jointed 24 in. from the floor to fold. A row of ⅜-in. holes is drilled in the upper edge of the bar for insertion of bent rods, which support the puppet controllers when not in use, Fig. 35.

Masking. Picture frame of the performance is the masking or proscenium, detailed in Fig. 34. In four parts, it is cut from a sheet of plywood. Three of the 45-deg.-angle joints are piano-hinged, but the fourth is attached with a butt hinge having a removable pin. The stage supports or brackets, Figs. 27 and 34, are hinged and fold flat. Legs are permanently attached with ⅜-in. bolts, the ends being peened over. Angle braces or clips in the upper corners attach to the traveler upright, and there is a strip of cloth tacked to the bottom to which the lower drape is hooked. Removal of the hinge pin permits the frame to fold flat.

Bushings. At all bolted joints where the parts are separated for packing, and on the parts permanently hinged, holes in wood members will eventually wear loose. To prevent this, drill the holes in the wood twice as large as required for the bolt, then fill with molten type metal, as in Fig. 29. Drill holes for the pivot pins or bolts in the metal.

Grand drape and traveler. The grand drape is attached with wire hooks over the supporting bar, Figs. 21 and 24. The drape is 162 in. wide and 55 in. deep, with allowance for fullness and hems. Side or traveler drapes are 37 in. wide and 75 in. long. Any dark, heavy material that does not permit light to shine through from the back is suitable. As can be seen from Figs. 21 and 24, the drape bars fold in the middle for packing. The grand-drape bar is adjustable for height on a support which is tongued and grooved, Figs. 21 and 30. The three sections of each support are held in place with metal plates on each side, and at the bottom of each support are loose-pin hinges for pinning the parts to the stage supports, Fig. 24. Although screws will serve, it's perhaps better to rivet the hinge butts in place, as in Fig. 31. Similar hinges are riveted to the traveler bar to fasten ends of the rail, Fig. 24. Tracks for the stage drape slides are screwed underneath the traveler bar, Fig. 25. The slides are made from telescoping curtain rod.

Curtains may be of a lightweight material, as compared with the drapes, but should be lightproof. They are about 57 in. long and with sufficient width for pleated fullness. A hook is sewed in each pleat for attaching to the homemade slides, Fig. 28. Side-by-side lapping of the slides or tracks will bring the curtains together for a complete closure. They are controlled with a continuous cord which passes over a pulley at each side. The border light strip, Fig. 26, consists of a curved sheet-metal reflector mounted on a batten bolted between the traveler supports. Tubular showcase lamps, lacquered in different colors as well as clear, are turned on according to the color desired by means of separate switches on the outlet panel, Fig. 24. This is a self-contained unit with switches controlling current to plug-in outlets and arranged so that the rheostat may be connected into any circuit for dimming any or all of the lights. General overhead illumination is also provided by a 50-watt lamp in a painted reflector made from a No. 2½ tin can. A similar lamp mounted on a music stand provides any degree of floodlighting from the side. It also can be covered with colored Cellophane for special effects. It has been found that a 50-watt lamp is ideal as a stronger illumination overlights the puppet characters and "washes out" detail and color. Footlights are not used.

Backdrops. These are of unbleached muslin, 5 by 8 ft., held on a curtain stretcher while the scenery is painted on. Use oil colors thinned with gasoline as this mixture will not stiffen the cloth or crack after repeated use. A hem at the bottom of each drop permits insertion of a narrow piece of

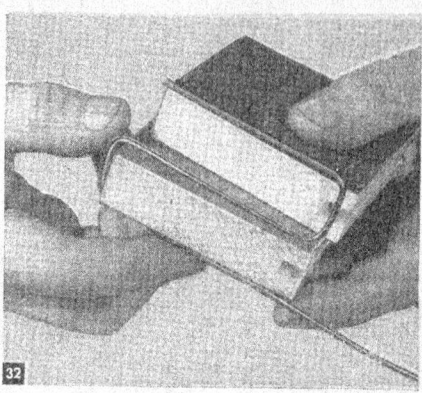

Above, the jig for forming the wire hangers which support members of puppet cast on the guard rail while awaiting their cues. Below, loops of leather attached to the controllers are slipped over the wire hooks to hold the figures securely

covered, but ordinarily hair simulated with paint will be adequate. Finishing of the head is done with artists' oil colors, Fig. 11, the features being painted in with a fine brush after the ground coat of flesh-colored paint has thoroughly dried. The latter also is used for the body. Characterization and personality, developed by the use of paints, is important for a professional performance. Costumes can be as simple or as elaborate as you wish, of your own design or reduced to scale from regular patterns. It is important to note that, for these small actors and actresses, clothing must be reduced in weight and texture by several times, as nothing could be more unnatural than to use cloth of standard weight which will not drape properly. As an example, to simulate the appearance of a velvet robe, use silk jersey; for a fur coat, use velvet. Clothing is attached with an adhesive or with very small tacks.

Stringing and controlling. Use fine black fishline for stringing the marionettes, attaching ends to parts of each figure with small tacks. Avoid loose string ends at the figure and replace broken strings rather than knot them together. The controller is convenient to handle and does not require separate controls as used with the customary airplane type. It is cut from ¼-in. plywood with coping-saw cuts for the strings as in Fig. 13. Surplus string ends are wound around the handle. Use of the controller is shown in Fig. 14, with the strings shortened to include the figure in the photograph. In this illustration Mr. Stevens is demonstrating how the loose leg strings are grasped in the left hand to control walking movements. Entire support of the figure is by the shoulder strings, which form a yoke ending 1 ft. above the head with a single string connecting the yoke with the controller. To maintain natural balance, it is important that the center of the yoke be exactly above the center line of the figure. Head strings are taut when the controller is horizontal. The head turns when controller is tilted to either side and with the controller tilted forward the head nods. The back string is loose to permit it to be caught with the little finger. This causes the figure to bow naturally.

(TO BE CONTINUED)

Eggshells Clean Narrow Vases

When narrow-neck crystal vases and bottles need cleaning and a bottle brush won't do the work, break several eggshells into the bottle or vase, add a little water and shake until all film and dust disappear from the glass. After rinsing, the vase will be crystal clear.

Ruth C. Buck, Jackson, Miss.

Harrow Disks Make Ice Planer To Surface Skating Pond

For removing skate marks or other roughness from the surface of a skating pond, one ice enthusiast found that a number of discarded harrow disks, bolted to a heavy plank, made a planer that would do the work. The device can be pulled by hand or towed behind an automobile.

Handy Self-Feeder for Rabbits

Made from a tall can and a cake tin, this self-feeder for rabbits is anchored to the hutch but can be removed for cleaning. The top of the can is cut away, and a portion of the side is removed to provide access to the food. Wire hold-downs are at each corner and cross wires are run through these.—E. Y. Wormuth, El Cajon, Calif.

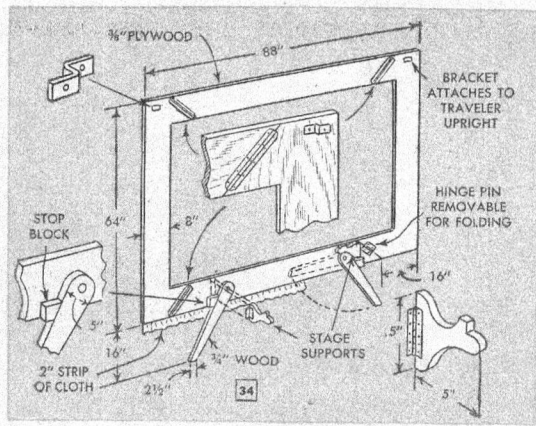

Above, the proscenium or masking frame which is placed directly in front of the stage. It's made of plywood and hinged at four points so that it folds. Below, the whole affair all set up complete and ready for the show

ALL SET FOR THE SHOW

wood which will serve as a weight to hold the drop taut. The top of each drop is fastened to a batten, the last scene being on top. Before the performance each drop is rolled up and fastened to the bar with lengths of cloth tape tied in bow knots. Then when changing between scenes, the operator pulls the free ends of the tapes and the drops fall into place. A kick rail, Fig. 21, prevents the operator pushing a foot into the scenery during a performance. Clips made from flat iron hold the rail in place.

The guard rail. Figs. 23 and 24 show how the guard rail is fitted to the puppeteer's bridge. This rail keeps the operator from accidentally stepping off the edge of the bridge and also serves as a hanger for the marionettes awaiting cues, Fig. 33. Wire hooks for hanging the puppets are formed as in Fig. 32. Back section of the guard rail is in two parts, with a lap joint so that the entire unit will fold. Two vertical supports hold the back section in place, the lower end of the supports being bolted to the bridge as in Fig. 24. Professionals generally use a sound system such as a record player with a loud-speaker located under the stage. If you use this added refinement, then the support post shown in Fig. 21 will be necessary. A piece of plywood is grooved into the upright and fastened to the bridge with a loose-pin hinge. Back section of the guard rail fits in the notch cut in the plywood, and the whole thing is held rigidly in place with guy wires fitted with turnbuckles. This simple arrangement takes little space and supports the record player securely.

(To be continued)

STAGE YOUR OWN SHOW

PART III

By Kenneth Murray

MOVEMENTS of marionettes on the stage are really projections of the actor-personality of the puppeteer—the fellow pulling the strings. Thinking that over, it won't take you long to conclude that marionettes will capture instantly the skills and emotions of the manipulator and convey these to the audience. The puppeteer then is the real actor, although of course the attention of the audience is always centered on the marionettes, for in a well-conducted marionette show the customers never are intentionally made aware of the puppeteer during the actual performance. All this means that one must practice until the controllers and strings perform as extensions of the muscles and nerves and impulses of the operator. Only in this way can the puppeteer acquire that smooth proficiency and sense of complete control which gives a marionette show its appealing reality.

At first you use a mirror as in Fig. 36 where the operator is demonstrating the correct position to take for early practice. The mirror should be as large, or larger, than the one shown and should be placed at the correct angle so that the manipulator can watch every movement of the puppet. The purpose of the mirror, of course, is to enable you to see the puppet just as the audience sees it. The figure must stand, walk and gesture with perfect naturalness. And right here is where you begin to think puppeteer-wise, keeping both your mind and your eyes on the doings of the miniature figure whose movements you are originating and directing. When it commits an error, an unnatural pose, gesture or method of walking, you can detect it instantly in the mirror. During the first few hours of practice, you should list all errors immediately they are made, writing these in detail on a sheet of paper for later reference. Then, during subsequent practice sessions, go through each bit of movement in which an error was committed time after time, on succeeding days, until you are sure that the corrected movements have become quite automatic to your fingers. Like the music student, you should allot yourself a regular daily practice period.

A practice stage is next set up as in Fig. 37, the purpose of this being to give one

Above, the operator is demonstrating a practice position before a mirror. Mirror enables you to see the puppet actor just as your audience will see it. Below, the operator is working a marionette on a practice stage

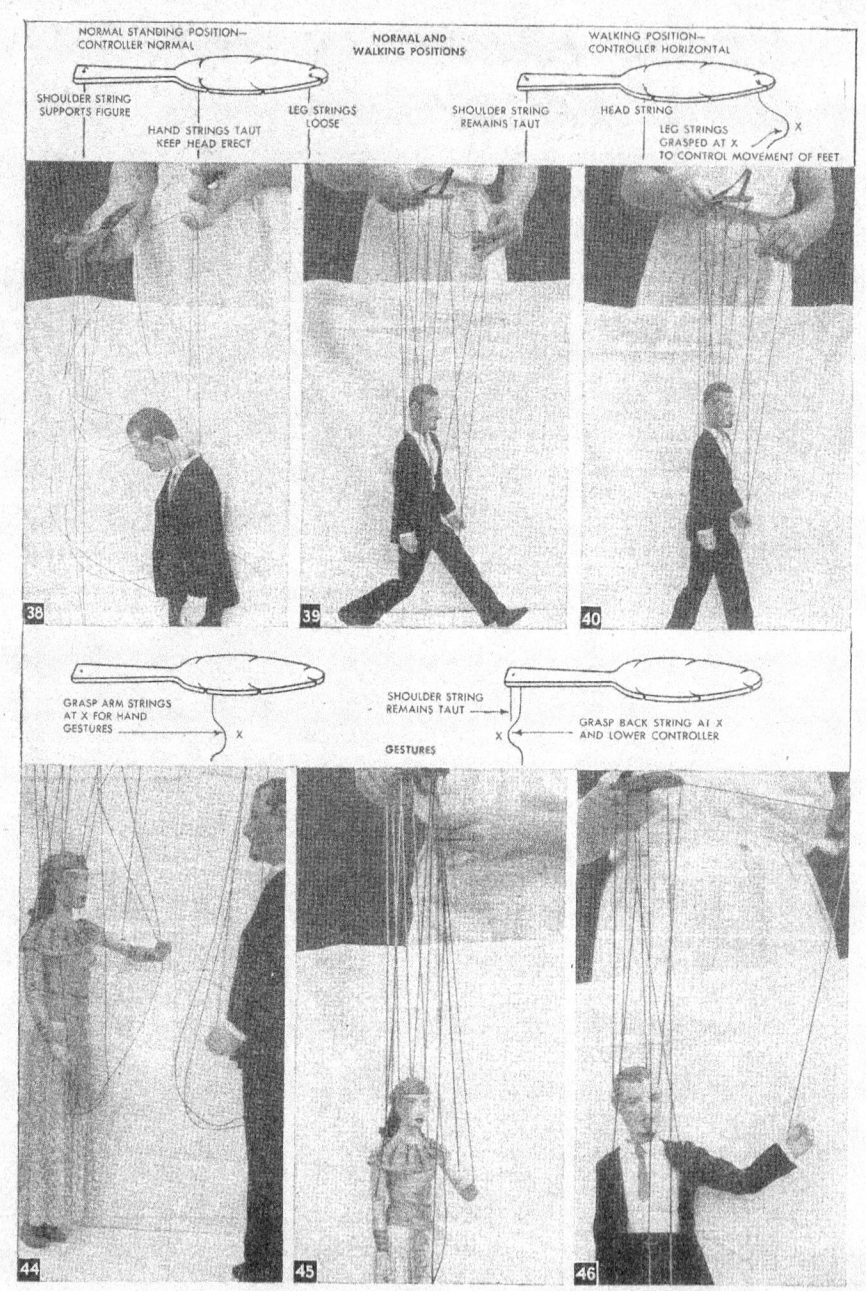

POPULAR MECHANICS

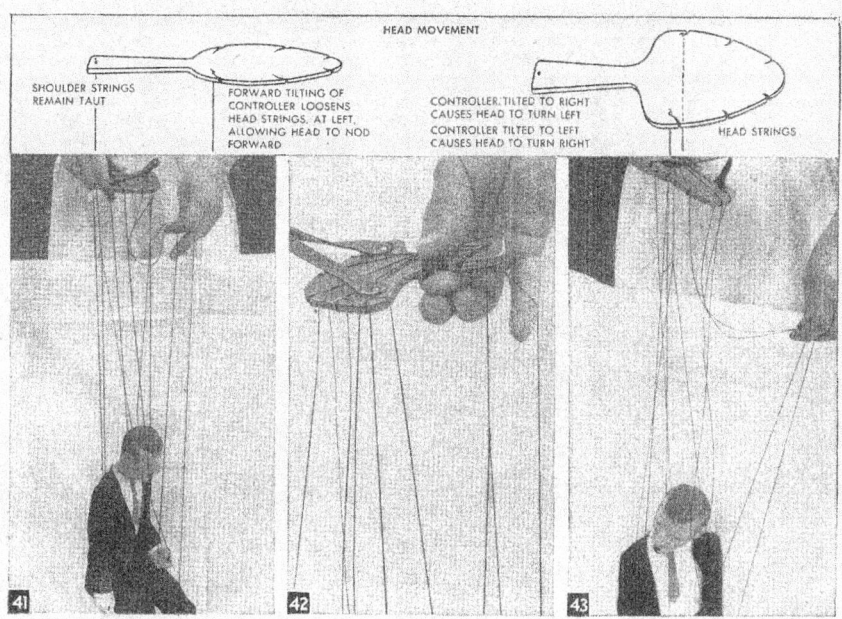

new at the trade the "feel" of the height and width of a marionette stage. Use a low bench on which to stand, and before it set an unopened card table on edge to serve as a background. If you wish you can still use the mirror in front of this informal setup. Mark off the stage dimensions on the floor with chalk or tape. Small wood or cardboard boxes can be substituted for props such as chairs or benches.

With this advanced setup, you work for the first time with full-length strings and enter puppets from the stage "wings," have them sit down, bow, gesture, talk and walk. From this you gain a feeling of proper distances, the stage size will become familiar and you'll get onto the trick of keeping the figures in a standing posture without sagging or "flying," a term puppeteer pros use to describe some of the grotesque positions the puppet may assume if you let things get out of hand.

Voice of the puppet is your voice, for you are the voice as well as the action of your marionette show. It is assumed that you will either use a professionally prepared script or write your own, which is preferable, as this makes the entire drama, comedy or other type of production entirely and originally yours. The script should feature the usual "sides," parts and cues, and particularly the different characterizations. From this point on you become an actor or actress on your own, with your own script. It is not difficult to learn to change your voice to distinguish one character from another. Practice this with a friend acting as your audience and mentor. Yours is the inspiration but in the end the marionettes do your acting before the customers. Only consistent practice can perfect the illusion but once you've convinced your audience that you've mastered the art of puppetry, they'll forget all about you, and they'll enjoy your show.

Now the mechanics of the thing: To begin with, study the steps demonstrated in Figs. 38 to 53 inclusive. Notice Fig. 38 particularly, and the detail of the controller directly above it. Remember, of course, that the operator is only demonstrating the more common movements and, besides, is using shortened strings. Because of this the hand positions cannot be shown exactly as they would appear in normal manipulation from the puppeteer's bridge. Fig. 38 reveals the real inside trick in stage-managing a puppet actor. The string yoke, looped over the operator's left forefinger, is attached to the handle or "heel" of the controller by a single cord as you see in the detail. Thus, even though all the other strings go slack for any reason, the figure will remain upright so long as you hold the controller in

FEBRUARY 1947

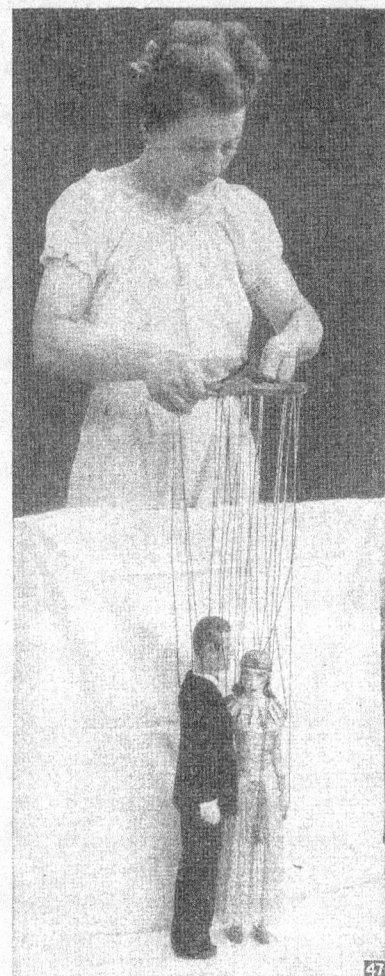

Puppeteers learn to be ambidextrous, that is, they become equally proficient with the right and left hand. Here the operator is working two puppet actors

a horizontal position. The important thing to learn is to keep the controller always a given height above the stage while your actor is going through his lines. These two simple rules take care of the fundamental mechanics of puppeteering. The rest is merely an elaboration of procedures. Figs. 39 and 40 are examples of this. In Fig. 39 the dapper puppet gentleman is being put through an undignified "bounce," as the puppeteers call it, which is an approved method of practicing the walk. Here the "lift" of the normal walk is purposely exaggerated. The controller is lifted slightly while at the same time the controlling fingers are "teetered" or alternated in height, which causes the legs to reverse position, spreading on the downstroke of the controller and reversing on the upstroke. Lessen the exaggeration until the bounce of the torso is scarcely perceptible, then take the slack out of the strings and you have the gentleman strolling casually across the stage as in Fig. 40. That's all there is to it, in essential. The naturalness comes with prolonged practice. Always the figure should have the feet on the stage floor with just enough weight to give a slight drag to each foot. Actually the walk is little more than a shuffle. Puppeteers refer to the advanced leg as the "lead" leg, the other as the "lag" leg.

When more puppets than you can handle are on the stage at one time, those not performing are suspended by attaching the controllers to the puppeteer's bar. Hooks are provided for both sitting and standing distances and you have to determine the positions by trial after studying the set required by the script.

Bowing is one of the easiest practice movements and is accomplished by hooking your little finger underneath the string attached to the back of the actor as in Fig. 42. Support the figure with the shoulder string, as usual, while allowing it to take a bow. With each of these actions, practice until you can make the required movements with the fingers while keeping attention on the puppet.

Actors are made to kneel by grasping the leg strings with the fingers of one hand as in walking, advancing the lead leg and permitting the lag leg to bend by slightly lowering the controller heel. At the same time the controller is tilted forward as in Figs. 41 and 51. Fig. 41 is mentioned in this connection because of the head movement required in the kneeling procedure. Be careful not to allow the head to fall too far forward at the start of the manuver. However, it should be inclined slightly as in Fig. 41. Complete the kneeling position by lowering the figure to the stage. These movements are indicated in Fig. 51. They are reversed to raise the figure to its feet.

The head pivot permits the head to swing in either direction while you are maintaining support of the body with the shoulder string. If you tilt the controller forward there will be sufficient slack in the head strings to permit the head to nod. Tilting the controller to either side will cause the head to turn in the opposite direction, Fig. 43. Practice until the movements are familiar, as they will be used frequently.

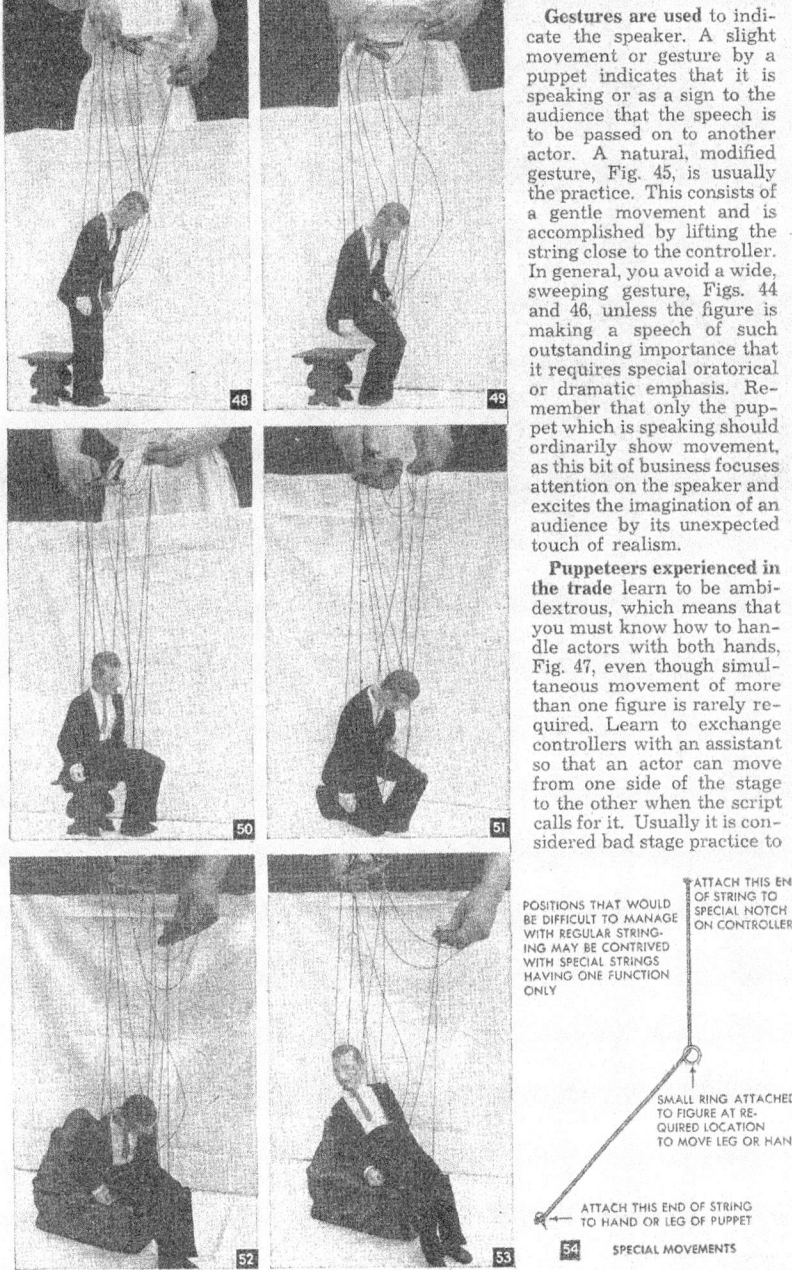

Gestures are used to indicate the speaker. A slight movement or gesture by a puppet indicates that it is speaking or as a sign to the audience that the speech is to be passed on to another actor. A natural, modified gesture, Fig. 45, is usually the practice. This consists of a gentle movement and is accomplished by lifting the string close to the controller. In general, you avoid a wide, sweeping gesture, Figs. 44 and 46, unless the figure is making a speech of such outstanding importance that it requires special oratorical or dramatic emphasis. Remember that only the puppet which is speaking should ordinarily show movement, as this bit of business focuses attention on the speaker and excites the imagination of an audience by its unexpected touch of realism.

Puppeteers experienced in the trade learn to be ambidextrous, which means that you must know how to handle actors with both hands, Fig. 47, even though simultaneous movement of more than one figure is rarely required. Learn to exchange controllers with an assistant so that an actor can move from one side of the stage to the other when the script calls for it. Usually it is considered bad stage practice to

POSITIONS THAT WOULD BE DIFFICULT TO MANAGE WITH REGULAR STRINGING MAY BE CONTRIVED WITH SPECIAL STRINGS HAVING ONE FUNCTION ONLY

ATTACH THIS END OF STRING TO SPECIAL NOTCH ON CONTROLLER

SMALL RING ATTACHED TO FIGURE AT REQUIRED LOCATION TO MOVE LEG OR HAND

ATTACH THIS END OF STRING TO HAND OR LEG OF PUPPET

54 SPECIAL MOVEMENTS

FEBRUARY 1947

If marionettes are to make a well-groomed appearance on stage they must be stored between shows in cloth bags to protect costumes from grime and wrinkles

stand one actor in front of another and, unless required by the script, the performers never turn their backs to the audience.

Allow your actors to sit down occasionally during a show. People tire of watching a play in which the actors are always standing. Everybody relaxes when a player walks to a chair or bench and seats himself naturally without a flourish or fault. Figs. 48, 49 and 50 show the procedure. Of course, miniature chairs and benches, instead of practice props, are desirable for a public performance. After maneuvering your actor easily and naturally into position before a seat, tilt the controller sharply forward, holding leg strings slack so that the figure bends over. Then bend the knees by lifting on the leg strings as in Fig. 49. Lower the controller until the figure is almost level with the seat, then gently drop him into it. If the performer is to remain seated for any length of time, fasten the controller on a hanger. A slight tug at one of the strings will effect any bit of movement that may be called for meantime.

A lying-down procedure is seldom resorted to unless essential to carry part of the story. Although marionettes are constructed with the balance required to simulate the movements of a human being, they lack muscles and it is difficult for them to lie flat on the stage floor, or to arise naturally from this position. Moreover, you always risk the clatter of a loosely-assembled mechanical device. The rule is, generally: Don't try it. However, in rare cases where it must be done, puppeteers use a compromise, providing a miniature couch or divan. Figs. 52 and 53 show the use of such a prop. Begin with the sitting posture and seat the actor at a slight angle. Then allow the figure to relax slowly backward by lowering the controller until the strings are slack. As you see in Fig. 53, the gentleman is in position to arise when you reverse these movements and the action will seem perfectly natural. Sometimes the script will call for movements of the puppet-actor's legs or arms that are difficult to manage with the regular stringing. Fig. 54 shows how this usually is handled by means of a special extra string. Extra stringing, however, should always be kept to the minimum. More than two extras are difficult to handle at best and you should practice handling even one until you feel complete confidence.

Marionettes must have good care between performances if they are to make a fresh, crisply pressed appearance on the stage. Experienced puppeteers store them in heavy cloth bags fitted with drawstrings like that in Fig. 55. After the marionette is gently dropped into the bag and the drawstring pulled, excess string is wrapped around the handle of the controller so that it will not become tangled. Both the controller and bag are marked with the name of the performer. Bags should be sufficiently large to avoid cramping and possible loosening of joints. They can be stored in a trunk or hung on wall hooks.

THE END

Trick Matches That "Burn" Twice Will Amuse Company

The next time you have guests at your home, you can amuse them with matches that apparently burn twice. Pick up from an ash tray several matches that appear to have been burned. These are the wooden, strike-anywhere type that are commonly used around the house. After asking the guests whether they have ever seen such a match burn twice, and receiving negative replies, strike the match on a rough surface and it will burst into flame. The secret, of course, lies in the fact that the match had been prepared beforehand. The heads of unburned matches were dipped in black ink and allowed to dry thoroughly before placing them in the ash tray. Be careful not to stain the stick.

Waldemar J. Gydesen, Milwaukee, Wis.

Appendix B The Great Stevens Marionette Stage

Fig. 164

Designed by Margi & Martin Stevens out of 40 years of performing experience!

8'6" high by 11'8" wide when set up, it is contained in a box 7-1/2" by 26-1/4" by 40", and a roll of battens and tubes 48" by 24" (circumference) when packed! It sets up in fifteen minutes, tears down in ten. And the stage floor is table height, and projects 12" beyond the proscenium making for perfect sight lines from anywhere in the auditorium.

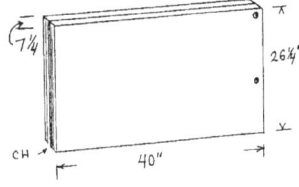

Fig. 165

Its total weight is under 70 lbs! And it fits in most any car. A practical, professional stage.

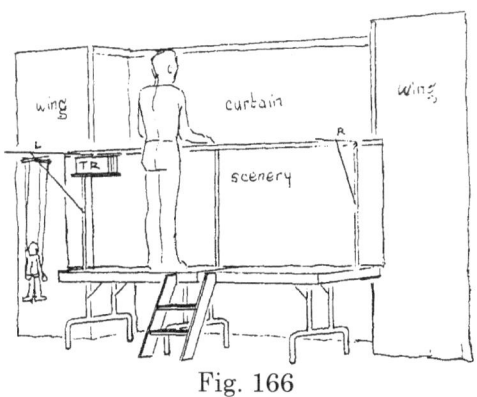

Fig. 166

Here it is backstage. Built for two people and a tape recorder. Puppets hang on racks R & L. Tape Recorder at TR. The area you stand on is on a level with the puppet stage and this platform with the legs folds into this box hinged at one end with a continuous hinge (we used to call them "piano hinges") CH.

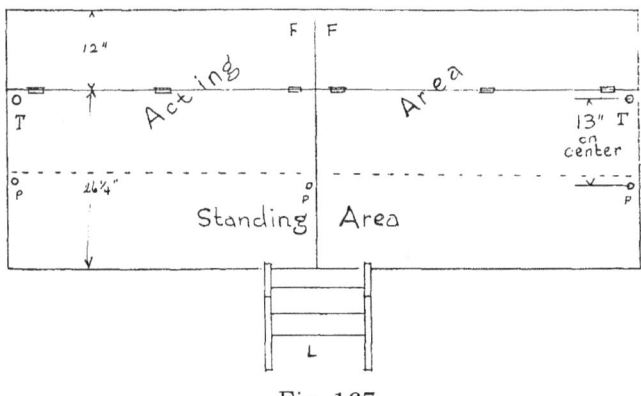

Fig. 167

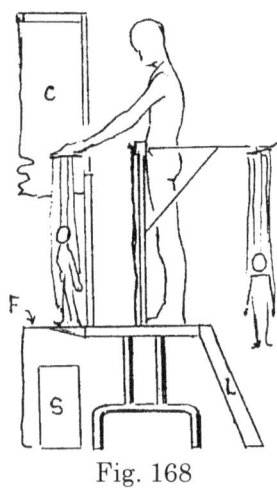

Fig. 168

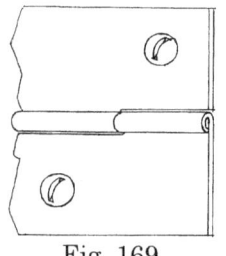

Fig. 169

Looking down at the stage. F & F are flaps that extend the acting area forward. L is a two-step ladder for mounting the stage. T & T are holes in which to insert 1-3/8" conduit (outside dimension – referred to as O.D.) to support the front curtain. p, p, & p are holes in which to insert "13/16" O.D. pipe to support the scenery rail. The dotted line is where the scenery hangs. Total distance front to back is 38-1/4" and from side to side is 80".

Figure 168 is the side view of stage. C is the inside of the front curtain. F is the front flap. S is the speaker which lives in the center of the stage under the flap, back of the "apron" – the cloth that masks the space from the Estage to the floor. L is the ladder.

The hinge (CH) is a brute. It's 3" to 3-1/2" is wide and 26" long.

Figure 170 is what you do inside the box. Three folding steel legs (I got mine at Sears Roebuck) are bolted to the 3/8" stage floor (plywood) which is glued and screwed to the 1 x 4" white pine side boards which are mitered, glued, and nailed. The continuous hinge is bolted to the end pieces (CH). Figure 171

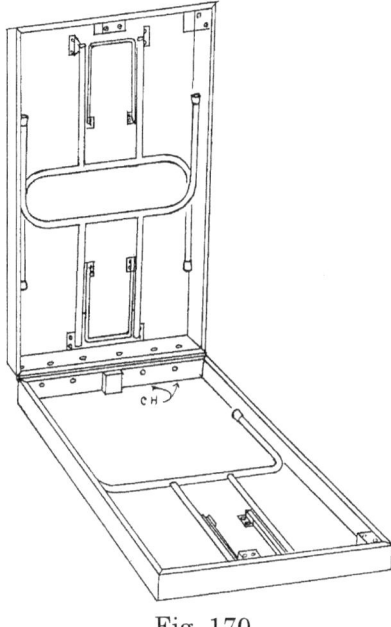

Fig. 170

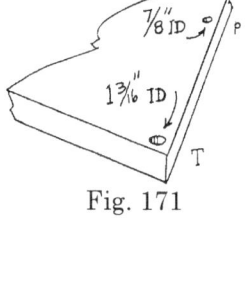

Fig. 171

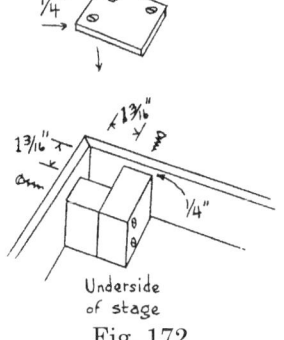

Underside of stage
Fig. 172

shows the placement of the holes into which are inserted the upright tubings that support (T) the front curtain and "wings", and

(p) the scenery rail. These holes must be made precisely. They must fit the tubing closely, and they must be absolutely vertical. T is drilled in the corner where the two side boards come together. p is drilled against the end board.

Figure 172 is the underside of the hole: make a square space directly beneath each hole the same outside dimension as the hole, using the corner for two sides, and two hardwood blocks for the other two sides, as shown. Glue and screw. This must be very strong as it supports the curtain, the wings, and the lights. The 1/4" plywood Q closes what will be the bottom of the hole and keeps the tube T from going on through.

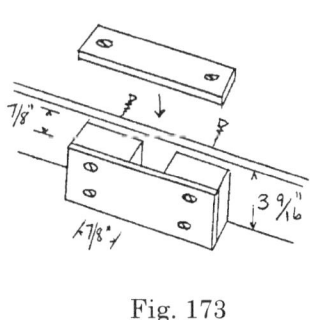

Fig. 173

Figure 173 is the manner of making the square holes for p. these support the pipes that support the scenery rail which supports the scenery, the tape recorder, the hanging puppets, and you, too, if you lean on it as you will at one time or another. So make them as strong as you possibly can!

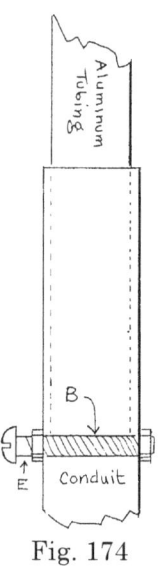

Fig. 174

Now the tubing to make the uprights. At the electrician's get two pieces of conduit 1-1/8" O. D. by 38" long. At the hardware get one 8' piece of aluminum tubing 1" O.D., have them cut it in two, making two 4' pieces. At the plumber get three pieces of pipe, 13/16" O.D., 43-1/4" long. These last three will support your scenery rail. Nothing needs to be done to them. The conduit will fit into the holes in the corners of the stage. The aluminum tubing will slide into the conduit. Do it, until the over all length of the conduit and tubing is 6'3-1/4". Drill a hole in the conduit where the bottom of the tubing comes (B) and insert a 1/4" bolt to stop the tubing from sliding any farther down the conduit. Do it as the drawing shows, and use the excess (E) to hold the curtain when you pull it up.

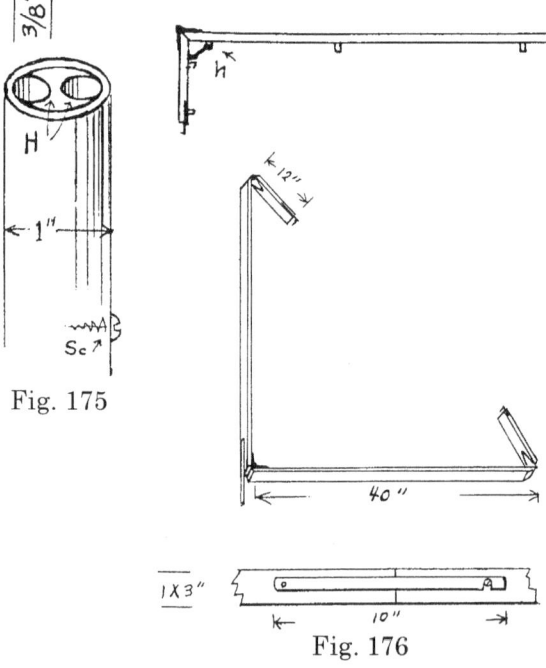

Fig. 175

Fig. 176

Insert a wooden dowel snugly in the top of each aluminum tube, fasten it (flush with the top) with a screw (Sc), then drill two 3/8" holes in the dowel (H) as in Figure 175.

Figure 176 is the batten on which you permanently fasten your curtain. Out of 1 x 3" stock (clear white pine is nice) cut two pieces 1' long, and two pieces 40" long. Miter the corners as indicated, and put the hinges on the outside so it can fold as indicated at the left.

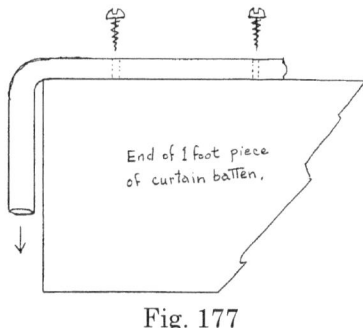

Fig. 177

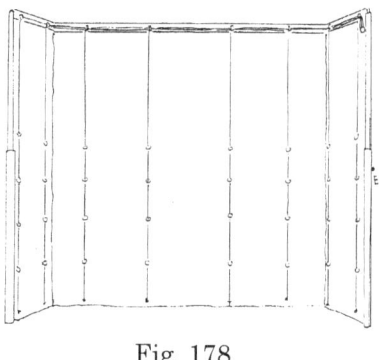

Fig. 178

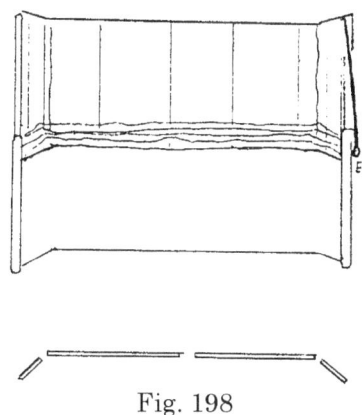

Fig. 198

While you're at the hardware store, get a 3/8" aluminum rod. It will bend easily in a vise; bend an angle like the one pictured in Figure 177. Drill two holes as indicated (I flatten the top horizontal edge with a hammer) and screw it on the unmitered end of the 12" piece leaving just enough space between the rod and the board so it can slip down into one of the holes in the dowel in the top of the aluminum tubing. Put a screen door hook across each corner (h) to keep from racking. A piece of strap like this will keep the batten from buckling in toward you at the center hinge. A bolt on the left will let it pivot so a notch on the right can engage a round head screw. The shape of the batten matches the shape of the flap extending the front of the stage for better, wider visibility.

Staple or tack the curtain on the front of the batten.

Put eight 5/8" screweyes on inside of the batten. Sew rings on the back of the curtain.

Fasten woven nylon twine at the bottom of the curtain, thread it up through the rings, across the batten, through the screweyes, and knot the ends together. Tie on a ring. To raise the curtain, pull the ring down and hook it on bolt E (Figure 173). Four 1/2 x 1" sticks in the curtain hem will keep the bottom level when it is raised.

We light the stage with two 150 watt reflector floods (NOT spots) available in hardware and drug stores. They fasten on the pipe uprights

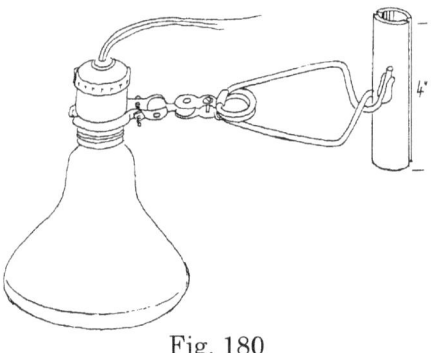

Fig. 180

that support the curtain by the devise shown here. Cut a 4" piece of conduit in two lengthwise and weld the ends of a clamp fixture to the two halves. Squeeze it and it will clamp around the pipe. Place it as low as you can behind the raised curtain without showing.

The wings are straight pieces of cloth supported at the top by a 3' piece of the 3/8" aluminum rod we used on the curtain batten, bent at a right angle. The long part fastens into the top hem of the wing – the short part drops into the other hole at the top of the upright. (Now you know why there are two.)

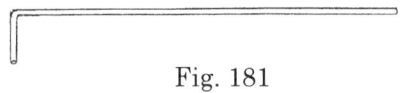

Fig. 181

The scenery rail is made of 1-1/4" x 1" clear stock. Holes are bored to match the holes in the stage. The hinge is on the top. A metal strip across the top of each hole will keep the pipe from coming up through. Backdrops (scenery) painted on unbleached muslin have #2 grommets in the wide top hem and hang on right-angle hooks placed on the front of the rail.

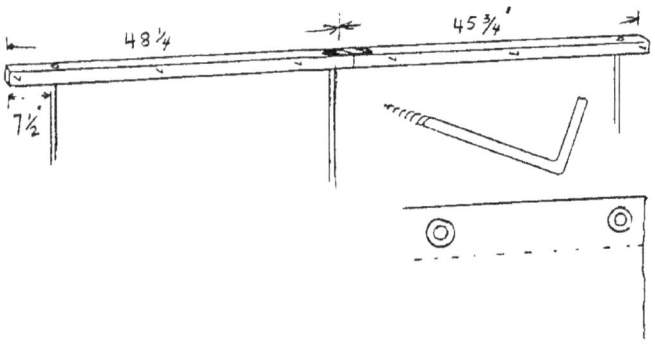

Fig. 182

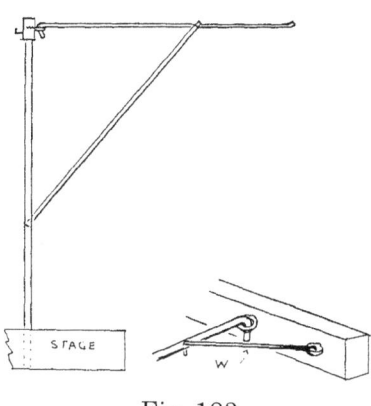

Fig. 183

The rod for hanging puppets backstage is made of two pieces of 1/4" iron rod. Cut the top one a yard long and bend as shown. A screweye in the rail slightly to one side of the pipe. The diagonal rod is riveted to the horizontal one loosely enough to swing up parallel for packing. Drill a hole in the back side of the pipe to insert the bottom end of the diagonal rod. To keep the rod from swinging from side to side, make a long hook of heavy wire (W), put it permanently in a screweye near the end of the rail. Drill a hole in the horizontal rod and drop the straight hook in. The hook stays on the rail. The rod lifts out to pack in the roll.

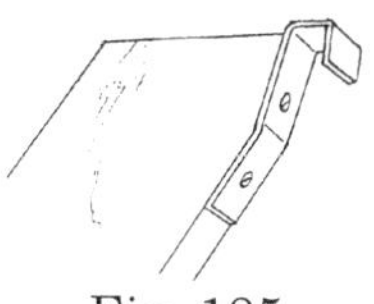

The ladder (really a set of steps) is made of four pieces of 1 x 6", four 3" hinges, and two 7" pieces of strap iron. The hinges bolt on the top of the steps on the left but on the bottom of the steps on the right, enabling the steps to fold nearly flat for packing. If you make the treads 8" wide instead of 16", it will fold completely flat, but will be less convenient to go up and down.

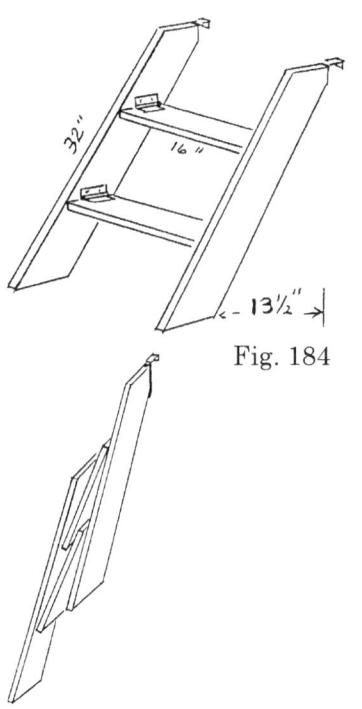

Fig. 184

Fig. 185

Bend the strap iron as shown in Figure 186. The lip drops into a slot in the stage floor.

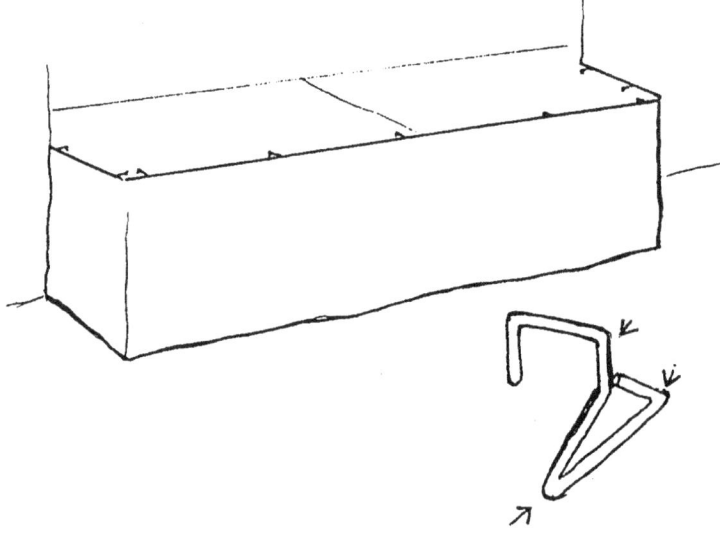

Fig. 186

The cloth that masks the space from the stage to the floor (called the apron) has webbing sewn around the top edge. Hooks made of coat hanger wire are sewed with fishline to the webbing at these three points, and dropped into loose holes drilled in the flaps. The top of the hook is just below the top edge of the webbing.

Something is needed to keep the puppets' feet from clattering on the wooden stage. We use black rubber (or plastic?) Matting. Roll it up for packing.

Fig. 187

Bolt four casters like this to the bottom edge of your stage. At least 2" wheels, of soft rubber rather than brittle plastic. Attach the castors as near the outside edges of the box as possible.

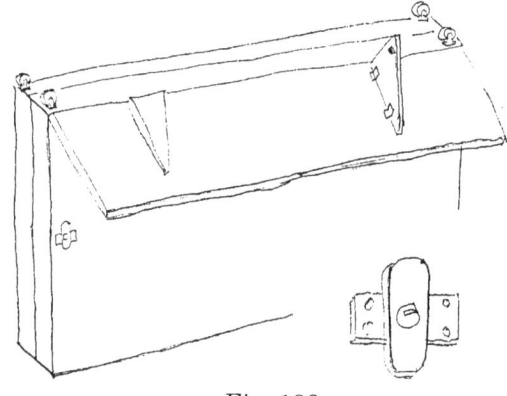

Fig. 188

The flap is permanently hinged to the box. The brackets that support it are 1/4" plywood. When folded flat, they are held against the flap by 1" squares of Velcro glued and stapled as indicated. The flap is held against the stage by turning latch, thus. Use only one to each flap, and put it on the off-stage side of the box.

- 210 -

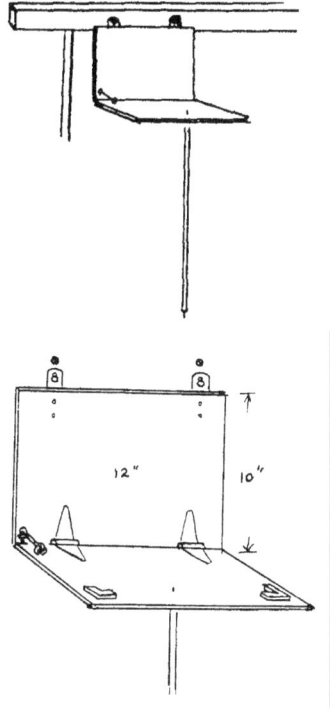

Fig. 189

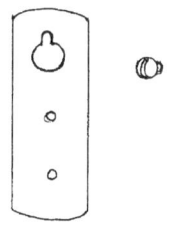

Fig. 190

It's handy to have the music where you can reach it while you're performing so here's a stand for your tape recorder fastened to the back of the scenery rail. Two pieces of 1/4" plywood 10" x 12" fits my machine. Two angular pieces on the near edge keep it from slipping off. Screen door hook steadies it. A dowel from the horizontal "table" to the stage floor has a finishing nail in each end, matching holes in the "table" and the stage to support the weight of the tape recorder. Two a '°metal hangers have keyholes which slip over the head then slide down to fit the shaft of round-headed screws on the leaning rail.

A 25' extension cord with three outlets suffices. Such things as won't pack in the stage box are rolled up in a tarpaulin (we use black denim) secured by two webbing straps.

And there you have it – a practical touring stage without a single bolt or nut to fiddle with! We use it ourselves – we know it works, and we hope you'll be very happy with it.

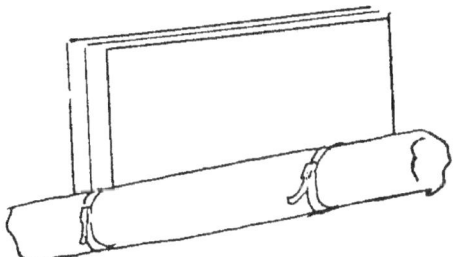

www.ingramcontent.com/pod-product-compliance
Lightning Source LLC
Chambersburg PA
CBHW060511300426
44112CB00017B/2630